Storming
the
Fortress

How Canadian Business Can
Conquer Europe in 1992

To Rob Mackenzie
Thanks for everything
Gordon Pitts

Gordon Pitts

Harper Collins
Toronto

First published 1990
by Harper Collins Publishers Ltd.
Suite 2900, Hazelton Lanes
55 Avenue Road, Toronto, Ontario   M5R 3L2

Canadian Cataloguing in Publication Data

Pitts, Gordon
   Storming the fortress: how Canadian business can conquer
Europe in 1992

ISBN 0-00-215986-4

1. Canada - Commerce - Europe.   2. Europe - Commerce
- Canada.   3. Europe - Economic integration.
4. Europe - Economic policy.   I. Title.

HF1480-15.E97P5 1990   382'.097104   C90-094059-X

90 91 92 93 RRD 10 9 8 7 6 5 4 3 2 1

For Elaine, Martha, and Katie

Acknowledgements

A book on Europe's Project 1992 and its implications for Canada has to be a "multilateral effort," with research in several countries on two continents. Many people helped.

I owe thanks to the Canadian Mission to the European Community in Brussels, particularly to Ambassador Daniel Molgat and Industrial Counselor Peter Campbell. I must also thank Robert Mackenzie, commercial counselor, and Marie-Lucie Morin, first secretary, with Canada's High Commission to the United Kingdom.

The Financial Times of London played a big part in the making of this book. I have drawn extensively on its clipping file, and the insights of its editorial staff. I must single out David Buchan and Tim Dickson of the Brussels bureau who made me feel so at home in "Europe's capital."

All this would not have been impossible without the support of my employer, The Financial Post, and its publisher, Neville Nankivell. Many people at The Post contributed to this book, but special thanks go to London correspondent Mathew Horsman who provided a home away from home.

My profound appreciation to the Nuffield Foundation for giving me the opportunity to research the European single market at Cambridge University. I owe a great debt to Cambridge's Wolfson College, David Williams, its president, and Bill Kirkman, director of the press fellowship program, for making those three months so worthwhile.

I am grateful to my editor, Marq de Villiers, for his guidance and good sense.

Finally, I must thank my family for its patience, support and love.

Contents

Chapter 1

The European Challenge

Europeans have a vision for the year 2000. The European Community (EC) will be the world's economic superpower. Its markets will be the richest, its citizens the most prosperous. Europe's companies will be the most innovative and competitive in their home markets and abroad. The Europessimism of the 1970s and early 1980s will be replaced by a giddy Euro-optimism.

This dream of a resurgent Europe is pushing closer to reality. The driving force is the EC's ambitious and far-reaching project to complete the single market among its 12 member states — Britain, France, West Germany, Denmark, the Netherlands, Belgium, Luxembourg, Italy, Greece, Spain, Portugal and Ireland.

Customs duties among these states have already been eliminated. This new wave of reform is leveling non-tariff barriers that have kept the so-called common market fragmented and weak. The program of reform and deregulation is called Project 1992, because the official deadline for creating the integrated market is December 31, 1992.

It will not be all smooth sailing towards this Europe of open borders and a seamless market of 324 million consumers. The EC is forging its new consensus against a turbulent backdrop. The world trading system is a battlefield between forces of liberalization and protection. Business and finance are undergoing a revolution of globalization, but nationalism remains an unyielding influence in the policies of individual governments.

The most remarkable development has been the collapse of Communist hegemony in Eastern Europe, including in the Soviet Union. The chaos and uncertainty that ensued present formidable challenges, particularly with the onrushing unification of West Germany and East Germany. But the liberalization of former Communist regimes is also a glorious opportunity, commercially and politically. That single market could yet extend from the Atlantic to Russia's Ural mountains — or even to the Pacific. The EC could form the nucleus of a much wider union than its leaders expected when they embarked on the single-market path in 1985.

Where will Canada end up in all this? This country has been handed an opportunity and a challenge by the 1992 reforms. Canada is well-placed to share in the European experience. But unless we move boldly and quickly, we could be watching from the sidelines.

This book is a guide for Canadians on Europe 1992. It explains what the project means and why it should matter to all Canadians — and particularly to the owners, managers and employees of businesses, both large and small.

The 1992 project is one important stage in a long process to knit together a continent. This book describes the historical background of the single market, and the people who made it happen. It lays out the framework of new rules for the free movement of goods, services and people. The emerging EC supergovernment in Brussels is mapped out. Canadians are told why they should be concerned about European business preparations for 1992.

Canada's relations with the EC are discussed from several angles. Why has the Canadian government been so slow to react to the changing geopolitics of Western and Eastern Europe? How valid are American concerns that the EC will use its single market reforms as building blocks for a Fortress Europe? What explains most of Canadian business's casual indifference towards 1992, compared with its Asian and American competition?

This book offers guidance on strategies and tactics for both beginners and seasoned veterans in the European market, with examples of the more notable efforts. It shows that even small and medium-sized companies can succeed.

Western and Eastern Europe can no longer be discussed as separate entities. This book analyzes the challenge of Eastern Europe, both for the EC and for Canadian companies that want to get their feet in the door.

There are three major aspects of 1992. First is the regulatory reform, the 280 changes in EC law aimed at eliminating non-tariff barriers in the community. This program is already well advanced. It won't be finished on December 31, 1992, but there will be enough of it in place to call the project a success.

Another part of 1992 is the corporate revolution, the wave of restructuring, mergers and acquisitions aimed at getting European companies ready for the single market. That, too, is well on the way. Canadian business can expect to confront tougher European competition in the 1990s — in Europe, in North America and in third-country markets.

Also on the agenda after the single market is a single economic and monetary policy, including a common currency. Jacques Delors, the president of the European Commission, is eager to move quickly towards a true federation of states with a strong, directly elected European government.

It is no longer a question of *Will the single market happen?* The major political compromises have been made. Many of the reforms are in place. The adjustments are underway in boardrooms, factories and offices. The challenge is no longer Europe's — it is Canada that must respond. Will we be losers or winners from 1992? Will it increase our trade or undermine it? Will Canada lose markets or seize investment opportunities? Will we have an important role in the shaping of Europe? The outcome is in our hands. It could go either way.

Chapter 2

Monnet's Vision

Winnipeg in 1906 was a bustling frontier town. Its dusty streets teemed with immigrants from Scandinavia and Eastern Europe who had ridden in on the railroad to find a better life. Taking in the sights, smells and energy of the Canadian West was a wide-eyed and thoughtful young Frenchman who had come to Canada to visit clients of his family's business.

Jean Monnet was only 18, just out of secondary school, not much more than a boy. But his father, the head of a cooperative of brandy producers in Cognac in Southwestern France, was eager for his son to learn every detail of the business. He was also determined that the boy gain an international experience, a useful qualification if he was going to sell the newly branded J.G. Monnet cognac into a world market. The young Monnet had already spent time in London's financial center, the City, learning the secrets of international finance. Now he was in remote Western Canada, finding out what customers were thinking of the company's fine smooth brandy.

Monnet heeded his father's advice: "Don't take any books. Look out of the window, talk with people. Pay attention to your neighbor." He found that the hard-working, unrefined people of the prairies appreciated good brandy. He took in the atmosphere of the young West. Coming from a Europe of tradition and conservatism, he reveled in the new Canadians' unbridled optimism. "What was going on in Europe had no interest for these Europeans making for the West, turning their backs on the Old World. Their efforts, their vision of a broader, richer future, that was what we talked about nearly all the time. I soaked myself in these impressions," Monnet later wrote in his memoirs.

"At Winnipeg, from the Station Hotel of the Canadian Pacific Railway where I was staying, I saw train loads of Scandinavian immigrants pulling in. They were not refugees: they were not starving. They had come to hard rewarding work — the conquest of new lands."

Monnet loved the fields along France's Charente River where he was born and raised. But he recognized the limitations of his homeland. His neighbors in Cognac were naturally suspicious of change. He was impressed by Canada's unlimited space and the confidence this seemed to foster in its people. Here, individual initiative could be accepted as a contribution to the general good. Many years later, he recalled how in Calgary a Scandinavian immigrant blacksmith, on meeting Monnet for the first time, didn't hesitate in lending him a horse. "His confidence was perfectly natural; and if I had shown him how surprised I was, he would certainly have been hurt," Monnet wrote.

His experiences in the Western provinces could be considered Canada's contribution to building the European single market. Monnet returned to France and the fertile banks of the Charente. He became the most influential European of his generation, widely known as "The Father of Europe." In the dark years after the Second World War, he rallied the leaders of a devastated continent around his vision of an integrated Europe. He built institutions that formed the building blocks of today's European Community. The 1992 project, aimed at breaking down the community's non-tariff barriers, is simply another stage in the evolution towards Monnet's dream of a United States of Europe. Jacques Delors, the brilliant and mercurial Frenchman who as current president of the European Commission has pushed forward this latest integration, is often described as the Jean Monnet of the 1990s.

In his memoirs, Monnet looked back on his time in

Canada as an important factor in his development as a world leader. He was impressed by the connection between physical space and confidence, between wider vistas and economic hope. He became a committed internationalist, a man unburdened by chauvinism and narrow parochial interests. His trips into the Rockies gave him a taste for long and arduous walks that, throughout his life, allowed him to concentrate and prepare for action. Monnet developed a capacity for single-mindedness, an ability to isolate himself from the background noise and concentrate on the job at hand. Whether he was talking to Winnipeg merchants about the cognac quality or forging the destiny of Europe, nothing distracted him from the goal at hand. "As far back as I can remember," he wrote, "I seem to have been busy at some unquestioned task. I have no imagination for anything that does not seem necessary."

It is impossible to pigeonhole Monnet — statesman, businessman, politician, diplomat. He was a bit of each, but that doesn't do him complete justice. He was a man of action, not an intellectual. He never went to university and rarely read books. Yet this self-educated man was in the middle of every important development in European history from 1914 to the end of his life in 1979. The great men of his age, Churchill, de Gaulle, Roosevelt, Adenauer, Kennedy, knew and learned from him. But he remained a background figure, never crowding the centre stage. In one official photograph during the war — of de Gaulle, Churchill, Anthony Eden and others — he stands off to the side, a stocky little man with a narrow brush of a mustache.

Monnet's long diplomatic career was launched with the outbreak of the First World War in 1914. Exempt from military service for health reasons, the 26-year-old businessman threw himself into the organization of the allied forces' transport and supply operations. (As head of the allied transport effort, he was able to call on his old Winnipeg contacts at the Hudson's Bay Company for help.) After the armistice, he was a key official in the new League of Nations, but grew disillusioned over the lack of progress in world cooperation. He quit the league, went back to Cognac, and worked in the family business. But he kept his hand in world affairs, conducting special diplomatic missions for the French government. When the Second World War broke out and France was overrun by the armies of Nazi Germany, Monnet was back in the thick of things, working in London with General Charles de Gaulle as an organizer of the Free French.

When Germany surrendered in 1945, he returned to his battered homeland. de Gaulle, now the French president, gave him the formidable task of rebuilding the country's industry and Monnet went at it with the single-mindedness that had served him all his life. But his vision could not be restricted to France. It was not enough for one country to rebuild; to be effective, reconstruction had to be on a European scale. Furthermore, Monnet, like many Europeans, was deeply shaken by the devastation of two major wars in 30 years. He was determined it would never happen again.

Monnet believed that the only hope for preventing future wars was to tie national economies together in a single market. "There will be no peace in Europe if states are reconstructed on the basis of national sovereignty, with all that implies in terms of prestige politics and economic protectionism," he said in 1943. He was also convinced that "prosperity and social progress will remain elusive until the nations of Europe form a federation or a European entity which will forge them into a single economic unit." These words could have been spoken by Jacques Delors in the late 1980s.

The making of a common market

Every breakthrough in world history flows from confluence of the right people at the right time. Monnet's dream of an integrated Europe was shared by two other men, French Foreign Minister Robert Schuman and the chancellor of a new West German republic, Konrad Adenauer. Monnet was the architect, and the other two the builders; together, they laid the first brick in the European structure. Their creation was the European Coal and Steel Community, which in 1951 pooled the coal and steel production of France, Germany, Italy and the three Benelux countries into a single agency. The idea grew out of the former Allied powers' concern over the future of the Saarland, the source of German industrial might through two world wars. The French feared that Germany would again dominate Europe through its control of this rich coal and iron area. The pact buried those fears, and linked French and German steel production in a spirit of reconciliation.

This crucial Franco-German alliance, forged by Monnet and Adenauer, remains the firm foundation of the European Community today. It legitimized the new West German republic as part of the Western family. What's more, the six member countries actually ceded pieces of their national sovereignties to a supranational agency, the community's High Authority headed by Jean Monnet. This dramatic surrender of powers sowed the seed for the deeper unity to come.

Monnet was a patient man; he believed great things were achieved in steps, one rising on top of another. Five years after the coal and steel community was formed, the six nations met again at Messina, Italy, for a conference that laid the groundwork for a full-blown European customs union. With that union, goods and services would move free of customs tariffs among the six members; the external tariffs of the six would be merged into one common duty on imports into the community. The conference also set up Euratom, a co-operative effort aimed at developing peaceful uses of nuclear energy. These initiatives were the substance of the Treaty of Rome, signed in 1957, the founding statute of the European Community.

Jean Monnet died in 1979 at 91 after a full and satisfying life. Many of his cherished goals had turned into reality. Internal tariffs and quotas had disappeared in the community. The club of Europe had expanded to nine countries, including Britain, the longtime holdout. Greece, Spain and Portugal would join in the 1980s. In the early 1970s, the EC forged free trade links with a smaller grouping of countries, the European Free Trade Association, consisting of Sweden, Switzerland, Norway, Finland, Iceland and Austria.

The community had developed its own institutions,

including an executive body (the European Commission), a parliament, a law court and a council of ministers from the member countries. It had created an integrated Common Agricultural Policy of subsidies and price supports (which turned out to be horrendously costly and wasteful.) A common trade policy and a shared program of aid and trade with the Third World had been established. In 1979, the year Monnet died, German Chancellor Helmut Schmidt, French President Valéry Giscard d'Estaing and European Commission President Roy Jenkins took leadership roles in developing an exchange rate mechanism, whereby values of participating currencies were closely linked.

It appeared that Monnet and his colleagues had achieved by peaceful means what Charlemagne, Napoleon and Hitler could only accomplish, rather imperfectly, by force — the unity of Europe.

However, that wise old man couldn't have been entirely satisfied with the Europe he left behind in 1979. The road to unity had been a rocky one, and was still far from complete. One roadblock was what Stanley Hoffman, the American historian, describes as "a quasi-theological debate" about the community's institutions. In this debate, Monnet lined up against his old comrade-in-arms, General Charles de Gaulle, who as France's president throughout the 1960s resisted the idea of a more integrated Europe.

Monnet had a vision of a supranational government, whereby member states ceded areas of authority to the community, with an independent European Commission serving as the main decision-making body. But de Gaulle envisaged something much less significant — a "Europe of states" in which sovereign nations would be continually negotiating common programs on the basis of balanced interests. The states would not give up their authority in these negotiated areas. De Gaulle was the ultimate French nationalist who had saved his country twice in 20 years — in the Second World War and during the Algerian crisis in the 1950s. He feared the surrender of French sovereignty to uncontrollable and irresponsible European Commission bureaucrats. He also suspected those Eurocrats would be susceptible to influence from another force he distrusted, the United States.

The tall and imperious general bent the community to his will. The Council of Ministers, a committee representing the nation states, became the ultimate decision-maker. The more independent European Commission took on a vague, shadowy role. The European Parliament remained toothless; for many years it wasn't even elected by popular vote. The principle of unanimity ruled in the council of ministers. Each country had a veto on major initiatives.

That Gaullist principle was a thick obstacle in front of any expanded federalism. de Gaulle, for example, was able to block Britain's entry into the community throughout the 1960s, because he feared the heavy hand of the U.S. in British government. This has a deliciously ironic twist in today's deliberations about 1992. It is British Prime Minister Margaret Thatcher, with her resistance to the community's incursions into national sovereignty, who is considered the only remaining Gaullist among Europe's leaders.

The general rode off the world stage in 1969, but he left a legacy of veto and paralysis. Efforts to forge a common foreign policy for the community foundered. A plan for economic and monetary union collapsed. Britain joined the community in 1972, but remained stubbornly ambivalent about its role. For 10 years, it continually complained about the community budget, arguing that it had been cheated in its contribution level.

Historian Stanley Hoffman calls the period from 1973 to 1984 the European Community's Dark Age. While the six — now 12 — countries had lowered their tariff barriers to each other, they erected ever higher non-tariff barriers against their fellow community members. They set up restrictive national standards and testing procedures that excluded imports from the other countries — and created wasteful inefficiency. The first cellular telephone systems, for example, were based on varied national transmission bands. A business person traveling from London to Paris to Rome needed three mobile phones to keep in touch with head office. Also, government procurement programs favored domestic companies over competitors from the outside. Truck drivers faced hours of delay and yards of red tape at customs posts.

When the world economy was devastated by the oil shocks of the 1970s and the recession of 1981-82, Europe's nations only reinforced these defensive national practices. They subsidized their "national champions," the local companies which had become favored instruments of industrial policy. When unemployment soared, they opted for fiscal tinkering, and poured money into retraining, job creation and unemployment insurance. It was the worst of both worlds: the single market became even more fragmented, and the strategies were not working. Inflation and unemployment climbed; major industries, such as shipbuilding, were lost altogether.

European companies, protected in their homelands, were losing big chunks of global markets to the Japanese and newly industrializing countries of the Far East. Between 1973 and 1985, Europe's share of the world's trade in manufactured goods fell to 36% from 45%. During the 1981 recession, all the world's industrial areas suffered, but Europe was slow to bounce back in the recovery of the mid-1980s. Unemployment across the community was still 11.5% in 1985; economic growth lagged far behind that of the U.S., Canada and Japan.

Also troubling was the EC's weakness in the emerging new technologies of the 1970s and 1980s. Telecommunications was an engine of economic growth, but an area where Europe was lagging. Most of the 12 states had concentrated on developing national champions in telecom equipment. This was accomplished through blatant favoritism by state-owned telephone utilities in their purchasing practices. These policies splintered Europe into 12 telecom zones, retarded economies of scale in production and co-operative research efforts, and dumped heavy costs onto taxpayers and consumers.

The EC estimates that it cost $10 billion in Europe to create 10 different switching systems, whereas in the U.S. it cost $3 billion to develop three systems; and in Japan, only $1.5 billion for one system. Seven digital switching systems are being installed in the EC, five of which were developed by national champions supported by their governments. This wasteful duplication exacted a heavy price from consumers. In the mid-1980s, the price per line of a digital switching system in the EC was between $250 and $500, compared with about $100 in the U.S.

All this contributed to an odor of defeat that hung over the community. The fashionable view, in Europe and around the world, was that the continent was suffering from an incurable Eurosclerosis. There was a crying need for a new Monnet, a new Schuman and a new spirit of rebirth.

Right people, right time

They were the odd couple of European statesmanship: Jacques Delors, the short, dapper French socialist and Catholic intellectual, and Lord Cockfield, the ponderous and bulky old fogy, a British businessman and member of the House of Lords. However, both men carried the Monnet vision — that Europe's economies should be bound together in a frontierless union. They also shared the blend of idealism and pragmatism necessary to revive the dream. As in 1951 when the European Coal and Steel Community was born, Europe in 1985 was blessed with the right people at the right time in history.

At the end of 1984, a new class of European Commissioners was about to take office. There were no fanfare and no great expectations surrounding this particular group. Commissioners are the men and women who serve as the "cabinet ministers" for the European Commission. They have been traditionally a very mixed bag. Appointed by their national governments, they are usually veteran politicians who were being rewarded for their loyal service and, sometimes, distinguished careers. There have been some prominent and activist commissioners. However, the commissioner's job is often considered a just reward for a worthy past, or a comfortable way station before resuming a national political career. Besides, in 1984, Europessimism was deeply entrenched, even in Brussels, the home of the commission. There was the feeling that nothing was ever going to change.

Anyone looking around the table at that first Commission meeting would have sensed that this was a solid group, but hardly memorable. Cockfield, the senior

British appointee, was a Thatcherite Tory with a tedious manner of speaking that hardly inspired people to dramatic action. He was also 68, near the end of his public life. But Cockfield was blessed with an independent mind and real business experience as a taxation expert and former chairman of the Boots drugstore chain. Peter Sutherland, the Irish appointee, was an ambitious young lawyer from Dublin, but an unknown commodity. Similarly, the new European Commission president, Jacques Delors, a 59-year-old former French finance minister, was not a "name" outside French politics. Willy de Clercq, the outspoken Belgian, and Frans Andriessen, a thoughtful hard-working but bland Dutchman, stood out among the rest. But no one would have imagined that "these people were more ambitious, more courageous than any other commission" — a judgment delivered in retrospect by one of Cockfield's senior staff.

The key was Delors, a small man with a sharp, thoughtful face and thinning dark hair, who would soon display the same sense of mission and determination that infused Jean Monnet. However, Delors wasn't the behind-the-scenes draftsman and organizer of the Monnet style. His is a much more complex personality. While Monnet was a man of action, Delors is a driven, tormented idealist and intellectual. He is a devout Roman Catholic and a disciple of an obscure left-wing Catholic theologian, Emmanuel Mounier. Yet he is also a fanatical sports fan who loves soccer and bicycle racing.

Delors' intellectual hero, Mounier, attracted a following in the 1930s when many European thinkers were influenced by the ideas of Nazi Germany and Communist Russia. Mounier espoused a political philosophy called "personalism," that occupied a middle ground between free enterprise and communism. His message was strongly anti-totalitarian: "The state is meant for man, not man for the state." Mounier believed man is above all "a person within a community." He believed in the shared values of society, and the possibility of forging consensus. His followers sought to avoid the bitter divisions of right versus left, worker against employer, and people against the state that plagued Europe of the 1930s.

These views can be seen running through Delors' political career. He has blended idealism and a concern for social justice with flexibility — some say opportunism — and a capacity to work with diverse groups. He was born in a working class district of Paris of a devout Catholic mother and a father who was a mid-level manager at the Bank of France, the country's central bank. He was a very good student but his father counted on a practical banking career. Instead of entering university after high school, the young Delors joined the central bank in 1945, where he spent 17 years rising through the ranks, and gaining a grasp of economics that would serve him later on.

Delors carried on a parallel career as a social activist in the non-Marxist wing of Christian union movement. In fact, the trade unions elected him as their representative on the board of the Bank of France in the 1950s. After leaving the bank in the early 1960s, he worked as a social policy specialist in French government.

His pragmatism was evident in 1968 when, as a university teacher with moderate leftist views, he was recruited as a social affairs adviser to a right-wing Gaullist prime minister, Jacques Chaban-Delmas. That gave Delors a somewhat tainted background when he left government and joined the opposition Socialist Party in the mid-1970s. Yet that reputation for pragmatism may have worked in his favor. Delors was seen as someone who could maneuver between the extremes in the party.

When the Socialists rose to power in the early 1980s under President François Mitterrand, Delors was the party's choice as finance minister. He is credited with turning the Socialists away from the state-centered economic policies of its first few years and guiding it onto a deregulatory path. With the economy on the upswing, he had hoped Mitterrand would appoint him prime minister in 1984, but he was passed over. However, the president did come through with a lucrative and demanding consolation prize. He successfully lobbied the other 11 governments to have Delors appointed president of the European Commission. (Ironically, his current antagonist, British Prime Minister Margaret Thatcher, was one of his backers.)

Delors was, in one sense, a natural for the job, says historian Hoffmann. "A former official of a French trade union inspired by progressive Catholic thought, Delors exemplifies the synthesis of Christian democracy and socialism on which the community was built. His commitment to a united Europe is as strong as his obstinacy and energy."

The EC president has a huge ego and seems to thrive in the spotlight, making the dramatic speech and the flamboyant gesture. Yet he is often portrayed as a consensus leader who weighs the conflicting arguments of his colleagues before presenting a possible compromise position. A workaholic who spends 12 to 15 hours a day on the job, he occasionally crumbles under the pressure, lashing out at colleagues and officials. In one memorable speech, he told a Greek commissioner that he was not capable of running a tavern; he once referred to the West German Chancellor as that "fat-assed Kohl."

There is a school of opinion which believes French leadership is somehow indispensable for advancing the cause of European unity. French statesmen seem to possess that blend of bull-headedness, arrogance and diplomacy that gets things done in Europe. Perhaps it stems from their superb training in the arts of statecraft and bureaucracy. Or perhaps it is only because they have the best chance of overcoming the objections of the French government to deregulation and freer trade.

Delors was determined that he would not be presiding over the further decline of the European Community. He was intent on being more than a ceremonial figure. Before taking office, he lugged his briefcase around the continent on a tour of national capitals, searching for a way to revive the moribund European ideal. He wanted to spark what the French call a *fuite en avant,* an escape by leaping forward. Delors asked the national leaders to consider four possible ways to push Europe forward: greater cooperation in defence matters; development of the community's system of government; a renewed effort for monetary union, including a single currency; and the creation of a proper integrated European market without barriers to the free movement of people, capital and goods and services.

The last option appealed most to them, although all four elements eventually got pulled into the single market process. Margaret Thatcher's Conservative government liked the deregulatory spirit of the single market, a Europe of free and open trade. Besides, after years of quarreling about the EC budget — a debate that had been finally settled — Britain was eager to look like a team player. Germany, with a new center-right government, liked the idea of liberalized trade. As the strongest economy in Europe, Germany would gain the most from the single market. And Italy had emerged in the 1980s as a stronger, more confident economic power, with much to gain as well.

France's Socialist government under Mitterrand was opening up the economy after its experiment in industrial policy and *dirigisme*. However, France had a lot to lose from a freer market. Her industries and workers were among the most protected and subsidized in Europe. But this was balanced by the fact that François Mitterrand, himself a pragmatic politician, had undergone a serious conversion to Euroenthusiasm. His presidency of the European council of ministers in late 1988 had resulted in a number of impressive achievements. The French felt if they took a leadership role in forging the single market, they could control the agenda, and minimize the damage. The risk was worth it, they concluded.

The EC's leaders recognized that an integrated market would entail the surrender of some sovereignty. They felt they could accept that if it would lead to a greater control over their economic futures through a stronger Europe. They were encouraged in this thinking by key members of the European elite, including leading businesspeople who had undergone their own conversion in the mid-1980s, giving up on the national protectionist policies they had previously supported. Their industries had come under intense competitive pressure from Japan, the Asian up-and-comers and the United States. Men like Pehr Gyllenhammar of Volvo, the Swedish car maker, Giovanni Agnelli, chairman of Italy's Fiat, and Wisse Dekker, chairman of Philips, the Dutch electronics giant, were urging that Europe finally create an integrated "home market" as a base to meet these threats.

Just as Jean Monnet had drawn much inspiration from the wide-open markets of North America, these latter-day Monnets looked across the Atlantic to the United States of America for their model. They saw the U.S. as a wide-open home market, free of the diverse technical standards and local favoritism in state buying policies that fragmented Europe. (The Canadian federation also served as a model, but the EC has been unimpressed with our interprovincial trade barriers.) It didn't matter that this view was simplistic, and the U.S. itself was a declining economic power. This image still held attraction.

Recipe for rebirth

Delors looked down his commission table and spotted the men best suited to spearhead this bold new thrust. Lord Cockfield became the commissioner in charge of forging the internal market. Another of the new commissioners, Ireland's Sutherland, was handed the important portfolio of competition policy.

Cockfield, with energy uncharacteristic of a semi-retired English lord, threw himself into the task of preparing a White Paper that would outline an agenda of action for the single market. Within six months, in June, 1985, he had produced the list of almost 300 measures necessary for, as the paper's title indicated, "Completing the Internal Market." The paper was written with a sense of urgency. Lord Cockfield emphasized that something dramatic had to be done if Europe would ever dig itself out of its hole. "Europe stands at a crossroads," the White Paper declared. "We either go ahead — with resolution and determination — or we drop back into mediocrity."

The paper said the single market would allow the free movement of goods and services, capital and people among the 12 countries. To do this, reforms had to move forward along three planes:

• The elimination of physical barriers, such as border controls on the movement of people and goods;

• The scrapping of technical barriers, such as national product standards and the favoritism accorded national companies in awarding public contracts;

• The removal of fiscal barriers, mainly through a harmonization of valued-added and excise taxes in the community.

The paper outlined in plain language, 300 precise and practical things that had to be done to achieve this single market. Many involved obscure regulations, such as rules governing harmful organisms in seed potatoes. Others had huge implications, such as proposals to narrow the gap in value-added tax rates. But the paper gave no priority to the measures; that might have sparked endless quarrels among the countries. Cockfield also set a timetable for the passage of these measures, and an ultimate deadline for the single market to become reality — by December 31, 1992. That date gave the program a momentum and a slogan that captured the imagination of the public, although in fact many of the measures won't see the light of day until well after that. According to the Brussels bureaucrats, "1992 isn't a date, it's a process."

It was fine to have a legislative timetable, but it was another thing to get these measures passed by the EC's creaky institutional machinery. The ghost of Charles de Gaulle still haunted the meeting rooms of the Council of Ministers, which rendered the final decision on the important community matters. Ministers from the nation states, one from each of the 12, made up the Council. Each state had a veto over council decisions. Under such a system, the single market reforms were doomed to being pecked to death by national self-interest.

Delors's inspired solution was the Single European Act, a document that epitomized the massive transfer of sovereignty by the member countries to the community under the 1992 program. The act, prepared in parallel with the White Paper, strengthened the powers of the European Parliament and raised the level of funding for regional programs. But above all, it removed the national veto in the Council of Ministers on most of the nearly 300 measures necessary to complete the single market. (Tax changes are one notable exception; they still require unanimous agreement.) The measures could pass the Council, the EC's final decision-making body, by a "qualified majority" vote, a system that gives more weight to some countries than others. Once passed by Council, they become community law, although national governments must still pass legislation to put them into action.

The proposed Single European Act, which amounted to a sweeping reform of the Treaty of Rome, ignited a firestorm in European relations. It was hotly debated, particularly at a rancorous summit in Milan in June, 1985, when the whole process almost collapsed under Thatcher's withering attack. The next summit meeting in Luxembourg hatched an agreement. The act was watered down from conception to final passage. Ireland and Denmark ran referendums on it; in both cases, the act's supporters were victorious. The legislatures of all 12 countries eventually passed it in 1987. Charles de Gaulle's ghost was finally exorcised.

Some observers have suggested that Margaret Thatcher, Europe's most unregenerate Gaullist, did not realize the full implications of what she was signing. She has since battled against the extension of majority voting to many areas that would seem to be covered in Cockfield's White Paper. Her defenders say Thatcher acknowledged the need to surrender some state sovereignty through the act. It is on the specific lines of the boundary between Brussels and the nation states, that she disagrees with Delors and her continental counterparts.

The Single European Act embodied another principle that has allowed the 1992 reforms to speed ahead with the urgency of a French passenger train. The new team in Brussels decided that earlier efforts to forge a single market in Europe were being undermined by the painstaking approach of trying to harmonize technical standards and regulations among the 12 nations. That had been a goal of the community's founding legislation, the Treaty of Rome, in 1957. But the process has been laborious, because the commission tried to develop harmonized specifications that would be agreed upon by all member states. The process broke down in nit-picking as countries would try to defend their national preferences for pizza, light bulbs, or telephone systems. If Europe was to hit the ground running in 1992, the process had to be accelerated.

It is fascinating, in charting the history of Europe's

integration, to trace the central role played by French wine and spirits. It was cognac that sent Jean Monnet around the globe, acquiring that expansive internationalist spirit that would inspire the formation of the European Community. It was Crème de Cassis, the French liqueur concocted from black currants, that gave Delors and Cockfield the tool to sweep away the unseen trade barriers in the community.

In 1978, a West German company called Rewe-Zentral AG ran afoul of German laws when it tried to import Cassis de Dijon, a brand of cassis liqueur, into its domestic market. No way, said the German authorities. The French drink could not enter because its alcoholic content was insufficient for it to be considered a liqueur by West German standards. Little Rewe decided to take on the giant-killer role, challenging the ban in the courts. The case went up to the EC's court, the European Court of Justice in Luxembourg, which was itself starting to show its muscles as a European supreme court.

The court, in a ground-breaking decision, ruled that West Germany had no right to stop Rewe from importing a product that was legally on sale in France, unless the sale was blocked for reasons of health, fiscal supervision, fair trading or consumer protection. None of these reasons applied to Cassis de Dijon.

The Brussels law-makers, in assembling the Single European Act, must have toasted their creation with a glass or two of Crème de Cassis. The court judgment formed the basis for the principle of "mutual harmonization" that is enshrined in the act. Each nation had to recognize the technical standards and regulations of the other 11. A single country now cannot block the importation of a good or a service from a community partner unless the product fails to meet community-wide standards of health and safety. That simple principle cleared the way for a dramatic deregulation in Europe. It meant that instead of hiding behind regulations and standards, the members would have to engage in a kind of competitive deregulation.

So the single market now had a legislative program (the White Paper), the tools to achieve that program (the

Single European Act) and a slogan (1992). All it needed were some economic studies to show Europeans why it was all worthwhile. That was provided by a team headed by Italian Paolo Cecchini, a former Commission deputy director. His $5 million study, called "1992: The European Challenge," concluded that the single market could boost European gross domestic product by 5% to 7% over five years. If all the 1992 elements fall into place, prices could drop by 6%, exports could surge by 10%, and two million to five million jobs could be created. The scale of Cecchini's rosy projections were hotly debated by economists, but all agreed there will be positive results.

With the principle of mutual harmonization established, Delors, Cockfield, Sutherland and Company finally had forged the instrument for creating a single European market. However, other people — future commissions — would have to finish their task. Lord Cockfield was unceremoniously dumped as Britain's senior commissioner by the Thatcher government in 1988. His crime, apparently, was becoming too European in his vision and sympathies, particularly in urging for too-dramatic tax harmonization among the 12. He was replaced by Thatcher confidant Sir Leon Brittan, who shows all the signs of becoming similarly unreliable and pro-European. It must be the Brussels water. Sutherland left the commission for the life of a well-paid corporate director and lawyer in his hometown, Dublin. But continuity was assured with the presence of Delors, who was reappointed to another four-year term, and a handful of other holdovers.

The unlikely partnership of Delors and Cockfield had established the broad design of 1992. It had been an arduous, hard-fought and seemingly impossible task, but it was accomplished. However, there was no time to relax. The White Paper's 300 measures — eventually trimmed down to 279 — had to be passed by the 12 members in the Council of Ministers, and then implemented by each state. That process, still going on, has made the passage of the Single European Act look like a tea party. Whenever the countries of Europe begin to look at the details of the single market — the harmonization of taxes, the elimination of the border controls, the creation of new standards —

the old suspicions, phobias and national pride rise again to the surface. It has become clear that the fine details will not be ironed out until long after December 31, 1992. But the reality is that there can be no turning back from the overall thrust of the Delors-Cockfield program. Jean Monnet's dream of a united Europe is alive again.

Eighty-five years ago, the 18-year-old Monnet left Cognac, bound for the emerging markets of the New World. A middle-class Frenchman, he was not afraid of the mysteries of Winnipeg and Calgary; he was not condescending towards the rough lifestyles of the prairie settlers. Monnet admired their confidence, their openness. He wanted to learn, and above all, he wanted to do business with them. He wanted to sell them brandy.

Today, it is Europe that exudes confidence, that suggests expansive markets and boundless potential. North America looks tired and mired in defeatist thinking. What Canada needs now are its own Jean Monnets, fearless business people, politicians and public officials who are free from the old ideas of Eurosclerosis, or traditional phobias of European cultures, languages and practices. We need a generation willing to explore Europe with the vigor and curiosity Monnet demonstrated. Only then can Canada be successful in storming the fortress.

Chapter 3

The Fine Print of 1992

Gary O'Meara and his wife Suzanne Tevlin, Canadian teachers living in England, had slipped into Brussels on the first day of a motoring tour of the continent. Wandering around the splendid old central square, the Grand Place, they came upon a shop window displaying delicate handcrafted Belgian lace. The couple succumbed and bought a lace tablecloth for the equivalent of $300 in Belgian francs. A helpful storekeeper advised them to stop at the Belgium-Holland border to get their receipt stamped, so that they could apply for a refund of value-added tax.

O'Meara guided his car along the super-highway between Brussels and the Dutch border, the flat treeless landscape flashing past. It slowly dawned on him that all kinds of little things were looking suspiciously different. The highway signs were a different color; the car license plates had changed. O'Meara had traveled five kilometers inside the Dutch border, with no hint of customs posts, uniformed guards, or a "Welcome to the Netherlands" sign — and no VAT official slip.

Bewildered and bemused, the O'Mearas retraced their steps until they found a poorly signed office building on a side road just off the highway, where they got their receipt stamped, and resumed their vacation. A few years later, they still joked about it — the day Gary lost the Belgium-Dutch border.

The O'Mearas had been given a little advance peek at the Europe of the future. The border between Belgian and Holland is one of the most unobtrusive in Europe, the product of years of peaceful, profitable co-existence among the Benelux countries. But sometime in the 1990s, borders all around the European Community will have that same innocuous appearance, if, in fact, they exist at all.

The 12 nations of the community are rewriting Euro-geography. They are creating a Europe without frontiers. Already, the atmosphere is changing. The continent is becoming a crushing bore for tourists who get excited having their passports stamped at every frontier crossing. Customs posts are turning into casual places where uniformed officers wave on cars with a smile and a "Bonjour" or "Guten tag," never rising from their chairs. Customs people can still be hard-nosed when magenta-painted vans sporting hand-written slogans like "Peace" and "LSD lives" come rolling through the checkpoints. But the commitment to a "Europe sans frontières" is making a real difference.

This loosening of border controls isn't aimed at making life easier for tourists, although that's a welcome byproduct of the process. The big paybacks are for business. Border checks have become one of the most effective non-tariff barriers that the 12 countries use to protect their home industries against competitors from their fellow EC members. Some states, such as Italy, have turned the frontier slowdown into an art form. Trucks line up in long convoys at Alpine border crossings as documents are examined and reexamined. Truckers discover that two different customs officials have to look at the same documents. The red tape related to sanitary and health requirements is exhausting. Non-Italian suppliers eventually throw up their hands; protected local industries claim a quiet victory.

The result has been habitually cranky truck drivers, and staggeringly higher costs for business. A European Commission report compares two transport trips of 1,200 kilometers, one within the United Kingdom and the other from London to Milan. The first takes 36 hours, the second (excluding time for the English Channel crossing) takes 58 hours. The report goes on to estimate that the gauntlet of frontier delays between Britain and Italy add 50% to the transport costs between the two countries. Border delays and paper shuffling are estimated to add close to 2% to the cost of an average consignment of goods moving across a European border.

For community outsiders such as Canadians, border checks are the most visible, physical evidence of "Non-Europe" — Brussels's way of describing the bad old days of splintered markets and national protectionism. Part of the 1992 reforms is aimed at eliminating these barriers. But Jacques Delors and his strategists are also targeting subtler non-physical impediments to the EC's internal trade. These hidden barriers not only increase the costs of business, but allow governments to bar entirely competing goods, services, capital and labor from other countries.

Prominent among these are so-called technical barriers, including such time-honored ploys as national product standards and government regulation; local favoritism in state procurement policies; and restrictions on the cross-border sale of financial services. European business people rate the 100,000 or so national product standards as the most important internal trade barrier in the EC. They are estimated to add close to $160 billion a year to the costs of businesses. Most serve no purpose in protecting consumer health and safety; they are artificial devices shutting the door to competition. By slicing the community up into fragmented national markets, they prevent the efficiencies that come from large-scale production, centralized distribution and Pan-European marketing. They impede the competitiveness of European firms in their global warfare with the Japanese and North

Americans.

These barriers show up in all kinds of products. Consider the Italian regulations on "pasta purity." These aren't simply an admirable defence of food quality. They require that fettucini, linguine and other variations of Italian noodles must be made from a certain quality of durum wheat. Outsiders see it as just another blatant device to protect Italy's cozy cartel of pasta-makers. They don't understand why Italian families shouldn't be able to slurp down different strains of noodles — and pay prices that might be as much as 15% lower.

Besides the physical and technical barriers, there is a third category of impediments to trade — national fiscal or tax measures. Most prominent are the widely varying value-added tax rates, which result in wide price variations for goods and services. Also targeted is the maze of excise taxes on cigarettes, alcohol and energy products. Protecting these sources of revenue has become a strong motivation for maintaining elaborate border controls.

The recognition that all these barriers have to go didn't suddenly dawn on the community in 1985 when the epochal Single Market White Paper was prepared. As discussed in Chapter Two, an unfettered single market was the great dream of the founders of the European Community in 1957. But national chauvinism and protectionism delayed this dream. Even when the European Commission decided to make some little move towards integration — such as its legislation to open public procurement markets in the 1970s — member states simply ignored their directives, letting them wither and die.

But now the 12 member states are generally united in their commitment to the single market. True, they disagree on the agenda after 1992, specifically, how quickly Europe should move to economic union and a single currency. But all have displayed a willingness to surrender once inviolate chunks of national sovereignty for the sake of the greater good of the community. The intensity of that commitment varies from country to country, depending on what issue is on the table. This combination of pliable flexibility and mulish stubbornness makes the 1992 process a generally exhilarating, but occasionally frustrating, thing to watch.

The British often seem to be the most recalcitrant Europeans, although in truth every country has balked at some aspects of 1992. Margaret Thatcher's grating style makes the British seem more intransigent. And there is a real British sense of isolation. That is apparent to any tourist who has discovered that the British ferry ports are the only places in the community where they can still be assured of getting their passports stamped. It is interesting to see plans for the London railroad terminal of the Channel Tunnel accommodating a handsome customs office. This does not look like a country preparing to dismantle border barriers.

There is a great deal of validity to the British concerns. As entrepreneurial, expansion-minded businessmen, Mafia leaders are known to be very excited about the 1992 reforms. Border checks have constrained their import-export business in heroin, cocaine, crack, prostitution and other illicit profit centers. The figures show that a high percentage of drug and terrorist arrests are at border points.

Continental Europeans maintain it is the fact the checks are being made — not where they are being made — that makes all the difference. Better co-ordination between police forces and vigilant policing within borders would be just as effective in detecting the Red Brigade terrorists or underworld drug smugglers, they say. They contend that border checks can be eliminated if there is harmonization of the diverse national laws that make such border checks necessary. These candidates for harmonization include visa policies, asylum and immigration laws, drug and gun laws, shared police data banks, and rules for police pursuit across national borders. No wonder the British don't like the sound of it all.

The area of Europe where the O'Mearas were roaming has set itself up as a kind of showpiece of European integration. Germany, France and the Beneleux countries agreed in principle to open up their frontiers to each other well in advance of the January 1, 1993 launch date of the single market. To do this, they have to harmonize those difficult national laws controlling people movements, policing and crime.

There has been, however, one little hitch — and it has neatly underscored the formidable obstacles to creating a borderless Europe. The five countries didn't count on the dramatic opening of the Berlin Wall in late 1989. At one point, the French got very worried that hordes of East Germans, who have automatic access to West German passports, would flood across its now open borders. The issue opened up a rift in Franco-German relations that put off the signing of the final border-opening agreement. It shows how forging a single market has become much more complicated with the Eastern European upheaval. Harmonizing immigration policies, never easy, gets even tougher.

The 1992 process will experience these occasional stutter steps, but it will move ahead. Not everything will be resolved before 1993. Very likely, Britain and the other 11 states will proceed at different speeds well into the 1990s and beyond. There will be battles over details, but the grand design is unstoppable.

Just what is this design? What kind of Europe will emerge in the 1990s? The following are the major elements of 1992 as embodied in the Single European Act, the 280 proposals of the Single Market White Paper, and in other legislation which, if not officially part of 1992, is at least affected by it.

TEARING DOWN PHYSICAL BARRIERS:

Internal border checks on goods and people will be eliminated (or if Margaret Thatcher has her way, at least relaxed). But external controls on non-EC visitors will be just as vigilant. The community will want to make sure that outsiders, such as North Americans, don't exploit its open frontiers for all the wrong reasons.

The strategy: As a first step, more than 100 different customs forms were eliminated in early 1988 with the introduction of a consolidated Single Administrative Document for importing, exporting and moving goods across countries. Individuals are now being issued Europassports, in addition to their national documents, to make border crossings easier.

As discussed above, there will be harmonization of national laws in areas such as drug enforcement, immigration and visa policy. Another important category is health protection. If animals and plants are to move freely within the community, the member states must move towards common veterinary and plant health standards.

Also up for reform are various national policies aimed at controlling imports from third countries, such as quotas on Japanese cars. These would be rendered useless when there is free movement of goods and services throughout the community. They will have to be replaced by community-wide import and quota policies.

GETTING RID OF TECHNICAL BARRIERS:

1. Streamlining standards

A product legally produced and sold in one EC country can be distributed freely throughout the community. The steepest barriers to such free flows have been national technical standards and testing procedures, such as rules on the purity of beer sold in Germany or the durum wheat rule in Italian pasta. These restrictions will be eliminated.

The strategy: Mutual recognition of standards. In the past, the commission tried to harmonize product standards by developing detailed common specifications, which had to be agreed on by all member states. The EC's new approach is "mutual recognition," whereby each country must recognize the others' standards. The consumer is free to choose a foreign product made of slightly different materials or composed of a somewhat different formula, as long it is healthy and safe.

Pan-European standards: The EC is engaged in the parallel process of constructing new European-wide standards in product areas where they are deemed necessary to protect consumer health, safety and the environment — or where compatible standards are necessary for technical reasons, such as for cellular telephones.

The European Commission defines the "essential requirements" for products in terms of health, safety, environment or consumer protection. Then, European standards organizations determine the exact specifications of the product to fulfill these essential requirements. The key organizations are CEN (the European Committee for Standardization] and its sister body, CENELEC (the European Committee for Electrotechnical Standardization).

Testing and certification: Just as standards must be streamlined, so must product testing and certification. The approach again is mutual recognition — that Germany would accept product tests done by a Greek laboratory. That isn't easy, given hard-to-kill national prejudices — or, from another point of view, justifiable concerns about lower standards. The commission is trying to hammer out common testing criteria.

2. Liberalizing public procurement

Discriminatory practices in the awarding of government contracts will be discouraged. It is estimated that governments, including nationalized industries, spend 15% of Europe's gross domestic product, but all but 2%-3% of that business goes to national companies. The European Commission projects that the annual waste from uncompetitive bidding practices could be as much as $26 billion.

The strategy: Opening up excluded areas. Some of the biggest savings will come from opening up four new procurement areas to EC-wide competitive tender. These areas — energy, drinking water supply, transport, and telecommunications — are all big-capital-spending sectors that have eluded earlier efforts to create a level playing field in public contracts.

Fairer bidding procedures: The EC is providing more "transparency" — or openness — in the bidding process, fulfilling one goal of the procurement code set down by the General Agreement on Tariffs & Trade. Public authorities must issue contract information well in advance of their purchases, giving outside companies time to react. Situations where only one company is asked to tender will be strictly limited. More complete reports on the awarding of contracts will be provided.

Tougher enforcement: Aggrieved companies will be able to take action against governments that have broken procurement laws. They will be able to pursue them through national and European courts. Judgments could result in the overturning of public contract awards, and new contract competitions. There are also plans to widen the liberalized system to include not only goods, but services too.

3. Free labor mobility

Citizens of each of the 12 countries will be able to live and work in any other member country. Laborers already travel fairly easily from country to country in search of jobs. But professionals have not been permitted such mobility. In the future, a doctor from Manchester will be able to practice in Lyons. A lawyer from Cologne will be able to hang out her shingle in Madrid.

The strategy: Recognition of qualifications. The community is working towards a mutual recognition of professional standards, training and experience, so that minimum qualifications of one country will be recognized as acceptable in the other 11. There has been stubborn opposition from professional bodies — associations of doctors, dentists and the like — which constitute the strongest forces for protectionism in Europe.

Mobility for professionals has been a goal of the Community for at least 20 years, but its approach was flawed. It tried to achieve harmonization of training and standards, but governments — and the powerful professional bodies — spent years in working towards a common framework. A directive on architects' qualifications took 17 years to work out. The new approach should speed up the process, but many years will pass before all professions free up their borders.

Education: Mobility will improve as professional training becomes more harmonized. Community-wide diplomas and education cards denoting a common level of training will be created. Some British universities, including Cambridge, are extending the classic three-year British engineering degree program to four years, which has been the standard period on the Continent. One steep barrier to free movement of professionals remains — the difference in languages. But that too may change, with the EC taking the lead in encouraging and funding foreign language education.

4. A free market in financial services

The 1992 reforms will create a single European market in services, including the crucial area of financial services. Until now, a welter of national regulations — from hefty costs for establishing offices to market-share quotas — has fostered protected national markets, with startling price differences.

For example, motor insurance premiums have been on average 100% higher in Spain than the average of the four lowest-priced countries in the community. Credit card charges were 90% higher in Italy than in other markets. The interest on a personal loan from a German bank was 136% higher. The cost of commercial loans was more than 40% higher in Britain and the Netherlands than the average of the four lowest-price markets. These price gaps should narrow as a result of 1992 reforms.

The strategy: Home country rule. The community's new principle of mutual recognition — that each member country has to accept the other's regulations — is being applied to financial services. A financial institution licensed to operate in one EC country will be able to set up branches and sell services throughout the other 11. The guiding principle is home country regulation. If a Greek bank moves into Germany, it will be regulated by its home Greek government, not by its host German regulator.

Minimum standards: Some Europeans worry about a possible deterioration of standards with all countries conforming to the lowest common denominator of regulation. But by and large, the financial services companies are swallowing their fears and their innate national snobbishness. The commission is allaying concerns by developing some community-wide minimum regulations, such as bank capital requirements.

Freeing capital flows: Capital will be allowed to flow freely across national boundaries. This is considered necessary if the single financial market is to thrive. A Spanish consumer would have trouble investing in British mutual funds if he continues to be limited in how many pesos he can legally convert into foreign currency.

All national exchange controls will disappear by 1993. West Germany and Britain abolished their currency controls long ago. The other senior EC countries — France, Italy, Denmark and the Benelux group — were to lift their controls in 1990. Four more vulnerable economies — Spain, Portugal, Greece and Ireland — don't have to scrap controls until 1992.

A single currency: Not part of the 1992 program, but it does flow naturally out of it. A single currency would take a lot of uncertainty out of doing business in the single market. But it would require a common economic and monetary policy, and probably one central bank for the community. Delors and 11 members want a carefully staged evolution towards this goal.

The British government, ever concerned about surrendering state powers, has been reluctant. This will be a big battle.

The EC already has a quasi-currency, the ECU (European currency unit), but it is a unit of account, not a circulated currency. It amounts to a basket of all 12 currencies. Many institutions use the ECU in budget statements, and it is the fifth largest currency in the international Eurobond market.

5. Deregulation of transport

The transport sector will experience sweeping reform, as airlines, shipping, railroads and road transport are exposed to more cross-border competition. The aim is more efficiency and lower costs. The community has been hamstrung in the past by 12 separate and largely unintegrated transport systems, knitted loosely together by quotas and bilateral market-sharing agreements. The result has been waste, over-regulation and uncompetitive markets.

The strategy: Trucking deregulation. The trucking industry carries more than half of the community's internal goods shipments, but it is mired in uncompetitive practices. The biggest obstacle to an efficient market is the community-wide ban on *cabotage* — the right of non-resident carriers to provide transport services within another country, thus competing with local haulers. Trucks that embark on inter-community trips come home empty because they are not allowed to pick up another cargo in another country. Along the German-Dutch border, it is estimated that 30% of the traffic consists of cargoless transports.

Haulage among member countries is regulated by a complex inefficient system of country-to-country and EC-wide licenses. These restrictions will be phased out, and the ban on *cabotage* will end.

Opening up the skies: The system of national airline regulation has kept a lid on new competitors and fostered high costs. The consensus is that ticket prices are on average 35%-40% higher in Europe than in North America.

Deregulation would break up scores of bilateral capacity-sharing agreements through which national governments negotiate the access of foreign carriers to their markets. It should also bring an end to the vetoes individual governments can use to block cheaper fares on flights between its airports and another country's. These single-country vetoes are in effect even when the fares originate in the other country.

High-speed trains: While not part of the 1992 agenda, the Channel Tunnel is in tune with the single market spirit. The "Chunnel" from Dover, England, to Calais, France, will provide passage for high-speed shuttle trains carrying cars, trucks and buses. When it is completed in the early 1990s (it has experienced huge cost overruns), travelers will make the London-Paris trip in less than three hours, making it competitive with air travel in terms of time.

The Chunnel is but one leg of a proposed integrated high-speed rail network that will link all 12 EC countries, plus Austria and Switzerland. The long-term cost estimate is $100 billion. One system will join five major urban areas — London, Paris, Brussels, Amsterdam and Cologne. Europe will be leaning heavily on the Train à Grande Vitesse (TGV) expertise developed by the French in linking Paris and Lyons by trains that can run at 180 miles an hour. The plan is to develop rail as an alternative to airplanes for business travelers.

Rail reform: The commission is planning rail deregulation to parallel reforms in air and road transport. The old national railway monopolies would end. The actual train tracks would remain in the hands of governments, but private companies would emerge to offer freight and passengers services that run freely across national borders.

6. Policies for new services

Emerging new cross-border services, such as satellite television and information services, will have access to a large, unobstructed market with common standards.

The strategy: Broadcasting policy. An EC directive on television broadcasting sets out community-wide rules on advertising, television violence, and pornography, and allows cross-border access of broadcasts from one country to another.

Telecommunication policy: The telecom service market will undergo deregulation. The basic telephone voice service will remain in the hands of the traditional utilities, such as the German Bundespost or France Telecom. But data communications and the new advanced services — such as electronic mail and computer data bases — will be open to cross-border competition.

7. Industrial policies

The community is preparing reforms that would help corporate Europe prepare for the single market. A top priority is to give home-grown companies the necessary tools — such as cooperative programs for technological innovation and an appropriate competition policy — to take on the Japanese, the North Americans and the new Asian players, such as Taiwan and South Korea.

The strategy: R&D spending. The EC is substantially increasing the amount of money it is devoting to research and development, through such community-wide programs as Esprit (for information technology) and Eureka (collaborative activity by companies in high technology). It has also established Jessi, a consortium of companies involved in semiconductor research. This is not officially part of the 1992 program, but it dovetails with the single market's aims of fostering stronger companies.

Merger policy: The EC has acquired the power and the tools to evaluate large cross-border mergers in Europe. In doing so, it has to balance two conflicting pressures — the desire to develop world-competitive companies that enjoy the efficiencies of size, and the danger of permitting mergers that reduce competition within Europe.

State aids: The community is taking stronger action to discourage the use of national government subsidies to prop up weak and uncompetitive industries. At the same time, it has been flexible in allowing governments to maintain programs which help balance regional disparities. The EC itself is committed to substantial increases in its regional funding to help cushion the 1992 impact on the poorer parts of the continent.

TEARING DOWN FISCAL BARRIERS:

The wide differentials in rates for value-added taxes and excise taxes among the 12 countries will be narrowed considerably. The European Commission believes that, without these reforms, there is great danger of large distortions in the single market, which would undermine the various countries' commitment to economic integration.

The strategy: Bringing the VATS together. Customs posts play a vital role in the collection of indirect taxes such as VAT or excise taxes. They give pause to people who would buy their suits, their cars, wine and their computer in neighboring countries with lower tax rates. The end of border checks would render VAT and excise rates unenforceable, and would mean big revenue costs for some countries. The solution is to bring tax rates so close together that evasion isn't worth the trouble.

VAT disparities are vast; some countries rely on the tax more than others. Italy and Greece charge as high as 36%-38% tax on some luxury goods, and 18% as a standard rate. Spain slaps a 33% levy on some expensive goods, but only 12% on most other items. Denmark charges 22% while neighboring Germany comes in at only 14%. A number of countries impose low rates — or no rates at all — on necessities, such as food and clothing.

Unless rates move closer together, some members

would be reluctant to cut back on border controls. So one of the steepest trade barriers would stay in place.

Excise taxes: As with VAT rates, the aim is to bring rates on excise taxes closer together. These are the pesky levies on alcoholic beverages, tobacco products and petroleum products. They also vary widely among the 12 member countries. Harmonization will, therefore, be a painful process.

Other taxes: Rates on corporate taxes will have to converge, but the issue is not as pressing as with VAT. There is a fear that, as trade barriers fall, tax levels will continue to distort corporate decision-making. Some worry that countries will engage in competitive rate-cutting to attract companies, putting pressure on state budgets.

"You cannot fall in love with a single market. Can a European consciousness be built on figures?" Jacques Delors has said this about his cherished creation. It is a self-effacing admission that there is nothing very sexy or glamorous about the 1992 project. It is a technocrat's dream, all about nuts-and-bolts details — technical standards, procurement policies, airline deregulation, the release of capital controls. At first glance, there seems to be nothing to stir the blood.

But this also explains the likely success of the single market. The project is defined by a list of small, incremental and achievable goals — the 280 items in the White Paper. By approaching the task in small steps, Delors, Cockfield and their people were risking that 1992 might seem a little ho-hum to the man in the street. They have tried to liven up the single market with snappy slogans and social policies that appeal more to the ordinary folk. But they have also recognized that lofty goals and sweeping statements of purpose create unrealizeable expectations.

It is important to look beyond the mundane details of 1992 to grasp the panoramic picture. The proposals amount to a sweeping surrender of national powers to a supranational European state. Even if not all the proposals become law by 1993 — or if some never get passed — the project will be one of the most stunning economic and political achievements of the century.

Chapter 4

Playing the Brussels Game

Along Brussels's dowdy little subway system, one platform stands out for its unusual flamboyance. Red, orange and yellow signs proclaim: "One community. Twelve countries. 320 million people." Posters praise the European Community's social programs, its research and development initiatives, its economic performance. On the rain-pelted streets above, determined-looking men and women rush about, sidestepping puddles, holding aloft their big blue umbrellas emblazoned with EC's distinctive emblem of 12 gold stars. A few blocks away, souvenir shops are hawking Euro-kitsch in the form of T-shirts, sweat shirts, handbags and pennants flashing that ubiquitous blue and gold flag. The strains of Europe's "national anthem" — Beethoven's *Ode to Joy* — can be heard everywhere.

Rising above this colorful subway stop, called Rond Point Schuman (after one of the EC's founding fathers, Robert Schuman), is a vast star-shaped 13-story office complex. This is the Berlaymont, home to the European Commission, the would-be super-government of Europe.

Brussels is a sober, understated city, distinguished by its magnificent old 17th century central square, the Grand

Place; its tasty but high-cholesterol french fries and waffles; the most unrelentingly wet weather in Europe; and appropriately enough in this city of drizzle, a small statue of a little boy urinating, called the Mannekin Pis.

But now this government-in-making is transforming Brussels, slowly but surely, into the dynamic "Capital of Europe." The polyglot melange of 12,000 bureaucrats, representing the 12 nations of the European Community, brings a rush of intensity to this sedate, crushingly middle-class city of a million people. Many of these Eurocrats carry a sense of mission, to rebuild their continent into an economic and political power. Sometimes they are impatient and move too fast, angering governments in London, Bonn or Copenhagen, but they never slow the pace.

The policies that matter are increasingly being shaped, or heavily influenced, at the community level. The trade policy of the 12 EC countries is formulated here. (Fisheries, for example, are a community responsibility, as Canadians know from our disputes with the EC over fish quotas in the North Atlantic.) With 1992 spawning more and more trans European companies, the EC has developed a competition policy to regulate large mergers and takeovers spanning two or more countries. Social and education policies are being formulated in the Belgian city, to Margaret Thatcher's noisy disapproval.

The EC is flexing its muscles in environmental matters. The 1985 Single European Act, which strengthened the community's powers, said all policies must reflect the need to protect the environment. The result has been a flurry of Green legislation. One law puts the onus on the polluter to pay for environmental damage instead of public authorities. Another would impose tougher regulation of automobile emissions, for which standards have been appallingly lax in certain states. A group of officials, tucked away in one of the office buildings near the Berlaymont, is preparing plans for a U.S.-style Food and Drug Administration with powers to impose health standards right across Europe.

This dramatic and sweeping transfer of powers from national governments to the community will not slow down. The occasionally indiscreet Jacques Delors kicked up a fierce controversy with his 1988 statement that, in 10 years, 80% of EC countries' social and economic legislation would come out of Brussels. Delors's vision of the future is much closer to the truth than his detractors would like to admit. The 1990s will see a further convergence of economic policies, and possibly a European central bank and single currency. Brussels will take an increasingly influential role in foreign affairs, notably in relations with Eastern Europe and in the construction of a separate "European pillar" inside the Western defense alliance (or whatever grouping evolves from the post-Cold War shakeout).

Margaret Thatcher, standing firmly on her free-market principles, has been the most vocal critic of this expansion of powers. "We have not successfully rolled back the frontiers of the state in Britain, only to see them reimposed at a European level, with a European super-state exercising a new dominance from Brussels," she said in a controversial speech in Bruges, Belgium, in September, 1988. Although harshly criticized for her contrary viewpoint, Thatcher was speaking for many European leaders who quietly resent the encroaching power of the Commission. But the others accept that by approving the Single European Act — and surrendering their rights to veto the 1992 reforms — they have passed the point of no return. They have conceded there must be a dramatic pooling of sovereignty if Europe is to take its place as an economic superpower.

If Canada and Canadian companies are to succeed in the EC, they must understand how this government and its institutions work. This is not an easy task; there are still big gray areas where powers overlap. The governance of Europe is constantly evolving.

The engine of the EC — its putative executive branch — is the Commission, and the highly committed bureaucrats who inhabit the Berlaymont. The 12,000 officials are organized into 22 government departments, called "directorates-general" — or DGs. The titular heads of the Commission and its DGs are the 17 Commissioners, who are appointed to office by the EC's 12 member states. These men and women are the cabinet ministers of Europe, ultimately responsible for the Commission's policies and programs. They are aided and advised by loyal personal staff, called *"cabinets," à la francaise.* On top of the Commission is its president, the individual who sets the style and agenda. This office has been occupied by Jacques Delors during preparations for the single market.

Despite the spreading tentacles of the Commission and its ambitious bureaucrats, the national governments of the 12 member states still call the final shots on the overall direction of the EC. They do this through the Council of Ministers made up of representatives, usually cabinet ministers, of the 12 national governments. The British magazine *The Economist* explains that "the Commission drafts proposals; the European Parliament chips in with opinions and amendments. But it is the Council which decides what the Community is going (or not going) to do." And ultimately, if the EC reforms are to have any force, the member states must adjust their own domestic laws to conform with them.

Of the key EC institutions, the Parliament, based in Strasbourg, France, is the only directly elected body. But it has lacked clout in influencing laws, until recently. Parliament's powers are increasing, and it may in time become a real legislature. More decisive has been the role of the European Court of Justice, based in Luxembourg, whose judgments have established a stronger role for the Community in relation to its member states.

The European Commission

There is no more persuasive evidence of the burgeoning authority of the EC than the managers, journalists and lobbyists who flock to Brussels from around the world — from everywhere, it seems, except Canada. In the taverns around the Grand Place, businesspeople from Charlotte, N.C., and Sydney, Australia, talk office politics as they quaff their fruity Greuze beer. The tables in the restaurants around the ritzy Place de Grand Sablon are overflowing with German, French and Japanese visitors. The Sunday morning antique market at the top of the square draws moneyed, discriminating consumers from around the world, who pick among the paintings, furniture and silverware. Brussels has become home to thousands of consultants — lawyers, accountants, management consultants — who have set up shop in the cold gray caverns of office buildings off the Rue de la Loi or on elegant Avenue Louise, the thoroughfare that swings south from the city center towards the huge Forêt de Soignes.

They come to Brussels to learn, to absorb and to influence. To do that, they have to penetrate the Berlaymont itself, situated on Rond Point Schuman, one of the busiest traffic intersections in Brussels. Outside and inside, the building is a hectic whirlwind of activity. The entrance, below street level in a plaza of chaotic sidewalks and columns, is a constant crowd scene. Black limousines disgorge parties of Commissioners, visiting heads of state and their officials. Inside, the bureaucrats bustle along narrow corridors, flanked by mundane brown-wood panel walls, to their tiny airless offices.

These officials prepare and propose community laws — or directives — which must be approved by the Council of Ministers and Parliament. It is also the Commission's responsibility to put these passed statutes into action. It is the protector of the community's treaties, and the creative source of 80%-90% of its directives. Its influence is wide, yet its power is circumscribed. In writing laws, the Commission is sensitive to input from the Council, the Parliament and the EC governments directly. It makes little sense to prepare legislation only to run into brick walls somewhere else along the decision-making process.

In addition to proposing and preparing legislation, the Commission has authority to make autonomous decisions in some areas, the most important being competition policy. It can also issue emergency regulations, such as its ban on goods from regions affected by radioactivity after the Chernobyl nuclear accident.

The bureaucrats who toil away in the service of the European ideal are a blend of the 12 nationalities that make up the EC. In its recruiting, the Commission tries to maintain a numerical balance of nationalities in all levels and departments. But the British are chronically under-represented, a product of their late entry to the EC, their poor language training, and the suspicions they have traditionally harbored towards Brussels and the continent. The Irish, Italians and French have done well, reflecting their commitment to the EC. Of course, the Germans are always influential.

The moving spirit in the bureaucracy is expected to be European, not national, but that is sometimes easier said than done. Outsiders say some officials are intense defenders of their native national interests. French-born EC officials often put French government interests first; Greek natives push Greek-favored policies. This tendency may stem from the recent practice of recruiting national civil servants who take up temporary residence in Brussels for a few years before returning to their own governments. The trend has some EC insiders worried about the independence of the European civil service.

For the most part, the senior ranks are comprised of committed and hard-working people, imbued with a strong sense of being European. They flash their credentials proudly on everything from their EUR licence plates to those ubiquitous blue-with-gold-stars umbrellas. Their healthy incomes, well in excess of those drawn by counterparts in national capitals, and comfortable spending allowances, free of value added tax, make them a highly visible presence in Brussels' best stores and restaurants.

All this conspicuous consumption is bitterly resented by more poorly paid Belgian professionals and civil servants. This is, after all, their capital too. "When I go into a shop and see an EC bureaucrat there, I just want to leave," says one disdainful university student.

What characterizes the Eurocrats more than anything is their openness. This is one of the most accessible bureaucracies in the world. Senior officials answer their own telephones; they seem to revel in bouncing ideas off journalists. David Buchan, *The Financial Times* of London's Brussels bureau chief, points out that the EC is an executive that is not part of any government. These civil servants do not have a captive audience, unlike counterparts in national governments who feed policies to cabinet ministers. Because power is so diffuse in the EC, Eurocrats have to sell their ideas widely — to their Commissioners, to the Council of Ministers, to the

European Parliament and, ultimately, to national governments that have to implement their legislation. It is
imperative to be accessible, particularly to the press and
public opinion.

Every weekday at noon, in a large auditorium deep
within the Berlaymont, about 200 journalists from 50
countries gather for their daily news briefings. (There are
no Canadians among them.) Commissioners and their officials, seated on a large stage, dispense pieces of
information, in English or French, to the scribbling
reporters. The press conference is followed by informal
scrums in the lobby outside, similar to, but much more
polite than, those conducted after Question Period outside
Canada's House of Commons.

Following the briefings, the really important communication takes place. Journalists and key officials peel off
together to the fine restaurants around the Berlaymont, or
they may meet later that evening at small dinner parties in
their homes. Brussels, because of its bad weather and fine
dining, is described as "an inside city." The streets are
generally free of joggers and skateboarders. The important
action takes place in restaurants and taverns. Here, the
selling of viewpoints never stops.

The Commission is also distinguished by its unusually
tolerant attitude towards officials' partisan political lean-
ings. The need to have friends in other high places means
that, unlike other civil services, the Commission encourages its officials to run for political office; it allows them
three months personal leave to campaign. A number of former civil servants sit in the European Parliament. Some,
after losing their elections, return to their old jobs. If they
are elected, they can get leave from their jobs for their
entire term in political office.

This mixing of partisanship with public service is
exemplified in the fascinating career of Stanley Johnson.
Johnson is an erudite, outspoken Englishman who 10
years ago was adviser to the EC's environment department. At that point he quit the commission to run —
successfully — as a Tory candidate in a European
Parliament riding in England. Many Canadians have
painful recollections of Johnson as a parliamentarian —

he led the campaign to ban the import of Newfoundland baby seal skins into the community. The eventual banning of the imports destroyed the island's controversy-plagued seal fur industry.

Five years after taking his seat at Strasbourg, Johnson decided to resign and slip back into his old job as adviser to the environment department. Along the way he wrote the only novel about the EC, a thriller set in the Berlaymont, called *The Commissioner*. What kind of issues has Johnson dealt with as a civil servant? He has been preparing EC policy on leghold traps, a form of trapping considered cruel by wildlife and environmental advocates. A ban on the import of furs obtained from leghold traps would have consequences for the livelihood of many native Canadians. Doesn't Johnson's political career suggest a certain bias? In Brussels, it doesn't seem to matter.

Outside the Brussels-based media corps, the Commission gets bad press, particularly in Britain where it is accused of meddling in areas that belong to national governments. David Buchan sums up the popular perception of the EC in many member states — and not just Britain — as "overpaid, overpushy and over there." The British tabloid newspapers are particularly zealous in characterizing the Commission as a bloated, greedy out-of-control monster. And it is true the Commission has no direct political master. Parliament is too weak and national governments often appear to be too divided and distracted to keep Delors and his crew in check.

But the reality is that, as a civil service, the Commission is very lean, particularly in light of its widening responsibilities. With about 12,000 bureaucrats, it is smaller than the administration of the city of Edinburgh, Scotland. The EC institutions combined have a budget equal to less than 3% of the budgets of the member states. (The funding comes from a portion of the national value added taxes.) Officials, defensive in face of accusations of profligacy, marshal convincing statistics to prove just how efficient and economical they are. The team coordinating efforts to deregulate national standards consists of only 30 people. Washington has about 550 officials to handle about 60 new anti-dumping cases a year, but Brussels makes do with only 96 — 40 of which are on loan from member states, to deal with the same workload. In fact, it could be argued that the bureaucrats are too thin on the ground to deal efficiently with the staggering workload.

Charges of scandalous overspending are more accurately directed at the huge subsidies handed out under the Common Agricultural Policy, which is, in fact, a sacred cow of many national governments (excluding Britain's). It alone soaks up more than 60% of community budget. The CAP is not only excessively costly, it is also the target of criminal activity. A recent study showed that three billion to six billion pounds a year — or 10%-20% of the EC budget — is being siphoned away through a criminal defrauding of the CAP, through such devices as false and duplicated documents. This is the real waste in Brussels.

Inside the bureaucracy, one of the biggest cost burdens is interpretation and translation. About 4,000 people are employed in translating the mountains of verbiage that must be made available in the community's nine official languages. At any Council of Ministers meeting, 27 interpreters might be at work translating the speeches of 12 ministers speaking nine languages. It makes Canada's language challenges look easy. It often takes weeks for many of the most important documents to make their way into the public domain, where companies and individuals can assess their impact.

The Commission has tried to save time and money by using an automatic translation system called Systran, but the results have been a running joke. One *Wall Street Journal* reporter quipped: "Systran is its name. Bloopers are its game." According to the Journal, when Jacques Delors once asked in French whether he could address a committee, Systran had him asking if he could "expose himself to the committee." On another occasion, a French writer used the expression, *"les agriculteurs, vis à vis de la politique agricole commune,"* which means "farmers, in light of the common agricultural policy..." Systran's English translation: "Farmers live to screw the common agricultural policy."

The EC has another language problem. It has created the most uncomprehensible jargon in the world, a vernacular so distinctive that it has its own name, Eurospeak. Many Commission documents have to be rewritten. Ministers occasionally reject a proposal simply because they don't know what it means. One example of Eurospeak is the popular term "subsidiarity" — that describes the principle that the EC shouldn't do anything that can't be done just as well by the member states. Then there is "derogation," the Eurocrats' word for an exception to the rules. "Monetary compensatory amounts" are paid to farmers. Whatever happened to cash?

The most influential practitioners of Eurospeak are the directors-general, the people who run the DGs and the equivalent of our deputy ministers in Ottawa. These are perhaps the most powerful people in Brussels. The typical director-general — along with his second-in-command, the director — is a veteran civil servant, who stays in Brussels long after individual Commissioners, his political masters, have come and gone. Fernand Braun, the Luxembourg native who retired from the industry DG in 1989, headed that department since 1973. A recent director-general of the competition branch held that position for almost a decade. Canadian diplomats negotiating the long-running fisheries dispute, for example, have had to deal with Eammon Gallagher, the Irishman who is director-general in the fisheries department, and Raymond Simmonet, his French second-in-command. These two were seasoned Brussels hands, who built up the fisheries department and have been intensely partisan and skillful advocates of the community's policies.

There are certain conventions that determine who occupies these key posts. The agriculture director-general is almost always a Frenchman; the competition job has always been held by a German. Another unwritten rule, says David Buchan, is that the director-general and Commissioner to which he is responsible should be of different nationalities. However, that rule seems to be weakening.

One of the burdens directors-general must bear is having to work closely with the Commissioners' private offices, or *cabinets*. These operatives have access to all the information coming out of the DGs; they influence the agenda at the Commissioners' meetings. The most important gatherings in Brussels are the meetings of *chefs des cabinets* — the leaders of the personal offices — to prepare for the weekly Commissioners' meetings. The important trade-offs and compromises are made at this level, then rendered official by the 17 Commissioners. One of the most influential people in Brussels is Pascal Lamy, the consummate French diplomat who has been Delors' *chef de cabinet* and his Sherpa at the summit meetings of the Western industrial nations.

This proximity to power makes the *chef de cabinet* a key target for lobbying efforts. But these advisers are mainly distillers of information and contacts. They set and manage their bosses' agenda; their interests are broad-stroke policy and how to get it done. They lack command of precise technical details, such as the exact wording of the directive on safety standards on power tools. For the details, they are more likely to refer business people and lobbyists to the directors-general and directors of the various DGs, or to the *fonctionnaires* below them.

At the apex of the DG structure are the 17 Commissioners themselves, the most visible human faces of the EC, the men and women who make the speeches and get their names in the newspapers. Appointed by their national governments, they are often former cabinet ministers or one-time leading politicians back home in Milan, Bilbao or Glasgow. These men and women, who inhabit the Berlaymont's 13th floor, are each given one or more departments to run during their four-year terms. The departments range from external relations, competition policy, to transport and fisheries.

Although Commissioners swear oaths not to be influenced by their member states, the governments that appoint them usually expect that they will toe the party line. The home government is almost always disappointed. It is an unwritten rule that Commissioners, once they get to Brussels, "go native" — they begin to talk and think like Europeans, not Brits, Italians or Germans. Knowing he cannot be removed during his term of office, an Italian environment Commissioner feels free to lambaste his country's polluting industries. That disloyal tendency is why Margaret Thatcher dumped Lord Cockfield as a British senior Commissioner after his first term in office.

The appointments may be short-term, but individuals can make an impact. Two of the Class of 1985, Cockfield and Peter Sutherland of Ireland, were indispensable architects of 1992. Of the group that held office in the run-up to 1992, Martin Bangemann of Germany, Frans Andriessen of the Netherlands and Sir Leon Brittan of Britain often carried the day on policy issues through their forceful advocacy of a free-market viewpoint. This Commission, in fact, often broke down into a tug-of-war between a liberal group and a forceful left-wing element headed by the social affairs commissioner Vasso Papandreou of Greece, with the pragmatic president Delors often navigating a middle course. But just as some Commissioners shine, others are nonentities, political hacks and has-beens who use their appointed position to ring up big expense accounts. Fortunately, there were few of these in the mid- to late-1980s, when the single market took shape.

The most powerful position in the European Commission is, quite naturally, the presidency. However, Jacques Delors cannot lay claim to the title "President of Europe." He is appointed by the national governments for a two-year term, which, by convention, is extended to four. The Commission's power is shared with other institutions, such as the Parliament and Council of Ministers. Therefore, the president carries quite limited official authority. Still, a forceful president, like Delors or Britain's Roy Jenkins in the late 1970s, can exert considerable influence — even power — through moral persuasion, skilled use of the media, and by controlling the agenda of discussion. Also, he gains stature by taking his place as Europe's voice at international meetings, such as the G-7 forum of industrial powers.

The Council of Ministers

Once Delors and his Commissioners approve a piece of legislation, it moves across the street from the Berlaymont to the Charlemagne Building, which is the official headquarters of the Council of Ministers. This is where the member states exert their influence on EC affairs. It is the Council that calls the ultimate shots on major policy decisions. It is, however, a hard concept for outsiders to figure out. The Council consists of cabinet ministers of the 12 member countries, who meet behind closed doors. The actual composition of the council varies from meeting to meeting, depending on what is actually being decided. On agricultural matters, the 12 EC farm ministers would convene; on industrial matters, the 12 industry ministers; and so on. The sessions with the heaviest clout are the monthly meetings of the foreign ministers.

Jean Monnet, the father of the European Community, intended that the Commission, being independent from the member states, should become the EC's main decision-making body. Instead, the Council has assumed the leading role, part of the legacy of Charles de Gaulle's concept of a Europe of states.

In their planning of the single market, Delors and Cockfield recognized the validity of Monnet's concerns. They worried that the council could become an obstacle to the single market reforms. Under the Treaty of Rome, each member country had a veto in the council on major legislation; put another way, every law had to win approval by consensus. This system had paralyzed earlier attempts to eliminate trade barriers.

The Single European Act was designed to overcome that impediment. A system of "qualified majority voting" now applies to almost all the 280 proposals related to the 1992 project. It was this reform that made the act so controversial and held up its approval by all member states. Its approval seems amazing in light of the tangible surrender of state sovereignty resulting from the act. Each country now gets a specific number of council votes based on its size and influence: Germany, Britain, France and Italy have 10 each; Spain eight; Holland, Belgium, Greece and Portugal five each; Ireland and Denmark, three each, and Luxembourg two. A measure must win 54 votes of the total 76 to gain approval. That means a bloc of the seven smaller countries cannot out-vote the Big Five. Nor can the Big Five gang up on the Little Seven. However, two big countries, plus any other country, can block a proposal by accumulating the necessary 23 votes.

It makes for feverish politicking inside the council, as increasingly controversial issues come up for discussion. *The Economist* once speculated on what might happen when the council votes on a measure ending national quotas on imports of Japanese cars. The toughest quotas are in Spain, Italy and France. If the Commission is too generous to Japan in its proposals, Italy and France would vote against them in council. But Spain might not because it wants to attract Japanese investment. So France and Italy would look for a partner, maybe Greece or Portugal. These countries might throw their votes to France and Italy in return for support on measures they don't like. And there are lots of those to choose from.

The old unanimous voting remains in effect for certain matters relating to Europe 1992. These include taxation, such as harmonization of valued added taxes. Other areas which carry veto rights are agreements between the EC and third countries, and legislation affecting workers' rights and the free movement of people. Given their fractious nature, these disputes could remain unresolved long after December 31, 1992.

The highest level of council meetings involves the 12 heads of state. These "European summits" normally occur twice a year, although they may be called for emergency purposes — such as the special Saturday dinner gathering assembled by French President François Mitterrand after the opening of the Berlin Wall in November, 1989. As 1992 gets closer, these summits are becoming progressively ill-tempered because of the wrenching surrenders of national sovereignty involved in the single market reforms. The June, 1989, meeting in Madrid, for example, saw a number of leaders gang up on Britain's Margaret Thatcher over the future of European economic and monetary union. This is Delors' vision that Europe should evolve towards a single central bank and single currency. Most of the leaders were in favor; Thatcher sputtered and raged, but agreed to proceed in 1990 with the first phase of the process — closer economic and monetary cooperation. Despite the occasional rancor, the summits usually blow away logjams that more junior ministers have been unable to pry apart through more polite negotiations.

One constant source of confusion is that the Council, like the Commission, has its own presidency. Whereas Commission President Jacques Delors enjoys a four-year term, the presidency of the council is rotated among the member states with each assuming the role for six months. No person actually sits as president of the Council. The country with the presidency chairs the meetings during its term. For example, when Ireland has the presidency, the Dublin agriculture minister gets to chair the agriculture meetings.

The head of the presiding nation acts as chairperson — and usually host — of the European summit. He or she also gets to press that country's priorities in EC legislation. When socialist countries assume the presidency, the agenda tends to be filled up with human rights and worker issues. With more capitalist countries in the driver's seat, liberalization of markets goes to the top of the list. It doesn't take much imagination to figure out the priorities of the British presidency in the second half of 1992, just before the dawn of the single market. It should be fun to watch.

An important background role is played by yet another Brussels institution — the ambassadors of the 12 member countries to the EC. This group, which meets as the Committee of Permanent Representatives, or COREPER, plays an important role in examining legislation that comes out of the commission. It convenes once a week to prepare the agenda for the actual Council of Ministers sessions, of which there are about 80 a year. They can speed the process because they often give approvals on minor matters, which are then rubber-stamped by the council.

Once approved by the Council of Ministers, new legislation is far from home-free. Even though governments of the member states might approve a directive, they must still incorporate the EC law into their own legislation. Here is where a lot of foot-dragging occurs. If a country doesn't like a particular law, it could simply ignore the directive, and not make its own laws conform with it. Some countries even support a measure in the Council of Ministers, but back down on it later. "A large gap has been shown to exist between the rhetoric of European leaders and the realities on the ground in the member states," says Allan Butt-Phillips, a British academic who has studied the implementation problem.

Ironically, Britain, that noisy skeptic of European integration, has one of the best records in implementing legislation on the single market. Italy, a vocal enthusiast, has been a laggard in changing its laws, as have Spain and Portugal. Whenever countries delay implementation, the Commission first tries to cajole them into action, then sends out a scolding "notice of infringement." If these fail, it takes the offending countries to the European Court of Justice. But all this takes a lot of time. In the final analysis, the effectiveness of 1992 may hinge on how vigorously national governments go about their implementation duties.

The European Parliament

The European Parliament is yet another player that must have its say before a directive becomes law. Like the council, it is little understood by outsiders, or even by many EC insiders. Until recently, the Parliament's 518 members were relegated to more of a consultative than real legislative role. They could recommend policy, but risked being overruled by the more powerful Council. Parliament had the right to reject the EC budget if the votes were by at least two-thirds majority. However, the common agricultural policy, whose farm price subsidies account for about two-thirds of that budget, was outside its authority. Parliament could also dismiss the 17-member European Commission by a two-thirds vote, but it has never come close to wielding this power.

At the same time, Parliament has served as an effective pressure group that has been impossible to ignore. As indicated above, the banning of Newfoundland's seal skin exports to Europe grew out of a Parliamentary motion. Proposed legislation against leghold traps has also emerged from a parliamentary resolution. A much toughened auto emission policy is a commission initiative that has emerged from the initiative of Euro-MPs.

But Parliament has been more famous — or notorious — for its free-spending MPs with their seemingly unlimited expense accounts and sometimes libidinous lifestyles. Many Euro-MPs in the past have been nothing more than recycled political hacks, rewarded for years of service to their national political parties. Free to roam the continent on expense accounts, their behavior has often been scandalous. The stereotype persists: A recent British movie about a woman Euro-MP focused on her prodigious sexual activities rather than her contributions to public policy. The well-publicized saga of the British Euro-Member who vociferously refused to do up his seatbelt on a cross-channel flight, has helped sustain this wacko image.

Europeans have responded to Parliament's limited role by staying home in droves from European elections, held every five years since 1979. The turnout in the three elections has hovered around 60% of eligible voters. Voting is on the basis of proportional representation, except in Britain which has carved out rambling Euro-constituencies. The tendency is for national political parties to run their own slates. As a result, the hot issues are often national and parochial, rather than European. The European elections often play the same role as by-elections — they send protest messages to the country's governing party, without imperiling its ability to rule. Protest parties of the left and right — such as Greens or German ultra-conservatives — tend to have larger representations in European Parliament than in their national legislatures.

But that's all in the past. The European Parliament of the 21st century may have real relevance. Many EC leaders are concerned about what they call "the democracy deficit." They see a loss of popular sovereignty resulting from the transfer of powers from popularly elected parliaments to the community, where legislation is "passed" by the Council of Ministers in secret sessions, and whose executive is the non-elected Commission. Jacques Delors talks of the need to strengthen the community's institutions, and particularly the directly elected Parliament. This need becomes more urgent as the countries of Eastern

Europe take the first steps towards applying for community membership. One possible approach is for the elected Parliament to exercise more direct control over the Commissioners, who are appointed by the states.

Michael Heseltine, the pro-Europe British Tory MP, is concerned about the shift of influence away from national legislatures, which are closer to the people and their lives. Heseltine believes national parliaments should have more direct influence on EC law-making. Therefore, he recommends the creation of an upper house of the European Parliament made up of members of the national legislatures.

Whatever the precise outcome, an evolution of Parliament's powers and structure is inevitable. Already, with its role strengthened by the Single European Act, Parliament shows signs of becoming more than a bit player. It has won the right to give "second reading" to laws passed by the council, which means it can propose amendments or reject a directive entirely. The Council of Ministers can only override Parliament's amendments by unanimous vote. Parliament also has the final word in commercial agreements between the EC and other countries, and the right to pass final judgment on any countries seeking to become members of the community. As time goes on, these powers will likely expand, with Parliament assuming more influence over the commission.

Eventually, political movements or parties that approach issues from a European standpoint, instead of a national perspective, may begin to emerge. At present, members of the Euro-Parliament do tend to coalesce into broad left, right and centre coalitions. The parliament elected in June, 1989, has a more social democratic hue than the previous one and has tended to favor so-called leftist issues such as the environment and social welfare. That could very well influence the spirit of 1992, providing more support for workers' rights, education and collective bargaining.

While the roles of commission, council and Parliament are being sorted out, the highly charged issue of where these various bodies should be located seems to defy resolution. Brussels has all the necessary ingredients to be

Europe's capital — a central location, easy transportation links to everywhere important, and a more than adequate infrastructure of offices, roads and services. But Luxembourg and Strasbourg could easily challenge the Belgian city's claim. The Council of Ministers' home is in Brussels — its 2,000 staff members are there — but it meets three months a year in Luxembourg. Parliament has its assembly hall in Strasbourg, but holds committee and group meetings in Brussels, and its staff of 3,400 is located in Luxembourg.

The result is horrendous duplication and cost. It is estimated to cost almost C$200 million — just to move papers and people among the three cities. The EC publishes a million pages of documents every year, and huge trucks cart them around the continent, following the caravan of itinerant Euro-MPs and bureaucrats.

The most sensible solution would be to centralize all functions in Brussels. Massive building projects are underway in the Berlaymont district to accommodate more growth. In fact, one new building happens to have enough space for a parliamentary chamber in its basement. But what makes sense doesn't always get done. The French are vehemently opposed to Parliament abandoning Strasbourg. And certainly, the Alsatian city is a powerful symbol of the post-war reconciliation and peace in Europe. This is clearly one dispute won't be resolved until long after 1992.

Not to be overlooked, too, is the European Court of Justice which plays an important role in defining what the EC can and cannot do. The court was influential in paving the way to the single market program. It delivered the ground-breaking ruling that Germany could not ban the import of French Cassis de Dijon liqueur simply because it failed to meet alcohol-content rules that, not surprisingly, German-produced liqueurs easily passed. That ruling against Germany smashed a stubborn roadblock to the integration of the Europe. So did judgments ruling against German rules on foreign beer imports and Italian restrictions on foreign pasta.

The court consists of 13 judges, one from each of the 12 community countries, plus a thirteenth rotated among countries. Decisions must be unanimous, unlike in Canada, where dissenting justices can deliver minority reports. The working language is French. Like the Canadian and U.S. Supreme Courts, the European model is the arbiter on jurisdictional disputes involving the EC and its nation states. The court's authority comes from the fact that community law prevails over national law whenever they conflict. And the court's decisions in such matters are final — there is no right of further appeal.

The workload of the tribunal has been steadily rising as the EC powers expand. Among its highest profile cases are trade and competition disputes, often involving North American and Japanese companies. As the new rules of the Single European Act take effect, its caseload will multiply. Much of the new act contains generalities, ambiguities and outright contradictions. It leaves considerable room for interpretation. The court will be called on to put some meat on this skeletal framework.

Note that the court is called the "European" Court of Justice. Officials in Brussels toss that adjective around as if there were no other Europe beyond the 12. But as we now know, there are more than a hundred million people in Eastern Europe. Not to mention those other Western Europeans, the 31 million people who live in the six EFTA countries. Sweden, Norway, Finland, Iceland, Austria and Switzerland are the nations that didn't want to be part of the tighter community. But they are being drawn in anyway.

Since the early 1970s, EFTA countries have enjoyed a free trade relationship in manufactured goods with their EC partners. They are each other's biggest trading partners. Of the EC's exports, 25% go to EFTA; 55% of EFTA's external shipments go to the EC. The EFTA partners are probably as closely integrated with the EC as the EC countries are with each other. They share the same technical standards and testing procedures; EFTA members have access to EC research programs, like Esprit and BRITE. The two groups say they are part of a wider union called "the European Economic Space."

But project 1992 has created an identity crisis in EFTA. Its members are so dependent on the community, they feel vulnerable. They wonder whether they might lose their privileged access under the new trading rules. They worry that competitors from within the EC might win some of their EC markets. Would they have to sacrifice further sovereignty in order to ensure this access? There is also a fear that EFTA might dissolve as its members individually seek EC membership. (Austria tried but was rejected, as was Turkey which belongs to none of the clubs.)

The future of EFTA remains very much in doubt. It will be hard to resist further integration into the community without sacrificing some trade. The EC would welcome more formal, institutional links between the two groups, and they have been negotiating closer ties. Some EFTA states, such as Norway, have proposed a customs union between the two, with a common external tariff. However, these are probably half-way steps towards the inevitable union — and the creation of an 18-member community.

There is one other ingredient missing in Brussels. It is an economic powerhouse in the making, but it lacks an international political presence. There is no European foreign affairs ministry or defense department. National governments still jealously guard these sensitive areas. They have been slow in freeing up defense procurement to companies based in their fellow EC states. For most member states, multilateral defense efforts have been concentrated on the North Atlantic Treaty Organization, which is also headquartered in Brussels. Yet an evolution towards a European foreign policy has been going on. The pace has accelerated with the collapse of the Communist Bloc and the sweeping changes in Eastern Europe. A financially pressed United States is eager to reduce its sizable commitment of troops to Europe. The Western alliance is not falling apart, but it is being redefined, and there is a role for a concerted European effort.

The 12 foreign ministers of the member states already meet each month at Council of Ministers meetings. These sessions are the embryo of a common foreign policy. The meetings have been given an institutional-sounding name, "political cooperation," but the results have been unremarkable. Who can remember an important statement which has emerged from the political cooperation process?

There is another handy vehicle for a common defence policy. An organization called Western European Union was founded in 1948 to formulate such a policy. It now claims nine of the 12 EC countries — all except neutral Ireland, and Greece and Denmark. Although it has maintained offices in London and Paris, the organization has been almost moribund. But as the EC becomes more integrated, there is talk of strengthening the WEU.

While the Cold War was in force, the external policy of the EC was to a large extent defined by the East versus West tension. This provided a comfortable framework for relations with the rest of Europe and the world. The foreign ministers shared a consensus view; they were for the most part members of NATO. Ireland was neutral, but its sympathies were with the West. France dropped out of the NATO military effort, but not out of the club. One of the barriers to closer integration with EFTA has been the high representation of neutral countries in EFTA. Sweden, Austria, Finland and Switzerland couldn't qualify as members in good standing of the Western alliance.

However, these old assumptions are much less meaningful, as regimes collapse and structures like NATO and the Warsaw Pact lose their relevance. The European Community could help fill the geopolitical void by assuming a more meaningful international political role. If that happens, those Eurocrats would have much more to chew on than merger policies and telecommunications standards. There would be nothing hollow to the claim that their city is the capital of Europe. The confident stride of the commuters stepping off the trains at the Rond Point Schuman subway stop would take on a new urgency.

Chapter 5

Inside Corporate Europe

René Lamy, the white-haired chairman of Belgium's Société Générale de Belgique, had just begun his opening remarks to shareholders when there was a burst of movement behind him. On to the stage bounded Carlo de Benedetti, the irrepressible Italian businessman whose relentless pursuit of the Belgian holding company had forced the convening of this special shareholders meeting in Brussels. de Benedetti's entrance was greeted with wild applause and cheering from his supporters.

Lamy was visibly angry. He was not used to having his normally sedate shareholders meetings turned into something like prizefights. He regained his composure and ordered the crowd of photographers clustering around de Benedetti to leave the hall. "I hope this kind of arrival won't be repeated," he snapped.

De Benedetti's rude entry was grand theatre, but not enough for him to win control of Belgium's oldest, most influential company, La Générale. On that night of April 17, 1988, shareholders rejected his bid to put three directors on the board of the holding company. The majority voted for the slate of candidates put up by the French white knight, Compagnie Financière de Suez. In June, de Benedetti officially surrendered, cutting a deal with Suez to sell a major part of his shareholdings.

Almost every news story on Carlo de Benedetti describes him as a "tycoon." No one wears that label better. He is fleshy faced, impeccably tailored, with curly black hair, slightly graying at the temples, and a hawk-like nose. He is a showman, a ruthless stalker of corporate prey and a successful turnaround artist. After a stint at car maker Fiat, he emerged in the late 1970s to take control of the near-bankrupt Italian computer company Olivetti, which he guided back to spectacular good health.

The restless acquisitor climbed on to a bigger stage when he launched his bold bid for La Générale in January, 1980. He had dreams of turning the stodgy and underperforming holding company for 1,200 businesses, into a vigorous Pan-European holding company that could seize on the opportunities offered by the elimination of trade barriers under the 1992 program.

But La Générale was something special, the corporate center piece of the closed and comfortable Belgian establishment. The banking and business elite would not countenance Italian ownership of a company whose activities directly or indirectly affect one third of the country's economy. They eventually turned to Suez — for some reason, French suitors were more acceptable — which had prudently enlisted support from a consortium of local companies.

De Benedetti's dream died, but his rude and flamboyant entry into La Générale's shareholder meeting was a ringing signal that things had changed. Corporate life would never be quite the same under the common market. The age of good manners was over. The gloves were off in Europe.

Dumbarton Rock, the craggy promontory sticking out of the Clyde River in western Scotland, seems far removed from Brussels and the cataclysmic changes of the European single market. But the men and women who work in the shadow of the rock and its ruined castle know their isolation provides no shield from the impact of 1992.

Ballantine's scotch has flowed out of Dumbarton since 1938 when Hiram Walker Gooderham & Worts, a

Canadian firm based in Windsor, Ontario, built what was then the largest distillery in the world. Hiram Walker and Ballantine's are now part of the giant British food/drink producer, Allied-Lyons PLC. Sixty-five per cent of the production from the rambling red-brick distillery is sold into the European Community. The bulk of that goes to mainland Europe where Ballantine's has a dominating 20% share of the scotch market.

However impressive that market share, Mark Butterworth, Ballantine's prim, correct managing director, realizes all this could go awry if his company makes the wrong response to the single market and its elimination of non-tariff barriers. Until recently, Ballantine's was distributed through independent companies in each of the EC countries. But as the barriers come off, these distributors will no longer enjoy protected markets. Some, more efficient than others, will be tempted to poach on their former allies' territories. Butterworth can foresee truckloads of scotch being whisked across the border from Spain into France, France into Italy, Holland into Belgium. Ballantine's carefully cultivated "quality" image could dissolve in ruinous price cutting and cutthroat sales tactics.

With this vision in mind, Ballantine's is being proactive in the runup to Project 1992. "There is a real need for us to acquire distribution to control all of the EC," Butterworth says. "We are negotiating to acquire the companies we have worked with — often private family businesses — and bring them in to larger organizations. This is happening gently, quietly and without too much publicity."

Butterworth believes there are no national markets any more in Europe — "There are just customers." Traditional trading relationships are breaking up, and management has to be responsive. "We have to iron out these old regional differences to support the brand," he says.

Alongside the old distillery, squads of cranky white geese stand guard over the long, gray warehouses containing the precious bottles of aging scotch. But Mark Butterworth knows the geese cannot protect Ballantine's against a much more dangerous intruder — the new competitive pressures from the single market in Europe.

Corporate Europe gears up

De Benedetti and Butterworth, tycoon and product manager, are both part of the European corporate story of 1992. Across the continent, variations on their themes are being replayed. Companies are looking for ways to capitalize on the single market and defend themselves against heightened competition. In Europe, this is the age of the merger, the takeover, the joint venture, the strategic alliance, the Pan-European strategy.

Companies are awakening to the concept of Europe, and not separate nation states, as "the home market." They are reaching across borders to tie up with foreign players in joint ventures or mergers. Unfriendly takeovers, once associated with undignified North America, are now part of the European landscape. Companies are selling off marginal businesses, getting together on joint ventures in research and production, or pooling their buying power on a European scale.

Production is being ruthlessly rationalized, with some plants being mothballed and others being mandated as the sole European source of a product or model. Companies like Ballantine's are taking control of distribution channels, buying out local importers and exerting more hands-on control of their brands and pricing.

Fears of being left behind in 1992 have fostered a flourishing industry in conferences, seminars, pamphlets, books and online information about how to prepare for the single market. They have also encouraged clever scams, such as the solicitations for bogus fax directories that have plagued British businesses. Managers have been suckered into buying phony fax listings because the crooks appeal to their need to have wider exposure in the new Europe.

The responses to 1992 vary widely — they depend on the industry and its characteristics — but in every sector there is furious activity, and a lot of soul-searching. The business class is Europeanizing with more speed and enthusiasm than any other group in society, except perhaps the Brussels bureaucrats. It is moving far in advance of national governments, their politicians and civil servants.

As markets open up, a European version of the Wall Street mergers & acquisition specialist is finding a home in Paris, Frankfurt, Madrid and Milan. But he has had to tread carefully on his Gucci loafers. The European corporate world, particularly on the continent, is accustomed to operating more like a private club than a savage jungle. Top chief executives go to the same good business schools; they socialize with each other; they belong to the leading business organizations, such as Unice (the employers' federation) or the Roundtable of Industrialists. Powerful banks or investment companies hold interlocking share positions in many of the continental countries' industrial outfits. There are few major firms on the continent that are not controlled by a major institution or a family. In France, for example, more than half the top 200 industrial companies are family-controlled; of Italy's 200 public companies, only seven have a majority of shares held by the public, and five of these are still controlled by family groups. When companies change hands it is usually done quietly, privately, bloodlessly, within the club.

The cultural differences extend to the ethos of management. European companies put their emphasis on continuity of management and long-term strategy. In North America — and Britain — management is more vulnerable to takeovers, and more dedicated to enhancing shareholder values. The business focus is short-term, fixed on the latest quarterly results.

But Carlo de Benedetti's attempted coup at La Générale sent a cold wind into the cozy and genteel boardrooms of Europe. Since then, takeovers — both hostile and amicable — have swept like a brush fire across Europe, whipping erratically from sector to sector. The Générale affair had scarcely wound up when in mid-1988 a fierce bidding war broke out between two Swiss companies, Jacobs Suchard and Nestlé, for the reputable British candymaker Rowntree PLC. The tug-of-war — eventually won by Nestlé with a £2.55 billion bid — confirmed that it was not just EC insiders that were determined to participate in 1992, but also companies from non-EC Europe.

Once a takeover epidemic starts, it takes on a life of its own. No corporation wants to think that when the dust settles, it will be left as a small and weak player in a sector otherwise populated by giants. The Rowntree takeover was followed by more deals in the food and beverage sector. Nestlé was the most aggressive. Besides Rowntree, it gobbled up Buitoni, the big Italian chocolates and pasta producer. "We're out to win the battle of 1992," vowed Helmut Maucher, the Swiss food giant's managing director. The action spread to high technology and telecommunications, with the German-based Siemens conducting a flurry of moves to cement its position as the continent's leading telecommunications supplier.

The focus shifted quickly into chemicals — France's state-controlled chemical company Rhône-Poulenc made more than 15 acquisitions during 1988-89 — before spilling into automobiles. Small car companies, such as Sweden's Saab and Britain's Jaguar, forged alliances with bigger players, General Motors and Ford, respectively. Sweden's Volvo and France's Renault joined forces. Services were the final frontier but they too succumbed. The big noise in 1989 was in financial services, where the 1992 reforms are expected to create a single market out of 12 highly protected ones. One megadeal saw insurance giant Allianz of Germany pay more than US$1 billion for the insurance operations of France's Navigation Mixte. The German banks, confronted with an increasingly mature market at home, have been gobbling up bits and pieces all over Europe. The French insurance companies have been busy, with Groupe Victoire taking over Germany's Colonia and Axa Midi buying Britain's Equity & Law.

Airlines, spooked by the prospect of deregulation, have moved quickly to tie up alliances inside and outside Europe. British Airways was the first, taking over its major domestic rival British Caledonia in 1987. Germany's Lufthansa and Air France have combined some marketing, coordination of routes and schedules, and other operations. Swissair and Scandinavian Air Systems formed a partnership for joint marketing, combined with an exchange of shares. Holland's KLM and British Airways teamed up to snare 20% of Sabena, the Belgian national carrier. Air France has moved boldly to control the French domestic market.

The pace of activity is underscored by statistics showing that the number of mergers or acquisitions among the EC's 1,000 biggest companies reached 400 in 1988, more than double the number in 1985. A survey by Translink's *European Deal Review*, reported 1,300 cross-border deals in Western Europe in 1989 with a disclosed value of more than US$50 billion. The report said that the figures do not reflect the full extent of M&A activity, since they cover only deals reported publicly. Mergers and acquisitions that reach across borders now account for close to 50% of all such transactions in Europe.

This process is being aided by an EC competition policy, which can be accommodating when a deal strengthens a European industry in global markets, but increases concentration within the EC. A new competition policy gives the European Commission the power to veto big cross-border mergers. The big question mark is the extent to which national laws will still be able to block European takeovers to protect their local companies — and entrenched managers.

No country has been entirely immune from takeovers, but some have been more vulnerable than others. Britain, with its liberal, North American-style trading laws and widely held companies, has been highly susceptible. In 1989, Britain was by far the largest target of cross-border acquisitions. The takeover pace has quickened in France, as domestic firms scramble to nail down their local markets before 1993. French companies are both big acquisitors and popular targets. The Netherlands market has been fairly active, event though Dutch companies can hide behind some of the toughest anti-takeover laws in Europe.

An even more forbidding climate exists in West Germany, where the close ownership links between banks and industrial companies discourage outside raiders. An institution like Deutsche Bank, with its extensive shareholdings in core industries, discourages the most fearless outside raider. But German firms like Siemens, Daimler-Benz and Allianz are highly acquisitive elsewhere. So are

Nestlé and Suchard from Switzerland, where industry is sheltered by big bank control positions. Most Swiss companies also rig their share structures, so that the majority of shares can only be held by Swiss nationals.

Outsiders, particularly the British, accuse the Netherlands, Germany, Switzerland and others of operating a double standard — their companies roam Europe as aggressive buyers, but are immune from being taken over back home. Obstacles to foreign takeovers will become more relaxed in the future, although they probably will not entirely disappear. More pressure will be exerted on these countries to loosen their barriers to foreigners, barriers that are inconsistent with the single market.

In the European style

Despite the hype over hostile takeovers — to which the above paragraphs have no doubt contributed — European companies are still more likely to forge peaceful alliances. The old ways retain a stubborn grip on how business is conducted. European managers seem relaxed about joint ventures, where two companies share ownership of another company to pool their activities. Collaborative efforts among competitors are not unusual. One example is the US$1 billion co-operative effort by Siemens and Philips of the Netherlands to develop a one-megabit computer chip. The two companies are combining resources in one specialized area of research, while retaining their independence in the rest of their operations.

Competition authorities seem willing to look the other way when mergers or takeovers are driven by the demands of innovation. There is a realization that companies can undertake pioneering R&D only when sales can support the heavy expenses involved. That is, for example, what drove Institut Mérieux, the French vaccine and biotechnology company, to seek a partnership with its counterpart in Canada, Connaught Biosciences Inc.

The Europeans are much influenced by the Japanese model of industrial policy, whereby government brings together companies to work towards a common innovation goal. The EC organizes and funds programs in which governments, universities and companies pool their pre-competitive research — that is, in advance of competing products. These include Esprit for information technology, Brite in industrial research, and Eureka, under which consortiums are organized for ambitious high-tech projects. One example is the US$255 million Eureka project for research on high definition television, involving all the major European television manufacturers.

Such cooperation has been more difficult in North America because of anti-trust legislation and business's traditional antipathy to "industrial policy." But attitudes are changing — witness the Sematech consortium of U.S. companies in microchip technology. But it is also a question of attitudes. North American managers are obsessed with control, while Europeans are comfortable with more relaxed, ambiguous relationships, such as in the Siemens-Philips link-up.

Pan-European thinking is hardly limited to technology companies. Another approach is being taken by three big supermarket chains — the British Argyll (which operates Safeway stores), the French Casino Group and the Dutch Ahold chain. They have exchanged shares in each other, and set up a joint venture to explore opportunities for shared marketing, distribution, purchasing, production and information systems. The venture in Pan-European purchasing will be expanded to include supermarket groups in Denmark, Italy, Sweden and Switzerland.

By entering this large-scale joint venture, the companies have shied away from messy takeovers and the culture shock of trying to merge large companies of different backgrounds. They can exploit the potential economies of scale, particularly in purchasing and distribution, that are now available under the single market. But each company retains control of its local supermarket operations, recognizing that retailers can't lose that crucial sensitivity to national consumer tastes and habits.

There is one way in which de Benedetti's actions, while symbolically significant, don't really reflect the substance of corporate activity. The trend in Europe is actually away from the conglomerate, from the Pan-European holding company that is the Italian magnate's great dream. The

1992 project is sparking what Martin Waldenstrom, president of Booz Allen Acquisition Services in Paris, calls "the dediversification of European businesses." Companies are hungrily acquisitive, but only if the acquisition strengthens their core businesses. Meanwhile they are selling what they consider to be peripheral businesses to suitors who find these operations closer to their own core activities.

This is nothing new to anyone who has watched the upheaval in North American industry in the 1980s. The sprawling conglomerates of the 1970s fell out of favor. Managers lost faith in the canon that says by diversifying over a wide span of sectors, a company can insulate itself from cyclical troughs and peaks, and remain on an even course. The new orthodoxy says organizations have to be lean, focused and alert to maximizing shareholder value. That means shedding undervalued assets and concentrating on core businesses.

The prospects of a single market adds another dimension to this strategy in Europe. The fragmentation of the European marketplace allowed many major companies to produce a broad range of goods for the markets they served. They could do this because local markets were protected by non-tariff barriers. Now that protection is being eroded by the single market. So managers are trying to respond by producing a smaller range of goods for the entire European "home market." Products with small runs are being eliminated or sold off; core business areas are built up through mergers or alliances. Even smaller outfits are pursuing a strategy of segmentation, whereby they concentrate on one product sold throughout Europe.

Not all these strategies will be successful; some companies are reacting rashly, and have not thought out the implications. But the trend is underway, as confirmed by a Business International survey for the Canadian government. It showed that large European companies were overwhelmingly directing their M&A activities at horizontal integration (buying companies in their sectors) rather than vertical integration (buying up and down their production-distribution chain) or diversification (buying companies in other businesses). The report suggested that diversification was an important goal only for companies in the auto, chemicals and construction business.

As these preparations proceed, picking winners and losers from 1992 has become a favorite pastime. International investors are organizing stock portfolios accordingly, loading up on companies likely to succeed and discarding those that are lagging. The most favored stocks are companies with Pan-European presence, such as Nestlé, the Swiss-Swedish engineering company ASEA Brown Boveri; the French food giant BSN; the German insurer Allianz, and the Italian clothing retailer Benetton. North Americans have got into the act. New Europe 1992 mutual funds have been established, giving buyers exposure to the winning countries and companies from the single market. The opening of Eastern Europe has only fueled this interest, firing up demand for investment funds that hold West German stocks.

For the corporations themselves, the stakes are very high. A nerve-tingling mixture of fear and anticipation stalks Europe's management suites. Industrialists realize that Europe has far more companies than it could possibly sustain when the deregulated Europe opens up after 1992. The carnage will be greatest in those industries which have been most protected by national governments. After 1992, there will be nowhere to hide. Percy Barnevik, the chairman of ASEA Brown Boveri, points out that there are 13 locomotive builders in Europe, compared with two in the U.S. and three or four in Japan. Europe has 40 suppliers of car batteries, compared with four in the U.S. Most of these companies will have to go. Barnevik believes only only a third of European companies will be clear winners from 1992. Another business leader, Sir John Harvey-Jones, former chairman of Britain's Imperial Chemicals Industries (ICI), warns that half the European companies could disappear in transition to single market.

These predictions would seem extreme if they didn't come from two of the most informed business people. The fear is also borne out by the survey of 400 executives undertaken by Business International. About half of them believed the 1992 program will precipitate a significant shakeout of weaker competitors in their industries, and another 35% expected moderate impact. Only 13% expected negligible effects. This shakeout is most acutely anticipated in food, mechanical engineering and pharmaceuticals.

The game in Europe isn't just about being bigger and better. The corporations hungrily prowling around Europe just want to survive. Part of the threat is internal, from their fellow Europeans. But they are also eying the bigger jungle of the global marketplace.

The global perspective

Wisse Dekker, a modest man, is allowing himself some quiet satisfaction over the progress of Western Europe's economic integration. If Jacques Delors is the political father of 1992, Dekker is its corporate progenitor. He is chairman of the supervisory board of N.V. Philips Gloeilampenfabrieken, the largest electronics company in Europe and the 22nd largest industrial company in the world with 300,000 workers and US$28 billion in 1988 sales.

In the early 1980s, Philips was victim of the Euroslerosis that afflicted the continent. From its origins as a light bulb company in 1891, Philips had sprawled out into products as diverse as washing machines, defence electronics and electric shavers. It was the quintessential conglomerate, with parts worth much more than its amorphous whole. Sales were increasing but profits were uninspiring; by 1983, the company was earning less than in 1974. A pacesetter in consumer electronics — it developed the video tape recorder — Philips was seeing its markets stolen away by the late-coming Japanese and Americans. By 1985, the Dutch company was playing with the idea of getting out of consumer electronics altogether.

Dekker and his top managers recognized that Philips was hobbled by one handicap that was not shared by its Japanese and U.S. competitors. Despite its global pretensions, it was very much a European company, with half its plants and sales, and two thirds of its assets and workforce on the continent. The problem was that even though Europe called itself a common market, it was anything but one. It was still chopped up into small, protected national economies. That fragmentation deprived the big Dutch company of a wide open home market that could be used as a firm base to catapult into the broader global arena.

Dekker is one of those corporate-statesmen types who seem to flourish in the European environment. A sad-eyed, balding man, he has doubled as a professor of management at a Dutch university. As befits his status, Dekker rubs shoulders with the elite of chief executive officers — Pehr Gyllenhammer of Volvo, Carlo de Benedetti of Olivetti, Giovanni Agnelli of Fiat, Helmut Maucher of Nestlé. Meeting at conferences, these top managers realized they shared a common viewpoint — if European industry was to survive, the single market must be completed.

Out of these discussions, Dekker believes, the march towards a unified Europe entered a new dynamic phase. Until then, the pressure for integration had been all political, and results were decidedly mixed. Now, the business elite was getting behind the single market — the industrial phase had begun. "Europe's industries were confronted with developments to which they could not respond without an integrated European domestic market. It was above all the captains of industry who have added a new impulse to the process of European integration," Dekker says.

United by a shared sense of urgency, Dekker and 13 other top businesspeople in late 1984 formed the Roundtable of European Industrialists. The group, later expanded to 40, became the focus of business lobbying for a renewed Europe. Its plea that Europe's survival was at stake got a sympathetic hearing from Jacques Delors.

Dekker's company also played a critical role. Philips in 1985 produced a detailed proposal, "Europe 1990: A Program for Action," and presented it to the European Commission in Brussels. That proposal was in many ways the prototype for the European Commission's White Paper, prepared by Lord Cockfield.

Outsiders say that Philips, while pushing for the single market as a worthwhile goal for Europe, had all kinds of trouble dealing with it internally. Despite its problems as a global company, Philips had adjusted fairly well to the fragmentation of Europe. It had developed a network of plants that served local markets. "We had to have a factory in France for France, in Germany for Germany — we had to have local-for-local production," Dekker says. The organization was clumsy and inefficient, but it could be argued that Philips adapted to the non-single market better than most other European multinationals. However, the structure encouraged a narrow way of thinking, with managers intently focused on their tightly circumscribed markets. And Philips was still saddled with overdiversification, as managers at headquarters in Eindhoven, Netherlands, tried to keep track of hundreds of diverse products.

In the early 1980s, Dekker began the wrenching job of moving Philips away from the old ways. The emphasis shifted to concentrating production in a fewer number of plants which could supply larger areas. Once the company had seven television factories in Europe; in the future, there will be only one or two. Instead of four factories for video cassette recorders, only one remains in Vienna. The changes in corporate structure have required a wider management vision. Philips still has local managers, but they are more closely integrated into a global management team for their particular product line.

At the same time, top management has been cutting back to Philips' traditional core businesses, with a heavy emphasis on electronics, computers and lighting products. In 1988, they hived off the appliance business, selling a 53% control chunk to Whirlpool in the U.S. The company is pulling back from the defense industry "because we don't think we are big enough in that area." The shedding of workforce is extensive and costly. Through 1988 and 1989, Philips has spent more than $500 million on restructuring.

Dekker admits that "we were perhaps more local than necessary in the past. The process of restructuring for us, for the Philips people, was perhaps a little more frustrating than for others. But it was so evident that it was necessary and we tackled it successfully."

If Philips emerges from the 1990s as a stronger company — the jury is still out on that — it will be another testament to the vision of not only Wisse Dekker but the political leaders who have listened to him. Despite Jacques Delors' credentials as a French socialist, his vision of

Europe 1992 leaves lots of room for a stronger corporate sector. The reforms are expected to sweep away the barriers that keep companies small, unfocused, inefficient and uncompetitive. Stripped of national non-tariff protection, major companies like Philips, Siemens, Alcatel, ICI and Fiat will look at Europe as a big, rich home market.

This thinking is most enthusiastically expressed in the EC's forecasts of 1992's economic impact, laid out in the book, *1992: The European Challenge.* The EC's rosy predictions of 4.5% economic growth and 1.8 million new jobs rely heavily on a dynamic corporate response to the single market. Author Paolo Cecchini said profits might initially get squeezed because of greater competition. However, in the longer term, business would adjust by increasing economies of scale, by gaining experience on how to produce more efficiently, by eliminating management inefficiency and by improving the capacity to innovate.

Cecchini's arguments have a powerful simplicity. Market integration, he predicts, will allow business costs to fall. "Prices will follow as business, under the pressure of new rivals on previously protected markets, is forced to develop fresh responses to a novel and permanently changing situation. Ever present competition will ensure the completion of a self-sustaining virtuous circle. The downward pressure on prices will in turn stimulate demand, giving companies the opportunity to increase output to exploit resources better and to scale them up for European and global competition."

That, some critics scoff, is a tall order. The 1992 benefits could be easily be derailed by a recession. But even if it is remotely accurate, this scenario poses the greatest challenge to non-European competitors, including Canadian companies. If Corporate Europe breaks out of its traditional inefficient morass, it will be a tougher competitor abroad.

That point has been driven home by European industrialists in speeches to Canadian business groups. For them, defending the European market is not enough. The challenge "is not local competitiveness, national competitiveness or even European competitiveness. It is global competitiveness, in price, product characteristics and quality and service," says Sir Graham Day, the Canadian-born chairman of two British companies, The Rover Group and Cadbury Schweppes. An executive for Italy's Olivetti echoes Day: "Even if the Europe 1992 project should disappear overnight, the climate at company level will not change, because for European firms today, Europe is a must, not an alternative, if they wish to meet global competition."

This concept of European firms using their home market as a base for a stronger presence globally is expressed by Italian appliance manufacturer, Vittorio Merloni, in a comment to Business International. The approaching unified market will mean the survival of the fittest and biggest in his industry, Merloni says. Looking beyond Europe, he believes the world appliance industry will be reduced to no more than five players by 1992. He wants Merloni to be one of the survivors, possibly in alliance with a big German or U.S. group.

There is, however, one large body of European companies that has less to say on what 1992 will mean to the global game. These are the American multinationals in Europe, giant companies in their own rights. IBM's subsidiaries in Europe had total sales in excess of 17 billion ECUs ($24 billion) in 1988, making them the continent's 25th largest firm. Ford Motor Company's units also exceeded 17 billion ECUs. Countless other U.S. companies are almost as important in Europe as at home.

These companies are hardly diffident about Europe 1992 — it will make their operations easier. But for them, the single market is not the revolutionary event that it is for their European-based counterparts. They discovered the single market long ago, in the 1950s and 1960s, when they first moved into Europe in a big way. Unlike their European-based rivals, they were not national champions; they were not tied into national industrial policies that limited their thinking. In a strange way, the U.S. companies *are* part of the process — they are the models to which European companies now strive.

In the mid-1960s, the French journalist J.J. Servan-Schreiber, in his book *The American Challenge*, warned Europe that "fifteen years from now, it is quite possible that the world's third greatest industrial power, just after the U.S. and Russia, will not be Europe, but American industry in Europe. Already in the ninth year of the Common Market, this European market is basically American in organization."

Servan-Schreiber described how Americans were setting up "European-style headquarters responsible for the firm's continental business, with sweeping powers of decision and instructions not to pay any attention to national boundaries. . . This is true federalism — the only kind that exists in Europe on an industrial level. And it goes a good deal further than anything Common Market experts ever imagined."

"While all this has been going on, Europeans have done little to take advantage of the new market on the industrial level. Europe has almost nothing to compare with the dynamic American corporations being set up on her soil."

Servan-Schreiber's dire predictions were a bit off the mark, but not by much. Twenty years after his book was published, American industry in Europe is still a powerful force. Unburdened by the parochial thinking of many European firms, it already thinks in terms of rationalized production and centralized distribution across the continent. Ford is a consummate Pan-European operation — its cars are manufactured wherever it is most efficient and shipped all over. Long ribbons of "Ford trains" are ubiquitous on the continent. IBM is a master of shifting its organizational structure from national to continental, depending on the political realities. These American success stories only harden the Europeans' resolve to complete the single market. If European companies remain locked in the old narrow, national thinking, the game in Europe will be lost forever to the Americans, or now the Japanese. And so too will the global game.

The Japanese learned from the Americans. Their car makers are quickly gearing up to operate on a Ford Europe scale. Consumer electronics company Sony is determined to develop a strong stand-alone company in Europe, independently managed with its own integrated research, production and marketing operations. Japanese investment is partly driven by Fortress Europe fears that 1992 could build barriers to outside trade. But it also reflects an outsider's fresh view that Europe is already a single market.

Then there are the companies whose homes bases are inside Europe but outside the EC. Executives from the EFTA countries sit on all the big trade associations; they belong to the major standards bodies. Companies from Sweden, Switzerland, Austria, Norway and Finland have operations all over the continent. But they would be losers if the 1992 program somehow alters the terms of free trade between the EC and EFTA.

As a result, business leaders in Sweden and Austria have been urging their governments to seek membership in the EC. Austria has already applied, and been turned down. Among the biggest players in the European M&A game have been Swedish and Swiss companies, which are determined both to capitalize on the single market and protect their presence inside.

Swedish ASEA and Swiss Brown Boveri created the textbook Pan-European merger, combining their operations into a global power-engineering behemoth. The rationale was both European and global, offensive and defensive. The two companies could see that only a handful of global engineering companies would survive, and they wanted to be among them. They are now the biggest company in their field. The Swedish appliance maker Electrolux has been on a shopping binge, picking up companies throughout Europe. Volvo has always seen Europe as the home market, and has strongly argued in favor of Sweden's entry into the EC. The car and truck maker is prepared to move quickly to increase its operations within the Group of 12 if its home country does not move closer to the community. In early 1990, it took a large step in that direction by buying a stake in Renault.

The private sector in non-community Europe is voting with its corporate strategies for a closer relationship with the EC. Sweden is the classic example. For the first 30 years after the Second World War, the pattern of Swedish investment had been remarkably stable — 50% in countries that are now in the EC 12, and 50% outside.

However, since the prospect of 1992 arose, the pattern has shifted to 70% into the EC and 30% outside. The EFTA companies are taking no chances.

The European Mindset

Anyone reading the headlines would conclude the effects of 1992 on corporate Europe have been breathtaking. The prospect of a single market, free from non-tariff barriers, has triggered megamergers, takeovers, and a drastic rethinking of corporate strategies. But the connection between 1992 and European strategies is a subtle thing. Few leading chief executives are *au courant* with the picayune details of public procurement, technical standards, or tax harmonization. And yet they are caught up in the spirit of 1992 — and that alone makes all the difference.

Joseph d'Cruz, associate professor of management at University of Toronto, is a management consultant who helps multinational companies develop strategic game plans. He also teaches in executive education programs at the prestigious IMEDE business school in Lausanne. As d'Cruz talked to European managers, he realized that their corporate strategies were being driven by a host of issues, not all related to 1992. Some are concerned about their survival as a global business against North American, Japanese and other Asian competition. Others are adopting Pan-European strategies as a reaction to moves by competitors, suppliers, customers or other factors within their industry. But the specific details of 1992 are not "a driver of strategies," d'Cruz concludes. Not that they are being ignored: people at the operational level, in plants and offices, were absorbed in such issues as tax harmonization, new standards in construction materials and other 1992 details. But the heavy hitters plotting the overall game plans seemed to have other things on their minds.

However, d'Cruz sees the single market fostering "a European mindset — a way of thinking about strategies that is particularly European." Corporate managers are now viewing Europe as one market entity, rather than a collection of individual country markets. Their conception of a single Europe extends beyond relationships between suppliers and customers — it takes in the whole "business system" in which companies operate. Moreover, there is a tinge of Fortress Europe in this mindset. They are designing business strategies to deal with the threat of the U.S. and Japan.

John Kay, an economist at the London Business School in Britain, agrees that the 1992 process may be having more of a "mindset" impact than anything else. "There is a sense in which the real significance of 1992 lies in the hype rather than the program itself," he observes in the book, *1992: Myths and Realities.* "The marketing campaign has enjoyed a success far beyond its promoters' dreams in alerting business to the potential of European markets and the opportunities for European ventures and in restoring self-confidence in the European ideal."

However, Kay and others are concerned that this mindset may be driving European companies blindly into mergers and alliances that don't make economic sense. They see a danger that the 1992 mentality will spawn inefficient monopolies and oligopolies on a European, rather than a national scale. It could create bloated, uncompetitive Pan-European giants that offer little improvement over the national behemoths they replace.

Kay points out that Europe's government-inspired merger activity of the 1960s spawned national champions in areas such as telecommunications and power engineering. But the gains from economies of scale turned out to be largely illusory. Many of the the new champions were put in monopoly positions and had no incentive to exploit whatever efficiencies were possible. Furthermore, says Kay, "consumers are plainly uninterested in the limited and often shoddy fare such champions often offer to them."

Some observers see history repeating itself in the runup to 1992. They see the danger in the airline industry, where the threat of 1992 appears to be spawning not greater competition but more concentration. This challenge of bigness is a crucial one for corporate Europe. Will the single market breed a stronger, more dynamic business sector that can take on the world? Or is Europe losing the competitive challenge because panicky corporations are rushing blindly into alliances that don't make sense? Some of Europe's industries will benefit from the efficiencies of larger-scale production, but not all. Outsiders, including Canadian companies, may offer a competitive alternative.

But what is happening in Europe is far more complex than just a drive towards large-scale production. Some companies, like Siemens and Philips, are pooling their efforts in expensive, leading-edge research & development efforts. Others, like the three supermarket groups, are combining resources in distribution or purchasing. In certain industries, the proper response is Pan-European marketing, but relatively small production runs. The preparations for the single market take many forms; they vary from company to company, sector to sector. Many companies have made the right choices; some have not.

But whatever the final score of winners and losers, the emerging European mindset is a dramatic broadening of corporate horizons. A Dutch businessman, speaking in London to a group of Canadian businesspeople, tried to convey what was going on. In 1492, he said, "a European discovered America. Five hundred years later, Europeans are finally discovering Europe."

Chapter 6

The Social Dimension

David Lea sounds every inch the capitalist manager as he describes the benefits his countrymen will reap from the elimination of non-tariff barriers in Europe. "First you will get mergers, acquisitions and rationalization, then you get 5% economic growth," Lea intones. "All things being equal, you will get a flip to gross national product. People's real disposable incomes will rise."

This enthusiasm for the single market emanates not from the executive suite of a major multinational corporation. David Lea is holding forth in his circa-1950s, wood-paneled office in Congress House, the rambling and decrepit headquarters of the British Trades Union Congress in London's Bloomsbury district. Lea, the congress's assistant general secretary for European matters, is the only trade union official left in the building. A fire drill has emptied the premises, but Lea has defied the clanging alarm bell to sit and talk with a journalist about the 1992 program.

Lea is a round-faced, pug-nosed proletarian philosopher who mixes quotations from Hegel with working-class slang. He is something of an independent thinker. When the British labor movement condemned the country's entry into the European common market in the early 1970s, Lea was a lonely voice in favor of Britain joining the European club. Now in the early 1990s, he is enjoying a kind of vindication. Organized labor and the opposition Labor Party in Britain have shrugged off their old suspicions of the Brussels government and have come to terms with Europe. They have joined their union brothers on the continent in supporting the single European market.

David Lea speaks of the 1992 program as British labor's perestroika, an opportunity for unionism to recapture its momentum after a decade of retreat during Margaret Thatcher's rule. He says workers and unions will need hard information on European Community programs regarding health and safety standards, worker retraining, and the environment. They will want to know how their employers are preparing for the single market. Lea argues that the TUC can give workers the information they need to ask the right questions. This way, it can rebuild its membership after the losing battles of the 1980s.

David Lea's forceful endorsement of the 1992 program and its elimination of non-tariff barriers sounds strange to North American ears. Labor leaders are not supposed to express enthusiastic approval for liberalized trade. It is almost as if in the middle of the 1988 federal election campaign, labor leaders Bob White and Shirley Carr came out with ringing endorsements of the Canada-U.S. free trade agreement. Such a reaction would be unthinkable in Canada, considering the threat of freer trade to jobs in some sectors and many companies.

Yet it is happening all over Europe, where the labor movement is embracing the efforts to complete the single market among the 12 nations. Union leaders are partly motivated by the pragmatic realization that the dismantling of non-tariff barriers is a necessary antidote to the Eurosclerosis of high unemployment and low growth that has plagued the continent. Leaders like David Lea accept the need for a stronger corporate sector if Europe is going to compete with Japan and America on a global scope.

However, unions and their members are also counting mightily on Jacques Delors' great tradeoff: Industry gets its single market and room to maneuver in mergers, takeovers and rationalization, but workers get 1992's "Social Dimension," a Pan-European safety net of social benefits, workers' rights and minimum standards for work conditions. Europe should not be run as an economic club, labor and social democratic politicians maintain. There must be provision for the rights of working people too.

Just as the 1992 program promises to transform Europe's lethargic corporate scene, it is reaching down into the shop floor and the typing pool. The Social Dimension — also called Social Europe — is Delors' handy catch-phrase for a grab-bag of measures at various stages of discussion or implementation within the EC. Some are largely symbolic undertakings, but others have real teeth — or would have if they ever become law. Among Social Dimension's most important elements are:

• A European social charter codifying worker rights in areas such as collective bargaining, minimum wages and working hours, and working conditions.

• A company statute allowing companies to incorporate under a single European set of rules, taxes and reporting requirements, but also requiring compulsory labor participation in management decision-making.

• Measures giving workers and professionals the freedom to move and establish residence in any of the 12 member states.

• Strengthened legislation to ensure common European standards on worker health and safety.

• Delors' promise to initiate a "social dialogue" between employers and workers at the community level.

Not all these initiatives will see the light of day; if Margaret Thatcher's Conservative government in Britain had its way, hardly any would. Employment and social measures ranks up there with European monetary and economic union as the most contentious issues dividing the EC member countries. Delors and Thatcher hold sharply divergent visions of Workplace Europe in the 21st century. Their messy, extremely personal debate is a reflection of the differences in national practices, habits and political philosophies that continue to divide Europe. These differences will not be easily settled, certainly not by

1993, or even by 2000.

However, any Canadian company operating in Europe after 1992 will not be able to ignore the social policy thrust of Delors' commission. Whatever happens to the specific measures, they do reflect the thinking of the European Commission. On most of these issues, Brussels has the backing of the vast majority of national governments, with Britain and sometimes Denmark being the lone holdouts. Canadian corporations in Europe could be facing much heavier social costs and responsibilities than they reckoned on.

Sorting out the employment implications of 1992 will be a personnel manager's nightmare. For the next 10 years, they will have the messiest in-baskets in Europe, as they are bombarded with memos querying the "human resource" issues of the single market. The opening of Eastern Europe only complicates matters, as thousands more workers and professionals enter the community, either by migration or as new states join the EC.

Jobs versus Justice

To understand the Social Dimension, remember that Delors is first and foremost a French socialist, although a very pragmatic one. His pragmatism persuades him to support what appears to be a free-market approach to mergers, technical standards, open borders and a host of other details. But his instincts say this deregulation must be balanced by an activist European-wide social policy. Delors and his Brussels advisers are determined that the single market will be good for all types of European citizens, not just managers, investors and bankers.

The European Commission projects that the wealth creation and higher output from the single market could eventually generate more than two million net jobs. But in the early years of the reforms, most observers expect a rash of plant closings, heavy layoffs and severe dislocation. Companies are already rationalizing, giving one factory the mandate to produce one product for all of Europe, while closing down the supply of that product from other plants. One estimate is that 500,000 jobs could be lost before the community's 1992 project creates a single new net job. Europe already owns an unenviable unemployment record; in 1989, a strong year for job growth, the unemployment rate still hovered around 9%. If, as many predict, the early 1990s sees a severe worldwide recession, the job loss could be magnified.

The Commission believes that during that shakeout period, there must be progress on the social front to maintain political support from unions, the public and a number of national governments. Some union leaders are already warning that the absence of progress on workers' rights, minimum wages and job retraining could lead to massive strikes and demonstrations. David Lea, the British labor leader, says, "The aim of Social Europe is to create a more cohesive Europe. If pigs could fly and the world consisted only of yuppie managers, it would be quite different. But this is a package deal — there has to be political backing for 1992 from all groups in society."

As any multinational manager knows, imposing common standards on the fragmented and fractured European workplace is a daunting task. There is no typical factory or office in Europe; there is instead a rich diversity of approaches to work and management. In some countries, like France, companies are extremely hierarchical. Everyone knows his or her place and never presumes to rise above it. Yet workers in most continental countries have some right to participate in or be consulted on management decisions, either as members of a supervisory board or through consultative works councils.

The Germans are particularly attached to their *Mitbestimmung*, the system of worker participation in management. Blue-collared laborers sit beside pin-striped bankers on a company's *Aufsichtsrat* or supervisory board, the committee that keeps a close eye on how the executive board, or *Vorstand*, runs the company. Management turns to employee works councils for consultation on health and safety, overtime, introduction of new technology, layoffs and other work-related issues. Decision-making in a German company is often arduous and time-consuming. Labor and management often seem to spend more time in meetings than getting productive work done. However, defenders of the system say the process overcomes workers' deep-seated prejudices against change in the factory or office.

Other continental countries have systems for worker participation, although less extensive than the German model. The glaring exception is Britain, where there is no compulsory participation system, although employee share-ownership is encouraged on a voluntary basis by the Conservative government.

The diversity in Europe goes much deeper than participation. Standard working weeks vary widely. Statutory holidays and minimum vacation periods are much longer generally in Europe than in North America, but within Europe, there is a wide range. Britain has no legislation on minimum holidays. However, workers in Denmark, Spain and France have a legal right to six weeks of paid annual leave. In France, the *fermeture annuelle* — the annual closing of shops for a month — is a fact of business life.

Most countries in Northern Europe, such as Germany, Holland and Denmark, have highly advanced social security systems, with companies picking up part of the expensive tab for cradle-to-grave protection. There is a wide gulf in wage levels and social welfare benefits between these states and the traditionally deprived "southern" countries — Spain, Portugal, Greece and Ireland (which gets lumped in the south because of its relatively lower income levels.) Social security spending in Spain, for example, is 10% below the European average, and 25% of the labor force is on short-term contracts. However, the picture isn't that simple. Spain and Portugal are also among the fast-growing industrial areas of Europe, as corporations pour in to the Sun Belt zone to take advantage of lower labor costs and the burgeoning prosperity of Iberia's middle class.

The 1992 program would bring high-cost and low-cost countries together in a market without internal barriers. That makes governments and the powerful unions in Northern European countries fretful. They worry about what they call "social dumping" — that companies, faced with the costs of highly developed social welfare systems in the north, will accelerate their transfer of production and jobs to low-wage southern countries. This would result in higher unemployment in northern countries. German unions fear that they would have to take wage cuts or work longer hours to avoid losing jobs to their brothers in the south. Their hope is the Social Dimension would spread some of their high labor costs over the rest of Europe.

Cooler heads point out that companies choose their locations for more reasons than wages and taxes. A high-quality, well-educated workforce is crucial to the technology-based industries that every country covets. Indeed, there is hand-wringing over the exact opposite prospect, that the lion's share of 1992 benefits will flow to the high-wage centre of Europe where productivity and job skills are strongest. The "golden rectangle" defined by London, Paris, Milan and Frankfurt is expected to do very well by the single market. But the fate of Palermo, Galway and Athens is not as clear. The traditionally depressed pockets — regions within otherwise flourishing economies — could get much poorer. Europe could be looked at as a grouping of regional economies that cut across borders. Geographers talk of "rural Mediterranean Europe," an area consisting of Portugal, most of Greece and the Galicia region of Spain where per capita income is 55% of the EC average and workers earn only 41% of the mean. In the Netherlands and the northern provinces of France, average annual income is 40% higher than the norm.

Brussels is acutely aware of the danger that regional disparities may deepen after 1992. Accordingly, the commission is planning to double the allocations of ECUs to its so-called structural funds — its regional spending — in time for the birth of the single market. Areas of Ireland, Northern Britain, southern Italy and coastal Portugal will receive transfusions of money to spend on infrastructure development and worker retraining.

This spending won't create enough jobs or a high enough standard of living to keep all the population at home. Another feature of 1992 is the continuing relaxation of barriers to the mobility of labor throughout the community. Blue-collar workers are already allowed fairly free movement in Europe. The trek to northern Europe in search of jobs is a way of life for many southern Italians, Greeks and — from outside the EC — Turks. The advent of the single market is expected to unleash another north-ward exodus of workers. In early 1993, the EC will lift its restrictions on the migration of Spanish and Portuguese workers. At the same time, government contracts will open to bidding from all across Europe, not just from the home country. Many Spaniards and Portuguese will be on the road in search of a better life.

The commission worries that these workers won't be able to take advantage of the expanded job opportunities unless they can be assured of adequate education. If they do move to another country, there is the danger they may be deprived of their home country's pensions or other accumulated benefits. Or they may lose out on the social welfare benefits enjoyed by natives of their adopted country. Therefore, guaranteeing rights to lifetime vocational training, minimum pay and health benefits has become part of the Social Europe agenda. Similarly, the commission has concerns about the number of new jobs being created on a part-time basis. However welcome the new jobs, the workers involved may not receive a decent minimum of social benefits.

However, critics argue that these policies actually work against many of the goals Brussels' social reformers are aiming to achieve. They say laws that impose a minimum wage, minimum hours and other rights over the entire community add new rigidities to the labor market. By trying to bring about a "convergence" of working conditions, the reformers may discourage the natural creation of jobs in hard-pressed areas. Workers in northern European countries are, after all, more productive than those in the south. If there is a leveling of wage and working conditions across Europe, no company will bother creating jobs in low-productivity regions. The result would be more entrenched regional disparity than existed before 1992.

The Social Charter debate

The Social Dimension advocates are torn. They want to strike a commitment to workers' rights, not only because

they think it is right and fair but also to pacify the powerful unions and governments of northern Europe. However,
they do not want to put obstacles in front of future job creation in the single market. Vasso Papandreou, the former
Greek cabinet minister who has been EC commissioner for
social affairs, acknowledged that: "It is neither right nor
possible for German and Portuguese workers to enjoy the
same wages or special security." Faced with this dilemma,
the commission has chosen symbolism and vaguely word-
ed commitments. It has left it to member states to decide
how to implement these noble principles. But critics on the
left want the legislation to be strong and binding enough to
"bring bad governments and bad employers to heel."

The result has been compromise, which, predictably,
satisfies neither side in the debate. Consider one aspect of
the Social Dimension, a European Social Charter that was
to have enshrined basic workers' rights. The charter has
been pilloried by right-wing Thatcherites as Marxist inter-
ventionism and by labor groups and socialist politicians as
vague and unenforceable. For example, it gives every
European worker the the right to "decent" wages and "a
minimum income." Brussels officials have backed away
from legislating a continent-wide minimum wage. It will be
left to national governments to set exactly what is meant
by "decent" and "minimum."

The charter sets out a number of other lofty goals:
Citizens should have the right to freedom of movement
throughout the community; they should be able to enjoy
the social and tax advantages of any country they live in. It
talks about a maximum length of working week; a minimum working age; rights to social security coverage and
collective bargaining; and the universal right to strike.
Equal treatment of men and women is guaranteed in the
workplace. Anticipating the potential loss of jobs and
regional dislocation, it ordains that every worker should
have the opportunity to vocational training throughout his
working life. Finally, there is a vague commitment to management participation by workers, although any
participation mechanism would have to take into account
the habits and practices of the member state.

In the final analysis, there is both less and more to the

social charter than meets the eye. There is less because the charter has no legal force — it is only an indication of political commitment to certain ideals. Even its natural opponents, European businesspeople, seem mollified by that assurance. Wisse Dekker, chairman of Dutch electronics giant Philips, is pleased that the commission has rejected a "top-down" approach to enforcing social policy in Europe. The "bottom-up" strategy, giving member countries latitude to apply the charter, is more acceptable. "It is more of a statement now that we have to show common sense. It simply mentions a number of things that are important, that we should want to have," Dekker says.

But other Europe-watchers see the charter as a kind of stalking horse for later Brussels' initiatives that will try to usher in a Pan-European social policy. The commission has drawn up a "social action program," entailing a number of pieces of detailed legislation. The governments of the 12 countries will be asked to approve a raft of specific laws enforcing the principles of the charter. The right-wing editorialists and economists may yet be justified in their paranoia.

They also worry a lot about a proposal called the European Company Statute. At first glance, it would seem to be just the thing for European multinationals with subsidiaries in several community countries. It would give a company the option of incorporating on an EC-wide basis, instead going through the process in each country where it had operations. Multinationals now have to report to a number of governments, and comply with a range of corporate tax rates and tax bases, labor codes, and rules of incorporation. The result is layers of paper, legal costs and administrative headaches. The European company statute, with single reporting requirements, would erase much of this burden. Such a statute has been an aim of the European Community since the early 1970s. The commission took the planning a step further by proposing a possible framework.

The statute offers one particularly tasty carrot for corporations. Those incorporating under it would be able to consolidate for tax purposes. A British company with losses in an Italian operation could use these to offset profits earned in the parent's operations. Just how this would work hasn't been made entirely clear. Some states have resisted full integration because of potential loss of revenue. According to one study, the statute is "a back door approach for EC-wide corporate tax harmonization." Brussels and the national capitals would have to work out some compromise on the sharing of tax from the new Eurocorporations.

But the biggest obstacle facing the European company statute is its "back door approach" to worker participation. The Germans, naturally, insisted that some kind of participation be included in the statute. They didn't want the legislation used by German companies to evade their home country's elaborate system of worker participation and works councils. Brussels came up with a compromise that would allow companies incorporating under the statute to choose among three different worker participation systems:

• A German approach whereby workers are actually represented on management bodies, such as the supervisory boards;

• A French-Italian model, with workers' councils consulting management on major issues;

• A Swedish system, under which the exact form of worker participation would be negotiated by collective bargaining.

This feature is what really rankles the British, who see it as an attempt to impose continental corporatist practice on a sovereign, free enterprise Britain. However, companies would have the option of incorporating under the statute or under the rules of the national states. That means a company doing business in Britain could still avoid the participation rules in its British operations. Beyond Britain, it would comply with the national tax, reporting, merger and worker-consultation rules of the countries where it operates.

But to the Thatcherites, the whole idea of Social Europe is anathema. They say job creation and social progress can only be achieved through strong companies in liberalized markets. It can't be done by bureaucratic interference and regulation, which only ties business's hands in the struggle against tough global competition. Margaret Thatcher, in her controversial Bruges speech in September, 1988, declared that "We do not need new regulations which raise the cost of employment and make Europe's labor market less flexible and less competitive with overseas suppliers."

Opponents of the Social Dimension says its measures are an unnecessary diversion from the real business at hand — completing the single market. They say this debate only foments discord, and takes leaders' minds off such crucial market-integration issues as fiscal harmonization and border controls. They do not buy the Delors argument that the 1992 program must offer something tangible to employees. The working classes, they say, will be more impressed with lower prices, higher productivity and job creation as a result of free, unregulated markets.

Sir John Hoskyns, the outspoken former director of Britain's Institute of Directors, expressed this view in a controversial 1989 speech in which he bashed the European Commission for "sixties-style social engineering," incompetence and dishonesty. Sir John concluded that the 1992 initiative was doomed: "Today the air is thick with talk of things that have nothing to do with the Single Market and are likely to prevent the newer and less developed members of the community catching up with their richer partners." He cited Delors' social charter, the social dialogue and "our old friend from the seventies, statutory worker participation."

"Meanwhile on many of the hard and complex details of dismantling frontiers — tax collection, public health regulations, the movement of plants and animals, visa requirements, political asylum, drugs, firearms — the commission has not yet even reached the stage of making workable proposals for legislation." Hoskyns would probably argue that not much has improved since he gave that speech.

The British debate over Social Dimension is tinged by the power struggle in the early 1980s between the government and the unions. For conservative forces, it evokes fears of Britain sliding back into the "bad old days" of Labor governments. One business spokesman told a delegation of Canadian businesspeople that the European Commission "appears to be moving towards collectivism, protectionism and a self-destructive desire for a social equality of the kind which nearly destroyed the economy of this country [Britain] in the sixties and seventies. We have lived through all that and people at every level in society here know that it doesn't work and more importantly that they don't want it back."

The emotional response evoked by Social Europe seems out of proportion to the significance of the measures being debated. Margaret Thatcher once described the social charter as an example of "creeping Marxism," a label sure to offend West Germany's center-right chancellor Helmut Kohl who supports the charter. At the height of the debate, David Buchan, Brussels bureau chief for *The Financial Times* of London, concluded that the British government "has so far chosen to read far greater inflexibility and interventionist purposes into the charter than its framers intend. But wars often start precisely because the belligerents misread each other's intentions."

Every spat between Britain and the European Commission is, at its root, about the European Commission's challenge to national sovereignty. Social policy is no different. The British see these initiatives as another power grab from Brussels. They worry that it could be the thin edge of a very big wedge. Much of the tension arises from the commission's view that measures like the social charter should be approved by a qualified majority vote at the Council of Ministers. The commission argues that such laws are part of the single market reforms which, under the Single European Act, can be approved by majority vote.

Britain clings to the right of national governments to veto legislation on such matters as tax policy, social security, equal opportunity and worker participation. Behind this seemingly technical debate is the real fear of the Thatcher government that nations will lose the right to veto future community legislation on employment and social policies. Its fear is fed by suggestions that the commission will unveil more "social action legislation" as time goes on.

Jacques goes to Bournemouth

It was Jacques Delors' highly publicized pilgrimage to the British seaside resort of Bournemouth in early September, 1988, that sent the British into a choleric rage. The short, neat French socialist climbed the stage in a hotel ballroom to address thousands of trade unionists who make up the leadership of Britain's labor union organization. Delors and his message — the EC's commitment to a social dimension — were wildly applauded by British unionists who had formerly scorned Brussels as an undemocratic and alien force. It was clear that British labor had accepted European membership, and embraced the Social Dimension.

It was also a daring strategic move by Delors. He was taking his message on the social dimension directly to the British unions, bypassing the hostile British government. He won friends and influenced people, but he also won the enmity of the Conservative government in London. He probably realized that pursuing a British endorsement of his social policy would be a futile task anyway. For the Thatcher Conservatives, Delors' mission to Bournemouth evoked several horrors. Here was the personification of a power-hungry Brussels intruding into national politics in a direct and personal way. Here was the embodiment of European corporatism forging political alliances with the despised union leadership. The emotional symbolism of that visit won't easily die, as long as there is a Conservative government in London.

As the 1980s wound down, the social charter was about to become the law of the community. However, it is extremely unlikely that Britain will pay much attention to it. Neither will the other 11 countries pay much attention to Britain's lonely opposition. On social policy, as on many other policies, Europe will run on two speeds, with Britain cruising at a lower speed. Only a Labour government would ever pick up the pace.

The irony is that, despite the Thatcher government's savage opposition, many British multinationals have not found worker participation all that onerous. Although alien to Britain, it is a fact of life for doing business in Germany, France or Italy. Seasoned managers accept that it can be an effective way to communicate with employees and to prepare the workforce for change. Many British businesses are quite comfortable with such arrangements in their German subsidiaries, but would oppose them for their head office workforce.

On the continent, business leaders seem to have two minds on social policy. Most recognize that the European welfare state is here to stay, but they are not eager to see it strengthened and widened. But others express something close to a European sense of mission in the workplace. They see themselves as agents for delivering more humane values to factories and offices throughout the world.

This is where the seemingly distinct visions of corporate Europe and Social Europe converge. Business sees the single market creating bigger, stronger corporations, which can use their expanded home market as a base to vault into global markets. They envisage that these multinationals will export the distinctive European approach to worker participation, social welfare and collective bargaining. Bernard Esambert, an executive with the Paris-based Rothschild group, was asked why it is important that European-based companies should flourish. Esambert thought about it, then suggested that the European company has something of value to contribute the world. "In the Third World, the European company will help apply some policies that are different than U.S. and Japanese groups. We can show the European way of multinationalization in labor relations, management and other areas."

An Italian executive with the Olivetti company told a Canadian audience that Europe offered the capacity to search for "an improved quality of life" because of its "long historical insistence on human values." The statement sounds arrogant and presumptuous, it is one more indication of the new confidence of Europe's leaders.

One Big Union?

The labor movement in Europe is not sitting back and waiting for this promise of a social dimension to 1992. The unions want further confirmation that their members won't have to accept lower wages or a looser, more fragile safety net of social benefits as a result of the single market. These fears are contributing to a growing sense of common purpose among European trade unions.

The single market and its dismemberment of non-tariff barriers will allow employers to range much more freely across the continent. Capital will be more mobile; companies will have greater flexibility to shift production or distribution into any corner of the community. Union leaders, particularly in the north, have visions of bucaneering capitalists moving factories around Europe like pieces in a chess game, looking for the lowest common denominators of labor, capital and other costs. Unions are trying to meet this perceived challenge through international cooperation with their brothers in other countries. They want to avoid the scenario of ruinous competition, whereby a factory in Spain might increase production, while workers in that same company's British plants are out on strike .

The giant German metalworkers' union, IG Metall, is leading the way, trying to organize works councils that transcend national borders. There has been some progress. A transnational works council is in place at Airbus Industrie, the aircraft maker jointly owned by French, British, Spanish and German interests. Workers will be able to consult with management regarding work-related issues on a European-wide basis. There is also growing cooperation in developing common strategies between unions of similar character and makeup in different countries, such as Germany's IG Metall and Britain's Amalgamated Engineering Union.

Bill Jordan, president of the AEU, told a *Financial Times of London* conference of a pioneering European-wide contract he helped negotiate through his union's membership in the European Metalworkers Federation. The contract involves workers of a French-based company in five different countries. One achievement was the creation of two consultative bodies: a European committee which has the right to prior consultation on important structural changes in the company; and a permanent liaison committee for the company to inform the union of developments in commercial and research fields.

Such consultative bodies are good for business as well as labor, Jordan told the largely business audience. They are "an ideal platform for a multinational company to project its plans for the future — including the standards in quality, efficiency, and safety it wants as a minimum in all its operations. And, of course, it is an ideal sounding board for senior management, an opportunity to hear an unexpurgated version of what is occurring in various parts of the empire."

Despite this breakthrough, Pan-European labor contracts are still very rare. Cultures vary widely among national trade union movements. As corporate managers are painfully aware, culture clash can wreck the most rational merger proposal. But the steepest obstacle may be the single market itself, and the corporate restructuring it has spawned. The flurry of mergers, acquisitions and rationalizations may stimulate more competition among workers, instead of cooperation. Unions in high-cost northern Europe will not feel warm thoughts about southern European workers taking their jobs away. Workers in the south may not want to sacrifice a better standard of living for the ideal of "labor unity." These differences make the dream of transnational unions much harder to achieve.

Perhaps the Europeans will look towards North America for their models. The international unions on this side of the Atlantic have traditionally encompassed workers in both Canada and the United States. In recent years, however, there have been some Canadian defections from international unions. Most notable was that of the Canadian branch of the United Autoworkers Union, which broke away from the UAW in 1985 after failing to win more autonomy in its bargaining.

Now, North American advocates of the international union are taking satisfaction from the trends in Europe. Lynn Williams, the Canadian-born director of the United Steelworkers of America, sees "a greater sense of coming together in Europe." Williams argues that international unions are the best way for labor to meet the challenge of the multinational corporation. "As business becomes international, labor unions have not kept pace. Now, we have to move in the direction of more international cooperation." Not surprisingly, he predicts that the Canadian labor's flirtation with national unions will end, as workers come to grips with the increasing globalization of their industries.

However lofty the EC's goal of a common, uniform social policy, it seems like a frivolous pursuit when compared with the goals that the workers of Eastern Europe have been fighting for. The concept of free, independent labor unions is very new to that part of the world. The events in the Communist bloc have erupted so quickly that Western Europeans have yet to analyze them in any kind of management/labor context. What is clear, however, is that the Communist bloc will generate a new wave of workers and professionals to serve European industry. Some will see this influx of people as an added incentive to improve the framework for social protection in the community.

Industry looks on Eastern Europe in a different way. Companies are thinking about how Hungary, Poland and East Germany could be used for low-cost production to supply goods for the rest of Europe. They are eyeing Eastern Europe as an even more cost-effective alternative to Spain or Portugal. That raises an alarming possibility — that billions of dollars in European Community aid to Eastern Europe could be used to subsidize jobs at the expense of the community's own citizens.

The EC does not want to place its own regions at a further competitive disadvantage against these newly liberalizing economies. Yet it feels obliged to help build up their economic infrastructures by directing aid and investment in that direction. The events in Eastern Europe could accomplish what Margaret Thatcher has failed to do — they may slow down the evolution of the Social Dimension. With so many more pressing issues to address, it will be harder to maintain the momentum for change in the European workplace.

Northern Europe and Canada face similar challenges in social policy. Both regions have highly advanced social systems, reflected in public health care, minimum wages and regional subsidies. Both are feeling pressure on these systems from the global economy and multinational corporations. Free trade creates economic opportunities, but it also exposes a country — or a community — to the possible competitive erosion of its distinctive social systems. It becomes harder to maintain a high-cost social welfare system when jobs can be moved to South Carolina, Mexico, Spain or, at some point, possibly Romania.

Delors' efforts to keep the Social Dimension on track will be closely watched in Canada. If his adroit mixture of pragmatism and conviction is successful, it will give hope to those who worry about the fate of our country's social programs under the Canada-U.S. free trade agreement.

Chapter 7

Selling in the Single Market

Charles de Gaulle said it is impossible to govern a country with 385 cheeses. To hear some marketing gurus talk, the integrated Europe of the 1990s should be a cinch to govern. Gone will be the quaint confusion of France's many little cheeses — or Switzerland's or Italy's. Consumers from Toulouse, Turin and Torbay will want to nibble on a few dominant Eurocheeses, and wash them down with glassfuls of the leading Eurowines.

The enthusiasts are taking the concept of the single market very literally. With the collapse of national standards and other non-tariff barriers, goods and services will be able to move more easily, and at a lower cost, from one country to another. They look forward to the day that the 320 million folks in the 12 countries will be buying, eating, drinking, driving and dressing as if they were one big Euroconsumer with a voracious Euro-appetite.

But for Canadians who appreciate Europe most for its cultural diversity, this vision of a bland homogeneous continent is depressing. The relentless expansion of McDonald's, Pizza Hut and Burger King from the Cotswolds to the Aegean Sea is already troubling enough. So is the discovery of erzatz English pubs on Spain's Costa del Sol and pasta bars in Edinburgh. Now, growing numbers of young Spaniards and Italians prefer Dutch lager beer to home-grown wines. Will the Europe of the 21st century be entirely stripped of local delicacies, customs and habits?

It is easy to get carried away by the fervor of the European marketers. The fact is, much of this talk about a big melting pot of taste is pure froth, the fantasy of an industry that churns out superlatives as a staple product. The idea that all-powerful Eurobrands will totally win over the affections and checkbooks of once chauvinistic consumers is one of the overrated myths of 1992.

It is true that the elimination of non-tariff barriers will make national markets more accessible to foreign products. There may be some convergence of taste among some consumers in the community. More Pan-European brand names will likely emerge. But Europe will remain a sprawling expanse of 12 distinct societies and cultures, with a multitude of ethnic and linguistic groups. France's cheeses will be safe. In French towns, shops will likely remain closed at lunchtime. The British will continue to drive on the left side of the road. The German weakness for heavy cooked meals, the Danes' for open-faced sandwiches, will not disappear.

Markets for household products will remain a mosaic of custom and habit. Take washing machines: the French load theirs from the top; the British prefer to load from the front. West Germans want high-powered machines that spin most of the dampness out; Italians like low-powered machines and rely on the sun to do the drying. Then there are cleansers. In northern Europe, floor surfaces are small and detergent is scattered over the area to be cleaned. In the south, where tiled or wooden floors predominate, cleaning agents have to be dilutable in water for more extensive application. In Britain, households use bleach to clean sinks and drains; on the continent, they use it to clean floors. The single market isn't going to change these things for decades, very possibly forever.

Within nations, a variety of local customs will remain entrenched. Wales and Scotland, for example, have consuming passions that are quite different from those of London and southeast England. Bavaria in Germany,

Catalonia in Spain, Friuli in Italy, will remain islands of preference for food and drink. There is some evidence that 1992 might, in fact, reinforce these regional identities. As national governments become less important in the scheme of things, a united Europe of regions may emerge, replacing the present Europe of nations. Scottish nationalists, for example, support the Brussels connection because they see it as a way to escape London's smothering influence.

Even the supposedly cosmopolitan European manager has fairly parochial tastes. A survey of top business people co-sponsored by *The Economist* suggests these supposed jet-setters spend the bulk of their time in their offices — and more than 70% in their own countries. The odds are that a German businessperson still prefers to relax with a bottle of local brew than with a Eurobrand like Kronenburg or Stella Artois.

Many businesspeople are, in fact, ambivalent about the idea of a uniform Euromarket. A German banker, quoted in a Canadian survey of European business attitudes, says: "[Europe] will not be a harmonized market. Even within Germany, there is and will be a difference between north and south, between city and country. The larger EC will still have different markets, some more attractive than others, and never really one in structure."

Companies that have developed successful European or global products are also wary about going overboard. Parents all over the world stub their stocking feet each morning on those little multi-colored building blocks made by the Lego toy company of Denmark. Lego has built an amusement park beside its world headquarters in Western Denmark that attracts millions of budding little Euroconsumers. But this consummate marketer remains skeptical about the potential to build strong Eurobrands.

Its marketing manager told the consulting group, Business International, that a "European customer" has not yet developed. The differences in language, climate, culture and average income result in a mixture of preferences and buying power. "There is a general trend toward the creation of this customer but the trend moves very slowly," he says.

As the Lego manager suggests, consumer markets will retain a national flavor as long as there are vast income imbalances among, and within, the 12 countries. In 1987, for example, the difference in average income between the poorest and richest EC countries was almost 140%. Moreover, Europeans have one strong line of defense against a total leveling of taste — the continent's diversity of languages. The Community has nine official languages, and as many as 30 dialects. *Vive la difference* — or some equivalent in a local dialect — will likely remain the rallying cry in all markets.

The marketing conundrum

The challenge for European — and North American — companies is determining which products can be pitched to a continent-wide market and which must retain a local identity. An executive of a major food company, quoted in *Advertising Age*, says the best candidates for European, rather than national, selling are entirely new products and those not involving strong cultural ties. An established product like coffee is not easy to internationalize. "It is associated with different emotions and is more tradition-oriented," the executive explains. Coffee drinkers who have traveled from Britain to France would nod their heads knowingly. Nestlé, the biggest instant coffee merchandiser in the world, has to process 200 different blends of its Nescafé brand to serve its diverse local markets.

Companies are understandably divided on how to approach this conundrum of uniform-yet-diverse consumers. A survey of 400 chief executives undertaken for the Canadian government shows that certain industries expect the single market to fashion a more homogeneous Euroconsumer. These sectors include energy, metals, autos, electrical/electronics and insurance. However, others put their faith in a continuing differentiation between national markets. Among these are building materials, electronic data processing, banking and — significantly — consumer goods.

Even when a product would seem to have a wide European appeal, marketers must tailor their advertising messages to the local market. They must be alert to the dangers of turning off national consumers with advertising that is insensitive to their perceptions. They have to struggle with the chore of making an ad reflect the essence of a good European idea but remain sympathetic to national tastes.

Some have managed to solve that dilemma through powerful visual images. Youth-oriented consumer products such as Coca-Cola and Levi jeans are most effectively promoted this way. However, not all goods can be advertised through a formula of catchy rock music, attractive young faces, and no spoken words.

Even the style of advertising can differ from one country to another. According to *The Economist* magazine, the French like to play on style or sex; the British ads draw heavily on humor. Germans appreciate factual declarations in strong headlines. Italian advertisements are noted for displays of emotion. Spaniards have a tendency to use melodrama. These sound like simplistic national stereotypes, but they cannot be ignored.

The *Wall Street Journal* cited the case of Proctor & Gamble which decided to sell a new brand of laundry detergent across Europe. After giving careful thought, P&G ended up with five different commercials for five different markets. Each one shows a housewife in her laundry room telling her teenage son that Ariel detergent removes stubborn dirt even at low water temperatures. But each housewife looks different — the blonde and glamorous Italian; the perky Frenchwoman with curled hair and turned up collar. "The English mom is a cross between Mary Poppins and June Cleaver, with pearls, pretty dress and soothing voice," the *Wall St. Journal* article says.

And yet there is some hard reality to this mushy myth of the Euroconsumer and the pervasive Eurobrand. The 1992 project will break down national product standards, allowing products like food and drink to circulate much more freely. Regulations on food additives and package labeling will become homogeneous. The elimination of standards and border checks will allow more centralized production and distribution. Prices across Europe will generally drop, and price variations in different countries will narrow. The deregulation of transport will lower shipping costs. It should be possible to produce larger quantities of a smaller number of standardized products, and do it more efficiently.

Furthermore, there will likely be some smoothing of cultural differences, and that may allow certain products to gain wider recognition and sales. Over long periods of time, consumers may think and shop more alike, although they will be far from homogeneous.

And it is not just the 1992 program that is a catalyst for these changes. Europe, like the rest of the world, is undergoing a communications revolution. Satellites can beam television signals into every corner of the common market. The European Community has developed a common broadcast policy that removes many of the regulatory barriers to such Pan-European television. Newly formed satellite broadcasters, like Rupert Murdoch's Sky Channel, are counting on a burst of Pan-European advertising to complement their programming. Satellite broadcasters have suffered teething pains, and have lost tons of money, but they appear to be the wave of the future.

The looming competition from satellites is putting pressure on governments to permit licensing for more private TV channels. National standards for TV advertising are being replaced by community-wide standards. With this comes pressure to remove endearing local rules, like the Dutch requirement that television ads for candy display a toothbrush in the corner.

In the print area, there are increasing numbers of Pan-European journals, such as *Elle, The Financial Times* of London, *The Economist* and *The Wall Street Journal Europe.* Also, media companies, such as Britain's Pearson Group and its Dutch ally Elsevier, are setting themselves up as European entities.

Marketing people contend that the EC's big international selling job on 1992's benefits is itself contributing to a more Pan-European outlook among business people and consumers. The single market's looser immigration and residency rules will make it easier for people to live and work outside their home countries, exposing more consumers to foreign tastes and fashions.

With the media becoming Europeanized, consumer spending is "the big unexploited area, the big unknown" in Europe 1992, says Douglas Ritchie, managing director of British Alcan, the major European subsidiary of Canada's Alcan Aluminum. Ritchie expects that the single market will usher in a new age of consumerism, and companies will have to react: "As the media opens up, we will get economies of production, and possibly more standardization of taste." But he is unsure how far this trend will go.

Some companies are already looking at Europe as a single market. The U.S. consumer goods company Johnson & Johnson, in launching a new line of feminine hygiene products in Europe, developed a common marketing strategy for the entire continent. The Swiss food company Nestlé and the U.S. firm General Mills have teamed up with a joint venture to sell U.S.-style cold cereals right across Europe, not just in their English-speaking strongholds of England and Ireland. No doubt, they visualize breakfast waitresses at a French hotels asking, "Will that be croissants or Cheerios, monsieur?"

As they pitch their message on a continent-wide basis, big advertising spenders are streamlining their complements of ad agencies. They have smaller numbers of agencies, with individual agencies taking on a European-wide mandate for certain brands. The big Netherlands-based food company Sara Lee/Douwe Egberts, for example, has reduced its agency team to four shops from more than 40 in the past. These new Pan-European marketing campaigns will mean hefty increases in ad budgets. Total advertising spending, about US$50 billion in 1988, is running at less than half the level in the United States. This gap should begin to narrow. With all these pounds, francs and lira finally dangling before them, agencies are positioning themselves to market brands through the satellite television channels and European-wide publications.

Just as the ad industry is concentrating on a global basis to serve multinational clients, there is a trend towards cross-continental networks of agencies. Mergers and cross-continental alliances are becoming common, often with local firms teaming up with large international agencies. These links are vital for medium-sized firms that are in danger of losing out to the big global shops unless they can ally with like-minded partners in other countries.

Bring on the Eurobrands

These mega-agencies dream about snagging big accounts for products that are widely recognized and sold throughout Europe. What's more, the big consumer goods companies are betting heavily that there will be more of these Eurobrands after 1992. These expectations have been a driving force behind the explosion of takeovers and mergers over the past few years. Some of the biggest takeover deals have been inspired by the hope of acquiring a potential European or global brand. Such well-known names as Kit Kat chocolate bars, HP Sauce, Louis Vuitton luggage and the cognacs Martel and Hennessy have changed hands in the takeover blitz. The intoxicating appeal of well-known labels lay behind the French company Pernod Ricard's 1988 takeover of Irish Distillers, with its venerable whiskeys, Jameson and Old Bushmills.

The managers who hatch these deals are not acting just on the basis that 1992 will make it easier to distribute products, or that Europeans will become more uniform in their buying habits. They also recognize that 1992 has raised the potential payoff from a hot brand. The people of Europe will have a lot more money to throw around. The vast benefits expected to flow from the single market are largely consumer-driven. The consumer is the new monarch in Europe.

In the post-Second World War period, up until the mid-1980s, Europe's governments looked to production-driven solutions for their economic problems. If they were concerned about employment and the strength of the national economy, governments would direct aid and incentives to their national corporations. The corporations were expected to maintain or increase production and save jobs.

But corporate favoritism spawned non-tariff barriers and inefficient national industries. Ignored and underappreciated consumers footed the bill for the lack of competition by paying higher prices. Similar products are sold for a wide range of prices across the 12 economies. In recent years, the variation in before-tax prices — the difference between the highest and lowest prices across the 12 nations — has been 31% for women's stockings, 49% for books, 50% for telephone services, and 27% for tea. The average variation for all consumer goods was 15%, and for production equipment, 12.4%. Some of the difference could be attributed to "natural reasons," such as transportation costs and variations in tastes. However, the primary factor was lack of competition, and the absence of a true single market.

The 1992 project will knock the props out from under this system, allowing foreign competitors to slip inside national markets. Lower prices caused by enhanced competition should put more money into the pockets of consumers. The European Commission's report on the economic effects of 1992, spearheaded by Italian Paolo Cecchini, estimates that competition will drive down consumer prices by an average of 6.1% over the first five years. Economists say the reductions will trigger a more dynamic economy, higher growth and stronger European corporations. This in turn should generate another secondary wave of higher personal wealth.

The upturn in prosperity will not be uniform across Europe, however. Some companies, regions and workers will lose in the shakeout, as industry reorganizes over the next five years.

Still, EC economists maintain that over the long term, the majority of Europeans should benefit. Consumers apparently share these rising expectations. A forecast of spending patterns released in mid-1989 by the Economist Intelligence Unit, a consulting group, paints a picture of a much wealthier shopper in the mid-1990s. The report says total spending power of EC consumers will have increased by more than 50% between 1989 and 1993. It predicts that as a proportion of U.S. consumer spending, the spending power of Europeans is expected to rise to 97% by 1993, up from 87% in 1987.

This surge in spending will be accompanied by striking changes in consumption patterns. More will be spent on homes, health, leisure and "green and healthy products,"

110

the survey says. Products most frequently mentioned are washer-dryers, compact disk players, satellite TV equipment, prepared foods and low-calorie drinks.

Predictions like these are what cause Europe's corporate managers to lust after those all-conquering brand names. But the business response to 1992 troubles one observer, Paul Geroski, an economist who specializes in business strategies at London Business School. He sees an implicit assumption in the European Commission's 1992 program that the single market will be populated with "a small number of giant Eurofirms, each producing a small range of Eurogoods on a massive Europe-wide scale."

Even if it were possible to create such uniformity — and Geroski believes it isn't — it would not be a positive development. Writing in the book, *1992: Myths and Realities*, he says "it is hard to believe that it is in any one's interests to have a few large arthritic dinosaurs thrashing about on the European industrial landscape, and there is nothing at all anti-European about the shivers of apprehension that this visions sends up one's spine. What is — and always has been — distinctive about Europe is its rich internal diversity — the source of much of the joy and cultural enrichment that its inhabitants have come to value."

Geroski, like many corporate managers, believes the collapse of trade barriers will foster greater European affluence. But this affluence, he says, will lead to a demand for greater diversity of goods and services, not a narrowing of consumer taste that many managers are counting on. He is scornful of European companies that blindly pursue production economies of scale, assuming they will be able to produce and sell vast quantities of standardized goods.

Geroski believes the single market will create a massive market, but not necessarily a market for mass produced goods. "In the United Kingdom, for example, there are marked regional preferences for alcoholic drinks with Scotland, the Midlands and the Southeast consuming scotch, bitter and lagers in varying proportions. Across the Channel in France, preferences run more towards wine and further East, back towards beer (although not for a variety preferred by many British consumers.)"

"Unifying the internal market will not turn us all into wine drinkers even if the price of wine is halved by the exploitation of scale economies. What is much more likely is that the range of drinks consumed throughout Europe will widen considerably. Not only will more scotch be sold in Germany but a much wider range of whiskies are likely to emerge and be made available, even in Scotland."

"What will result from 1992 then is not a large mass market but a large market composed of very heterogeneous consumers. Further, as incomes rise throughout the community, the taste for diversity will if anything rise."

Geroski's analysis suggests that there may well be a proliferation of Eurobrands after 1992, but these won't necessarily be brands that are produced or consumed on a mass scale. In many cases, national products manufactured by small- to medium-sized companies may find a wider continental market as barriers to trade and taste fall away.

There is one category of product that might qualify as a Eurobrand. This is the expensive, high-quality item sold to the upper middle class, including affluent business people and professionals. This elite of big spenders constitutes an internationally oriented, highly mobile group of shoppers. They move easily from London to Paris to Rome. Many are multilingual. They build up an enormous appetite for a cosmopolitan mix of products — Aran sweaters, Rolex watches, BMW cars, Chateau Margaux wines, Glenfiddich scotch, Mont Blanc pens.

Corporate strategists are betting these big-spending Euroconsumers will become even more wealthy and more mobile after 1992. It is no accident that many of the mergers and takeovers involve luxury goods with internationally recognized brand names, like Louis Vuitton, Chateau Latour, Hennessy, Martel, Jaguar and Hermes. If the single market does generate more general affluence, this elite group of consumers should grow in numbers. Also, the population of Western Europe is aging, very dramatically in countries such as Germany. Some analysts believe that might accelerate the shift towards higher-quality, expensive items, and away from mass-produced goods for less affluent consumers.

Hill Samuel Bank Ltd., the British investment banker, concludes in its study of mergers & acquisition strategies in the single market, that "cultural differences are narrowing at the top where people are most mobile and wealthy and business more international. Affluent consumers are becoming more Europeanized." It cites the example of Scottish-based Dawson International, a woolen company which sells its Pringle and Ballantyne sweaters in all the well-off markets of Europe.

Companies like Dawson will satisfy these expensive, high-quality tastes on a continent-wide basis, perhaps creating some greater efficiencies in their production, distribution and marketing. Even quite small companies might be able to exploit these advantages as they expand sales across national boundaries. There may, in fact, be some golden opportunities for Canadian firms that sell specialized luxury goods. But at the household level, where washers, dryers, cleansers and cheeses are the staple goods, markets may remain quite national and fragmented for some time to come.

Besides the well-off, two other categories of potential Euroconsumers come to mind. One is the business buyer. Business purchases of computers, fax machines and power generators are less influenced by personal tastes or local custom than consumer shopping. Quality, price and systems compatibility are the big determinants of purchase decisions. With technical standards becoming more uniform, big Eurobrands could flourish in these markets, and mass, standardized production is more promising.

Another category of consumers is particularly susceptible to a Europitch in advertising. Teenagers, the Coke and Levis crowd, appear to have more in common in their buying patterns than other groups. They are the targets of trendy commercials that exploit fashion trends, celebrities and rock music. Their icons like George Michael and Michael Jackson are recognizable anywhere in Europe — and in the world. The coming generation may turn out to be more European than its parents. But that has been predicted before. Weren't the Beatles and their wide following in the 1960s supposed to usher in an era of global conformity? Well, it didn't quite happen that way.

Another stimulus to Eurobrands could come from the retail sector. Store chains have been slow in going European because of concerns that varying tastes in different markets would make such operations hopelessly chaotic. Only the stylish Benetton sweater shops have managed to pull it off. "Within Europe, there is no other retailer operating in global terms on the scale of Benetton," says a report by Nomura Research Institute.

Others failed to manage Pan-European expansion successfully, and have pulled back to their safe national markets. Now, the 1992 phenomenon is sparking a reappraisal of this idea. The hugely successful British department store Marks & Spencers is moving into the Continent, particularly to France. The German supermarket chain Tengelmann has ambitious plans for the Netherlands, Spain and Portugal. The French grocery chain Carrefour is on an expansion kick; so is the Belgian department store chain GB-Inno-BM.

The 1992 project is driving these decisions. The end of non-tariff barriers will allow retailers to rationalize their buying power and distribution networks. The relaxation of border checks permits stores in several neighboring countries to be served from a single warehouse. The chains also feel they must build up more purchasing clout to deal with the increasing Pan-European concentration of the wholesalers and manufacturers they must buy from. As they expand, these retailers will lead the way towards more uniform prices in the 12 countries. And chain stores with a wide presence in the EC are good vehicles to promote and sell European brands.

The interest in Eurobrands is in fact a subset of a wider phenomenon — the fascination with global brands. Both concepts have a simple, tantalizing appeal. Product names with wide recognition and franchises spanning the world are highly prized commodities. Those companies that don't have them are trying to buy or build them. Global brands are viewed as reservoirs of immensely valuable hidden assets. That thinking has sparked outrageously expensive takeover auctions for companies, such as RJR Nabisco or Pillsbury, that own these household names.

The appeal of globalization is captured by Kenichi Ohmae, a management consultant for McKinsey & Co. in Tokyo, writing in *Harvard Business Review*: "Whatever their nationality, consumers in the Triad [the U.S., Japan, and Europe] increasingly receive the same information, seek the same kinds of lifestyles and desire the same kinds of products. They all want the best products available, at the lowest prices possible. Everyone in a sense wants to live — and shop — in California."

This analysis is, of course, provocative and intentionally simplistic. Look beneath that simplistic image of global Californians and you can find a lot of regional diversity. Japanese, Europeans and North Americans are different in how they live, what they eat. The challenge for companies in Europe — and around the world — is how to sell products according to a global strategy but to respond locally at the same time. "Plan global but act local" should be the approach of any company with transnational ambitions.

The culture confrontation

Ohmae's image of pervasive American pop culture — fed by global advertising, movies and television — causes many Europeans to break into a cold sweat. They welcome the Pan-European broadcasting and community-wide advertising, but they are acutely concerned about the programs that will fill in the time between the ads. This thinking reflects a sensitivity, felt strongly on the the Continent, and particularly in France, that Europe may be in danger of losing its cherished cultures. They see this homogenizing threat coming not from their fellow Europeans — not from commercials or television shows produced in London, Paris or Frankfurt — but from the American entertainment juggernaut.

Their worry is that with the opening up of the European airwaves, the continent will be fed an even greater diet of "Dallas," "Dynasty," "Cheers" and "thirtysomething." They dread the prospect of the American soap operas marching inexorably across European TV screens, leaving the ruins of local cultures in their wake.

(The British might argue that a more critical threat to their culture comes from the Australians whose soap operas are the daytime TV craze.) The distinct cultures of Scots, Basques, Friulians and Bavarians are threatened more by Blake Carrington and "The Young and the Restless" than Asterix the Gaul.

Jacques Delors and the European Commission share these concerns. The new EC broadcasting directive gives broadcasters the right to transmit channels anywhere in Europe. But a key condition is that a majority of programs shown are produced in the European Community. Some community members, led by the French, had proposed 60% content rules, but these proposals were relaxed after furious lobbying by the U.S. and its entertainment industry, which characterized the directive as another building block of Fortress Europe. The U.S. entertainment industry sells about US$800 million of programming a year into Europe.

The EC's 50% content quota is not legally binding; it is more of a statement of intent. The rule calls for stations to broadcast a majority of European-made programs "where practicable." The directive, called *Television sans Frontières* also sets out the rules for advertising standards, television violence and pornography.

There is a good reason why American television is so feared. Home-grown programming, with the possible exception of some British productions, is uniformly bad in Europe. Even the French, the continent's cultural defenders, produce dreadful shows. But the cultural continentalists say this is precisely why European programming, still in its development years, must be protected and nurtured. European Commission President Jacques Delors, echoing many a Canadian cultural nationalist, asks: "Do we not have the right to perpetuate our traditions? We cannot treat culture as we treat refrigerators and cars."

Delors' statement reflects the great gulf in perceptions between Americans and the Europeans. The Americans see their television programs as simply products; when these products are restricted by quotas or content rules, they view these measures as barriers to trade. Their response is to threaten retaliatory trade action. But the Europeans see something more basic at stake, their cultures, languages and ethnic diversity.

In this debate, the Europeans tend to find a common ground with Canadian cultural nationalists. In defence of its rather token efforts to restrict U.S. programs, the European Commission cites the Canada-U.S. free trade agreement. The free trade pact, it points out, does nothing to tamper with Canada's broadcasting content rules, which requires 50% Canadian programming on radio and television. So why, the Europeans ask, are the Americans getting so excited about the single market's little exercise in cultural protection?

Despite the commission's efforts, the Americanization of European television will likely proceed, particularly among the young. This is one of many trends that the spirit of 1992 cannot alter. Marketers should take careful note of this reality. They shouldn't be approaching the 1992 reforms in isolation from the other significant social, economic and cultural changes that are shaping Europe. Some of these trends are stimulated by the single market, but others are often quite independent from the decisions being made in Brussels.

For example, many more European women are entering the workforce, raising the demand for prepared food and fast food restaurants. This is happening even in France, the home of the three-hour dinner. The population is getting much older, creating a demand for certain types of goods and services. Expectations of a better life are rising with incomes. Traditionally backward areas of Europe, like Spain and Portugal, are poised for greater industrialization which should put more wealth into the hands of their citizens. As in North America, Europe is undergoing a revolution in public attitudes to the environment, with "green products" in increasing demand.

Add to this stew a spicy new ingredient, the future consuming power of Eastern Europeans. At the moment, the economies east of the Elbe River are hampered by stagnant industries, overregulation, a tattered infrastructure and nonconvertible currencies. Yet they offer one thing that every marketer dreams about — vast potential for an upsurge in consumer spending.

Astute companies are not blinded by the dream of a homogeneous Euroconsumer. They keep their eye on the bigger picture, the larger trends. They recognize that some tastes and some products will be global, and their market reach will be broadened by the improvements in communications. At the same time, so much of what people buy, eat, wear and watch will remain parochial and culturally unique. Italians will continue to eat three times more bread than other Europeans; the Spanish will continue to devour fresh fruit and vegetables at twice the normal rate. And we should all be thankful for that.

Chapter 8

Inside the Fortress

Saturday morning meetings are rare at the Brussels head-quarters of the European Commission. Only matters of extreme urgency would require a high-level weekend gathering of the kind that took place at the Berlaymont building in the late summer of 1988. A number of the most powerful EC officials were on hand.

The commission was facing a public relations crisis. The 1992 project aimed at creating a single integrated market was under attack from the United States. The Americans' weapon was a simple slogan, Fortress Europe, with a powerful implicit message — that the Europeans, while dismantling non-tariff barriers within the community, were building stronger, higher walls against their non-EC trading partners.

The aim of the emergency meeting was to come up with the commission's own counter-slogan to minimize the effects Fortress Europe was having on international opinion. We kicked it around at the highest levels of the commission," recalls one senior official. "We wanted a slogan that was strong but not aggressive."

At one point, someone suggested the phrase, Leader Europe. But that was quickly discarded when it was pointed out that "leader" is translated into German as "fuhrer." "Fuhrer Europe" wasn't the impression the commission wanted to convey. Someone else mentioned Powerhouse Europe. That was rejected as too threatening. Finally, a consensus emerged in favor of Partnership Europe. Several months afterwards, the official wasn't sure the choice was right. "I still think Fortress Europe sounds better than Partnership Europe," sighed the British-born Eurocrat. "Our slogan sounds kind of wet, doesn't it?"

This urgent attention paid to a simple phrase seems all out of proportion to reality. But Fortress Europe became one of the hot geopolitical buzzwords of the 1980s, right up there with "Read my lips" and "Perestroika/Glasnost." It still gets cited in countless speeches. It is the title for a constant barrage of seminars and conferences on 1992. It has become part of the lexicon of business and diplomacy.

Fortress Europe is a U.S. invention, coined by some official in the Treasury department. But other non-Europeans, particularly the Japanese, have adopted it. Some of the 66 Third World countries that enjoy preferential access to EC markets have taken it up, as well.

As with all good slogans, it was never exactly clear what it meant. For some, it raised the specter of a deliberately protectionist Europe. The image of Europe as a fortress surrounded by a moat and thick walls, with Jacques Delors and François Mitterrand manning machine guns on the turrets, appealed to the paranoia and lack of understanding of 1992 felt by many outsiders.

For others, the fortress was made of subtler material. They worried about an increasingly inward-looking European economic bloc that looked to be taking a more independent stance in world trade diplomacy. The more pessimistic noted that the Canadian and U.S. economies were becoming more integrated under the free trade agreement. A nascent economic grouping was being formed in the Asia-Pacific region. With the industrial world splitting into blocs, there were fears for the future of the multilateral negotiation system that has so effectively resolved trade disputes since the Second World War.

The Americans, having invented Fortress Europe, often seemed unsure of how seriously to take the whole thing.

The White House under Ronald Reagan was generally suspicious of Brussels and Europe. But the more Atlanticist administration of George Bush began to take a softer line on the single market. Bush himself made positive speeches about the integration of Europe. He saw a more united Europe has an important bulwark of peace and security. As the Communist regimes of Eastern Europe collapsed, he recognized the importance of a strong anchor to hold a distracted Germany in the Western alliance. Fortress Europe seemed passé.

But a more parochial U.S. Congress still envisaged Europeans, trowels in hand, laying the bricks of a protectionist wall. Many business leaders remained skeptical of the EC's assurances that the 1992 measures are of net benefit to outsiders. Even cabinet members — particularly the 1992-sensitive trade and commerce secretaries— trotted out Fortress rhetoric when the situation demanded it. The European Commission's new broadcasting policy was such an occasion. The policy sets guidelines for 50% European content on television programming throughout the community. It was immediately blasted by senior U.S. officials as a Fortress Europe action.

The question remains: How accurately does Fortress Europe sum up the reality of 1992? Does it simply express outsiders' concerns about something they can't understand? Have they latched on to an effective slogan to deflect criticism from their own defensive, protectionist policies? Wisse Dekker, the influential chairman of Philips, thinks so. He sees the Fortress Europe label as "self-projection" by the Americans and Japanese. It is they who are assembling the bricks for their own protective fortresses, he maintains.

Indeed, the Americans and Japanese are far from blameless in the guerrilla war of trade disputes that was waged throughout the 1980s. Japan's own markets often seem all but impenetrable. The U.S. Omnibus Trade Bill, which gives Americans the power to "punish" what it considers to be unfair traders, is the height of hypocrisy. No one, including Canada, has been free of shameless protectionism. However, this hardly excuses the European Community for its own abysmal behavior. It is this track

record, more than the potential perils of the 1992 program, that causes the community's assurances to be met
with skepticism.

Building the foundation

The base of Fortress Europe was built long before 1992
was even a gleam in Jacques Delors' eyes. As the U.S.
declined as an economic superpower in the 1970s, the
European Commission took an increasingly aggressive
posture on trade policy, one of the areas on which it
speaks for all 12 members. As Europe became more forceful, the U.S. found it was no longer in control of economic
events, and became more defensive. The community's confidence only increased with the launch of the 1992 project.
Conflict was inevitable.

At the same time, Japan was emerging as an economic
colossus. The Japanese built their financial might on careful industrial planning, spearheaded by its Ministry of
Trade and Industry. It also had a facility for being subtly
protectionist at home, while aggressively exporting into foreign markets. Like North Americans, Europeans grew
alarmed as some hallowed industries crumbled before the
onslaught of first the Japanese, and then the rapidly
industrializing Tigers — South Korea, Taiwan, Hong Kong
and Singapore. They had already seen the continent colo-
nized by U.S. multinationals in the 1960s and 1970s. In
face of the Asian invasion, the community took bold measures to defend its besieged industries.

Ironically, the industry that Europe has protected with
the most zeal, and cash, is one that faces no threat from
Japan. Europe's Common Agricultural Policy is by now
legendary, a massive structure of import levies and support prices. Although its subsidies have been whittled
down over recent years — and its legendary mountains of
milk and cheese melted away — the CAP remains a huge
economic commitment to overproduction. The community's agricultural spending of 27 billion ECUs a year ($38
billion) still accounts for 60% of the entire EC budget.

Europe's heavy commitment to farm support triggered
a costly farm subsidy war involving the U.S., Canada and

the world's other food-producing countries. This competition was particularly damaging to the defenseless producers of the Third World, who saw their markets stolen by the subsidized farmers of the EC. Farm subsidies have been the major bone of contention throughout the difficult negotiations of the Uruguay Round of the General Agreement on Tariffs & Trade. They were responsible for the bitter breakdown of talks during meetings in Montreal in 1988.

The U.S., hardly saintly on the subject of farm subsidies, was an uncompromising hawk on the CAP, calling for a rapid dismantling of farm subsidies. The EC was committed to scaling back subsidies substantially, but argued that it could not meet the U.S. timetable. More than 10 million people are employed in the EC's farming industry, against 1.6 million in the U.S. Visitors to France or Germany are impressed by the vitality and relative prosperity of rural life. Going cold turkey on farm aid would throw large numbers of small, marginal farmers off the land, at an immense social cost. It is no wonder farm subsidies have been a source of bitter friction between trading partners.

Against this background of bad feeling, new disputes moved to the forefront in the mid-1980s, as the Japanese and the Tigers made inroads in such strategic industries as computers, consumer electronics and cars. The Europeans believed these new competitors were not playing fair. They saw the need for immediate action to protect their companies.

Protectionism 1990s-style is a subtle art. The weapons are not the highly visible tariffs; today's protectionists are skilled practitioners of the more oblique non-tariff barriers. One celebrated European example is the Poitiers case. One day in late 1982 — just before Christmas — the French demanded that all imported video tape recorders should clear customs at a small, undermanned post in the provincial city of Poitiers. Very few imported video tape recorders were sold in France that Christmas. This thoroughly illegal measure was withdrawn, but not until Christmas was over. Commentators couldn't miss the symbolism of France's actions. Poitiers was one of the bases from which

Joan of Arc began her tragic crusade to save France from an earlier invading army — in that case, the English.

The Japanese and the Tigers had to live with restrictive national policies. Most common are the voluntary export restraint (VER) agreements, whereby the Asian countries agree to limit their exports of a certain commodity to a specific percentage of the European country's market. There are an estimated 700 such agreements covering imports into the 12 EC countries, including such goods as textiles, televisions, bananas and shoes.

VERs have been particularly pervasive in the car industry, where worries about the Japanese invasion are most acute. Japanese imports have about 10% of the EC car market, but there is a large variation between countries. They are limited by VER to 3% of the French market and to only a few thousand cars a year in Spain and Italy. Britain has an 11% ceiling, while other countries allow unrestricted access. Japanese car makers supply more than 25% of the Dutch car market, 45% of Ireland's and 15% of Germany's.

The handiest protective tool the Europeans have found is the anti-dumping law. Dumping occurs when a company sells goods abroad for less than it sells the same goods in its home market. This form of predatory pricing is difficult to prove because of complex distribution networks and rapidly changing technology. Still, a number of governments slap duties on foreign suppliers which they say indulge in such practices. They justify this by arguing that dumpers drive domestic competitors out of business, so that they can then raise prices to much higher levels.

The world trade forum, GATT, has permitted countries to impose duties on dumped goods if they can prove the pricing tactics are injuring their own producers. The EC enthusiastically seized on this opportunity and became the most skilled anti-dumper — although Canada and the U.S. are no slouches in this regard. It has been particularly aggressive going after imports of consumer-electronic goods and office equipment from Asia.

The Asians may be dumpers but they are no dummies. In the mid-1980s, they began to circumvent the anti-dumping duties by establishing European plants, which would assemble products composed of parts imported from abroad. These got the pejorative label "screwdriver plants" — presumably, the only value added in Europe was to tighten a few screws. The EC quickly responded by extending anti-dumping duties to any parts used in such factories, unless 40% of the components used came from countries other than the dumper's own home country. Then one clever Japanese copier firm found a way around these rules of origin. It started importing entire photo-copiers assembled in California to avoid the extra anti-dumping duties. The commission then ruled that these products were really Japanese and subject to the duties.

The anti-dumping standoff made a lot of bystanders very nervous. It appeared that anti-dumping laws could cause injury to countries that were not the primary target of their fire. Consider, for example, the increasing number of Japanese car producers who have set up factories in Canada. If these plants were used to export autos to Europe, could they run afoul European anti-dumping laws? It would seem so.

Some disputes pitted one EC country against each other. With the Japanese establishing factories inside the community, some national governments were determined that an acceptable threshold of the products' content was sourced in Europe. An unseemly row broke out when Nissan cars built in Britain were classified as Japanese imports when imported into France. The French claimed the cars failed to meet their 80% European content requirement. The British Nissans were eventually admitted as European cars, but only after Brussels intervened.

CAP, anti-dumping, quotas, local content. They formed a pattern: the exercise of industrial policy through trade restraint. It is no wonder that, viewed from New York or Seoul, protectionism seems as European as croissants, tortellini and paella. For anyone aware of the EC's track record, the coming of the single market looked like an opportunity to raise the walls even higher.

The architects of the 1992 program let it be known that their objective was to strengthen European business. The single market was not intended to benefit outsiders. Non-

Europeans might draw some secondary advantage from the strengthening of the European economy, the 4.5% blip in economic growth. But they would have to pay a price for this reflected prosperity by allowing free access to their own markets by European firms.

Paolo Cecchini, the economist who prepared the commission's economic study of 1992's impact, explained that the dynamic EC economy would provide a much-needed shot in the arm for other markets and economies in much less buoyant shape. His report maintained that "in return, EC governments will have the right to expect appropriate responses from the Community's economic partners abroad, notably the U.S. and Japan. If the fruits of the European home market are to be shared internationally there must also be a fair share-out of the burdens of the global economic responsibility, with market-opening measures extended internationally on a firm basis of clear reciprocity." It was a clear enunciation of the principle of reciprocity. The world would be hearing that word again, and it wouldn't always like it.

As 1992 became better understood, the calls grew louder for reserving the major benefits for Europeans. Many business leaders view the world as a battle for survival with Japan and America. Europe could only win this battle by first providing a large protected home market for its own companies. It would be counterproductive to put the single market in place if the multinationals of Japan, the U.S. or the Asian Tigers were the big winners.

The concerns were acute in industries that had been zealously sheltered by their states. Makers of cars, textiles and shoes worried about what would happen when protection was swept away. This anxiety was heightened by predictions that the single market would foster brutal competition. There were predictions that consumers would benefit from lower prices, but companies would see their profit margins shrink. Many European companies would be stronger, particularly those that had prepared for 1992. But many others will find their survival threatened.

The cries went up for transitional provisions — say, protection for five to 10 years — to allow industry to prepare for this competition. The attitude was: Why let the

Americans come in and clean up, while our own companies are perishing in cut-throat competition? These calls grew more frequent the farther south you would go in Europe. Some regions of Italy, Greece and Iberia could be hit hard by industry's restructuring.

The strongest pleas came from the car industry, led by Italy's Fiat and France's Peugeot. Car makers were fearful because the old national import quotas were vulnerable. In an integrated market with little or no border checking, state quotas would be meaningless. Free-market advocates saw this as an opportunity to pry the car market wide-open, exposing it to unrestricted competition. That is what the single market is all about, they argued. Predictably, industry leaders argued for a highly restrictive community-wide quota for at least for the first five years of the single market.

Cesare Romiti, Fiat's chief executive, warned that the EC would risk "economic colonization" by Japan and the U.S. unless it developed a strong defensive industrial policy. Romiti said the car industry deserved further special Community assistance because it was "strategic for the economic future." He called for a transitional freeze on Japanese car exports to the EC, and local content rules on Japanese assembly plants. And Jacques Calvet, Peugeot's opinionated chairman, suggested that if the EC car market were completely opened to the Japanese, one in every three jobs in the continent's motor industry would be destroyed. Calvet made it clear he believed the quotas would have to apply to Japanese cars built in Europe, as well as imports from Japan.

These debates have become noisier and more heated as Europe has moved down the road towards its single market. The shaping of the market has become a balancing act between the forces for protectionism and those in favor of a free market. Neither side has been totally victorious or completely vanquished. This oscillation makes it hard for North Americans to read the final direction of the reforms.

The task hasn't been made easier by the EC's disconcertingly self-obsessed attitude. Thoroughly occupied with the single market, its leaders were more inward-looking, more self-involved than at any time since the Second

World War. The early preparations for 1992 were remarkably bereft of any consideration of the outside world. It took the EC almost three years after the 1985 White Paper on the single market before it explained to the world what is was doing and where everybody else fitted in. Even when it did, the answers were vague and unsatisfying.

Part of the problem also lay with the rest of the world, which was slow to recognize the scope of 1992. North Americans remembered earlier efforts by the Europeans to get their act together. The old petty nationalisms had prevailed, and little was accomplished. But suddenly, in 1988, it became clear that things were starting to happen. The other world players had to pay attention. Aspects of the single market were making them nervous:

Product standards: At first glance, Europe's ambitious overhaul of product standards and regulations looks like a plus for any company wanting to do business in the 12 EC countries — or in the six EFTA countries, which have the same rules. A business wanting to sell widgets has to conform to only one measure of width, strength or voltage, instead of 18. But some outsiders worried that new European standards could become the bricks of Fortress Europe. They had seen how the Germans had used beer purity laws to keep out competing brews from inside the EC. Why couldn't such techniques now be directed at non-European outsiders? "Standards are one of the better ways to get a hidden trade barrier in," warned Canada's High Commissioner to London, Donald Macdonald.

Outsiders wondered to what extent the Europeans would conform to widely recognized international standards, or set off on their own path. In a number of areas, the Europeans were dealing with new technologies, in which they would be establishing world standards. To what extent would they be open to representation and influence from outside the community? Companies from outside the community worried that they may fall behind their EC or EFTA competitors in changing production processes as new European standards are developed.

North Americans have been particularly uneasy about

the pivotal role played by European standards bodies, CEN and its sister organization, CENELEC, in the development of new technical standards. Under the EC's new approach to technical standards, the European Commission sets out only "essential requirements" for products in terms of health, safety, environment or consumer protection.

It is the job of CEN/CENELEC and other standards-setting bodies to decide the technical details — the exact voltage, the amount of insulation, the thickness of lumber, for example — to fulfill these essential requirements. These bodies are confederations of national standards organizations, and consist solely of European business interests — that is, the major associations and companies in the relevant industries. Non-European companies cannot make representations or sit on committees. The Americans have complained loudly and bitterly about being excluded from the process, and have actually received encouragement that they might have some input. Canada has quietly voiced concern, and is unlikely to get a seat at the table.

Canada's forest industry is one outsider with a lot at stake in the standards-setting process. Forest products are Canada's leading export to the EC, generating more than $3 billion a year in sales. The industry monitors a CEN committee which works on the sizes, performance standards and testing and certification procedures for lumber as a building material. Canadians have no direct input into the committee's work; yet our major lumber-producing competitors sit at the CEN table. CEN's representation comes not just from the EC but also from EFTA, which includes those forested Scandinavian nations, Norway, Sweden and Finland. Quite naturally, the "Scans" would want to impose their own standards on all of Europe.

Canadian forestry officials cite one example of how standards can block or discourage exports. In 1989, lumber producers exporting to European markets found they were increasingly required to dry their wood. It was not an EC-wide requirement, but some countries demanded it. The problem was that not all of Canada's lumber companies have easy access to drying kilns. It added another cost and a disincentive to selling in those markets.

The challenge often lies not in the standards themselves, but in the testing and certification procedures for those standards. If a Canadian producer encountered an unfamiliar test for the strength of lumber, it might cost added time and money to make sure its products meet the criteria.

So far, forest companies have been fairly content with proposals from the CEN committee. But as the standards-setting exercise gears up, other industries are unsure of how their products will fit in under the new codes. Telecommunications companies, for example, are closely watching the deliberations of the new European Telecommunications Standards Institute, a body established to speed up the creation of new telecom specifications.

Any Canadian company with an interest in EC standards should maintain a stance of knowledgeable concern. The information coming out of the CEN and CENELEC committees is often sketchy. Nasty surprises could slip into some of the new standards rules. However, that is not the European Commission's intent. Its officials make a convincing argument that setting standards for protectionist purposes would backfire on the community. The EC, with 20% of the world's trade, would not want to harm its chances of selling its products into the wider world. It would be defeating its own purposes to devise quirky regulations. It is in the EC's interests, the officials argue, to use international standards as their starting point. They would seem to have an argument.

Financial services: Outsiders also appear to have a lot to gain from the single market in financial services. A bank, broker or insurance company with a license to operate in a single EC country will be able to sell its services and establish branches throughout the other 11. The benefits are manifold: There would be no need to obtain local approvals in every market; a bank could operate on a single capital base without having to allocate capital to local branches; national reporting requirements would be reduced or eliminated. It would seem, on the surface, to be a win-win situation.

There is, however, one complication — the EC's doctrine of reciprocity. It first raised its head in the draft proposal for the Second Banking Directive released in 1988. That directive said non-community banks will gain access to the single market only if EC banks get "effective market access" in the applicant's home country. The community said this principle will also be applied to insurance and investment services — and to any aspects of the single market not covered by GATT.

At that point, the commission was in its head-in-the-sand phase; it wasn't paying much attention to how the rest of the world saw 1992. The wording of the banking directive was vague; the commission itself wasn't sure what it meant. That left the door open for much misunderstanding. The Americans sputtered in anger, characterizing the directive as the clearest manifestation of Fortress Europe. They felt exposed because U.S. banking regulations are more restrictive than in Europe after 1992. U.S. commercial banks cannot perform investment banking, and interstate banking is restricted. There are no such restraints in the European market. The U.S. banking lobby was concerned that its members might be denied entry to Europe because the U.S. could not provide the same degree of access to European banks.

Canadian concerns were less acute. Recent deregulation in Canada had allowed commercial banks to deal in stocks and bonds. However, foreign-owned institutions — other than U.S. banks, which have special status under the free trade agreement — were limited to 12% of the domestic banking market, although they have never come close to scratching that ceiling. On reading the banking directive for the first time, Canadian financial institutions were worried too.

Faced with confused, hostile reactions to its banking directive, the commission shifted into damage control. It issued reassuring statements that North Americans need not worry about reciprocity. The banking directive, in its final form, turned out to be less dangerous than feared. Canadian institutions have little to fear. As a Fortress weapon, the banking directive has been overrated.

The commission has the authority to deny licenses to outside applicants if its banks aren't getting "comparable or equivalent" treatment in the applicant's home market. But the commission sees reciprocity mainly as a bargaining tool in GATT negotiations for opening markets. Brussels has never intended that it be wielded against North America. Its targets are the Japanese and newly industrialized countries, where market access is much more restrictive.

The commission says it is not looking for "mirror-image reciprocity" — that is, tit-for-tat concessions which are evenly balanced, sector by sector, on both sides. In the final version of the final banking directive, it has moved instead towards "national treatment." Non-EC banks will be admitted to the single market as long as their home countries do not discriminate against EC-based banks. EC institutions should not face more restrictive rules than home-based companies. The directive says the commission will continually monitor how EC banks are being treated in other countries, and will issue periodic reports on the situation. With these reports in hand, the EC could decide quickly on whether or not to suspend an application from an outside bank if its home government was practicing discrimination.

Canadian institutions also heaved a big sigh of relief because the reciprocity test would not be applied retroactively. Any bank, insurer or investment dealer inside Europe before 1993 would not be subject to the test. That let most of our big financial players off the hook, since they were already in Europe.

Public procurement: Public procurement reforms are aimed at benefiting European companies first and foremost. Under the new rules, the whole government tendering process will become more open. National governments will not be able to let contracts out the back door to national companies; they will have to offer them to everyone in the community. The rules would open up EC-wide competition four rich procurement areas — energy, drinking water supply, transport and telecommunications — that were previously the preserve of national bidders.

So what's in it for non-EC businesses? The Europeans are making a big commitment to building up their telecommunications prowess, a potential source of economic growth that has been hampered by national favoritism. That makes Europe an attractive target for Canadian firms, which have built up expertise in the telecom area.

There are ways in which outsiders can establish European credentials. Under the Treaty of Rome, a company is "European" if it is incorporated in one of the member countries. That applies to both European-owned companies and to subsidiaries of foreign companies. For example, Northern Telecom, Canada's leading telephone equipment maker, has set up French subsidiaries for manufacturing and research in that country. It has 28% ownership of STC PLC, the British computer and telecommunications company.

But non-EC companies worry about the little details. The European choice of standards will play a big role in determining the openness of the telecommunications market. Also, how much European content must a product have before it, too, qualifies as European? The commission has suggested that public authorities would be able to reject a bid if more than 50% of the value of the goods or services were generated outside the EC.

Furthermore, the commission has decided that purchasers should have to award a contract to an EC supplier if its price is up to 3% higher than equivalent bids from suppliers from outside the community. That would give European companies a good head start. These rules may provide a powerful motivation for Canadian suppliers to do substantial production and possibly research & development in Europe.

This a dangerously fluid situation. The 50% content rule isn't written in stone. The more protectionist elements in Europe would like to see stronger provisions to strengthen the hands of EC companies. The commission itself sees the 50% content rule as a starting point for negotiations within the GATT to open up public procurement markets on a global basis — or, if that fails, for bilateral negotiations with other countries. It's yet another exercise of the EC's controversial reciprocity principle.

There are other areas of Fortress Europe concern. *The Economist* magazine talks about matters of "discriminating taste." The EC has been known to ban an import because it simply doesn't like it. The community blocked hormone-injected beef in 1989 even though laboratory tests showed that the meat wasn't harmful to people's health. Similarly, Canadian baby seal skins weren't injurious to Europeans or threatening to an industry, but the killing of seal pups was morally objectionable.

The flavor of the month — or the decade — seems to be environmental standards and animal and plant health regulations. These are hard to argue against because everyone agrees they are a good thing. The Green movement in Europe — as elsewhere — is causing governments to take a close look at the cleanliness, safety and healthiness of products and production processes. In this atmosphere, it is difficult to determine when an environmental standard is being wielded for protectionist purposes.

The pressure can extend beyond official product standards and into the realm of public opinion. Pulp and paper companies are being asked by their importers about their pollution standards in their own home countries. Do they dump dioxin into the waters? What are the local rules on reforestation? This may be the start of a whole new trend where exporters are judged according to their environmental standards in their own countries.

This is hardly the stuff of Fortress Europe, but it does point to a growing self-confidence by Europeans of their place in the world. As trade barriers, concerns over the environment and animal rights are sleepers. They begin as marginal issues, on the periphery of public policy, then ride to the center on a wave of popular concern. Non-EC companies are often slow to pick up these trends until they start affecting markets and products. In this age of green thinking in Europe, outsiders have to be more alert than ever before. The discouraging aspect is that Canadian business — with some prominent exceptions — seems unwilling to devote the time or the interest.

The Quiet Canadians

Derek Burney, Canada's burly, straight-shooting ambassador to the U.S., was giving a roomful of Canadian exporters the inside scoop on how Americans were viewing the European single market process. The political view in Washington, he said, was that the European Community was building, "brick by brick," a fortress around itself.

That flippant comment in fall of 1989 to the Canadian Exporters Association conference struck a raw nerve. Businesspeople in the audience were taken aback. Here was one of Canada's senior diplomats raising that old bogey of a protectionist, inward-looking European Community. Some of Burney's colleagues in the department of External Affairs felt that the tough-talking envoy had gone too far with his remarks.

The reaction was indicative of a peculiarly Canadian ambivalence towards the Europeans' project of tearing down internal trade barriers before 1993. Many Canadians, including a number of the businesspeople in the audience, were wary about what is going on in Brussels. But they had never displayed the passion and anger that American managers and trade officials have mustered so effectively. One senior Canadian diplomat, who takes a rather hawkish line on 1992, wonders why Canadian businesspeople seem so unquestioning about Europe 1992 while their U.S. counterparts have been noisily critiquing every directive, standard or regulation coming out of Brussels.

Indeed, there are a number of aspects of the 1992 program for Canadian industry to be genuinely concerned about. Reforms in product standards, financial services, public procurement and the environment are important to any nation which has a trading relationship with the EC. The community is Canada's second biggest trading partner with $26 billion in annual bilateral trade. Canadians are no less vulnerable than Americans to protectionist actions just because we are more polite, understanding and even-handed.

However extreme the Americans' rhetoric may seem,

they have been at least paying attention to 1992. U.S. business, alerted to the dangers of a closed, protected market, has been determined to leap the barriers and get inside that market. Japanese companies have been less boisterous but no less active in devising their European strategies. They have been quietly, painstakingly stepping up their investments and branch-plant formations inside the community. Business people in the U.S. and Japan are taking no chances on whether or not the EC becomes a fortress. They are going to be EC insiders in any case.

Canadians may recoil from the aggressive tone of the Fortress Europe rhetoric, but they cannot deny it has been, in its own way, effective. It has succeeded in focusing attention — both outsiders' and Europeans' — on the potential excesses of the single market. It has forced a distracted Europe to pay attention to the external implications of what they have been doing.

That became apparent on Oct. 19, 1988, when the European Commission, having finally debated the "external dimension" of 1992, came out with a four-page press release which tried to set the whole matter of external relations straight. The release argued that the single market would benefit community and non-community countries alike. In that release, the EC portrayed itself as "Partnership Europe," the slogan concocted at that Saturday morning meeting in Brussels. The 1992 process, the EC said, would not lead to protectionism; the community would continue to meet its international obligations. The release portrayed the EC's reciprocity principle as a benign concept, and consistent with efforts in GATT to liberalize international flows of goods and services.

It was a tardy defense but quite convincing. The EC made the point that any move towards protectionism on its part would be absurd. The 12 members were simply too dependent on international commerce. The community is the world's biggest trader, with its 1988 external exports generating 20% of all world trade, compared with 15% for the U.S. and 9% for Japan. Its export sales make up 9% of the community's gross domestic product, compared with 6.7% for the U.S. and 9.3% for Japan. Does this sound like somebody who wants to build a fortress?

The EC keeps pounding out the theme that its internal liberalization is good for everybody, inside and outside the community. This view gets support from independent economic forecasts. It is true that the elimination of non-tariff barriers within the community will cause some trade to be diverted away from non-EC countries. One forecast by Project Link, a global economic model supported by a consortium of international economic researchers, forecasts that about 8%-10% of the community's external trade — with outside countries such as Canada — will be diverted into internal EC trade over the next decade. Canadian exporters will get a smaller piece of the EC trade pie. However, that pie should be much bigger because of the 1992 program's shot in the arm for the European economy. Project Link's model shows that countries such as Canada should achieve a net benefit because of the dynamic effects of the single market, such as higher European living standards and greater consumer demand. All this assumes, of course, that there will be no further trade barriers erected against the outside world.

Fears of that now seem less justified. The final wording of the banking directive was a relief for most outsiders, although some observers are still suspicious about the potential abuse of the reciprocity principle. The standards-setting exercise seems to be progressing well, although it demands close monitoring. Furthermore, a shift in the political balance of the European Commission has helped reassure the outside world. The 17-member commission that held office from 1984 to 1988 had a decidedly protectionist tinge. However, the team that will occupy the Berlaymont's 13th floor in the crucial years leading up to December 31, 1992 contains a strong phalanx of free-trade advocates.

This has coincided with the election of an American president who seems to understand and value Europe. The debate over the broadcasting directive was just a noisy diversion. The Americans chose to ignore that, in the end, the directive's 50% European content rule for television broadcasting was not legally binding. The rule was more of a noble statement of community purpose. The U.S. government's protest reflected more than anything the lobbying clout of its entertainment industry.

Fortress Europe has come to look more like a chicken-wire fence than a real fortress with stout walls and unpenetrable redoubts. It is time to bury that slogan, which was never anything more than a PR trick — although a highly effective one. The Americans like to portray themselves as the world's only committed free traders, all the while relying on a bevy of countervailing duties, subsidies, quotas and trade restrictions to protect their industries. For many U.S. bureaucrats and some businesspeople, Japan-bashing and Europe-bashing is a substitute for curing the nation's more profound ills of uncompetitive manufacturing, urban decay and inferior education. (Canada shares this double standard, but at least we're not as belligerent about it.) There is some validity to the European contention that Fortress America is more likely than Fortress Europe.

That doesn't mean the European Community won't try to put its own people and industry first. Agriculture will remain a sore point. The debate over the future of the European car industry will be hard and bitter, because so many jobs are at stake. But the overall drift of the commission should be towards open trade. John Richardson, the articulate head of services in the EC's external relations directorate, says: "Unless something goes wrong, the economic interests are such that the EC can't go in any way but a liberal direction."

That "something," however, could be a severe economic recession. If the world economy turns bad, 1992 could possibly turn into a protectionist exercise. The competitive pressures on Europe's companies and countries might intensify to the point where demands for relief could not be ignored. In that scenario, a Fortress Europe could be constructed, as could a Fortress North America, and possibly a Fortress Pacific. A continuation of trade disputes and name-calling would raise the odds of that happening.

Some see the tighter integration of the EC as part of a growing trend towards the formation of big economic and trading blocs. Presumably, the EC might be the core of a European bloc, which would embrace the six members of the European Free Trade Association. Eastern Europe, including possibly the Soviet Union, might also join. The United States, Canada, and probably Mexico would constitute a North American grouping. Japan might be a member of this club, or it could dominate a Pacific bloc. In this divided world, major trade and economic bargains would be forged through negotiations among the most powerful economies. The multilateral body, the GATT, would decline as a forum for setting the world trade rules and resolving disputes. Middleweight countries like Canada would get hurt in this collision of superpowers. They would have less control over their destinies.

Economist Sylvia Ostry, Canada's former trade ambassador, identifies another area of uncertainty and friction. There is great interest in the West in the Japanese model of innovation policy: the government targets a strategic industry where it hopes to win a competitive advantage through collaborative research & development. She sees efforts in the the U.S. and the EC to emulate this approach by assembling groups of companies in projects such as Sematech (for U.S. semiconductor technology) and Jessi (its EC equivalent.) The result is competing "innovation systems," as all three blocs target the same strategic industries.

A world divided into blocs — or innovation systems — is a perilous place for a middle power like Canada. It is important that Canada continue to play a role as a bridge between North America, Europe and Asia. We should appreciate the crucial role of the GATT process in giving us a voice in world trading relations. Canadians have been correct in generally avoiding the Americans' noisy confrontational approach in dealing with the EC. However, they must take more interest in what the community is doing and thinking.

The European Community is not trying to build a wall around itself. But it is becoming a more self-confident and assertive player on the world arena. The challenges of creating a single market before 1993 have made the community more inward-looking than ever before. It will on occasion do things that annoy and confuse us. Canadians have to maintain an informed vigilance.

Chapter 9

The Uneasy Relationship

Maeve Doran is, for a rare moment, speechless. The usually loquacious European diplomat is searching for words to describe the complex web of relations between Canada and the EC. "Globally, the relationship is in good shape," she says finally, fixing her eyes intently on her visitor. "Emotionally, it is not doing as well."

It is late afternoon in Doran's narrow broom closet of an office in the Berlaymont, the Brussels headquarters of the European Commission. Doran, a tiny, white-haired Irishwoman, is a key official on the "Canada desk" in the commission's external relations department. She has just rambled through a half-hour analysis of the state of diplomatic relations between Canada and Brussels. It is not a happy story, and Doran, a highly partisan advocate for the EC position, has let her frustration boil to the surface.

Doran's outburst is indicative of a concern shared widely among European Commission officials. The view in Brussels is Canada has neglected its relationship with Europe, allowing misunderstandings and disputes to grow and intensify. Officials are frustrated and confused by the lack of attention Canadian politicians, diplomats and business people have been giving the community.

The relationship swings between benign neglect and outright hostility. Canadian cabinet ministers, on tours of Europe, tend to hop from Rome to Paris to London, but rarely touch down in Brussels where the critical policies on the EC's trade, environment and external relations are being formulated. Canada has done little to build a political profile in Brussels. The EC believes this apparent indifference has been a big factor in allowing Canada-EC economic disputes to hang around for years.

Among the difficult diplomatic disputes that have damaged relations during the 1980s, four have loomed particularly large:

• The two governments have been locked in a bitter fishing showdown in the cold waters of the Grand Banks off the coast of Newfoundland. Ottawa has banned community fishermen from Canadian waters, charging the Europeans are overfishing and dangerously depleting fish stocks in the area. The EC has argued that Canada is unreasonable and inflexible in its conservation policies.

• The Europeans complained for years about the heavy markups slapped on their wines by provincial liquor boards, and their meager listings in liquor stores. This dispute was eventually resolved through negotiation, but only after the EC won a judgment against Canada before a panel of the GATT.

• Canada in 1985 slapped a countervailing duty on European beef imports, claiming that subsidies were allowing the Europeans to grab bigger pieces of the Canadian market, thus injuring Canadian cattlemen. The EC won a GATT ruling on this issue too, but Canada did not accept it. As this book went to press, the countervailing duty was still in place with no compromise in sight.

• The Commission banned the import of furs from seal pups, effectively closing down the Newfoundland seal hunt. It has also threatened to ban furs from animals caught in leghold traps, although it will give trappers breathing space to find alternative methods.

Some of these disputes have severe consequences. Depleted fish populations in the North Atlantic, for example, are hammering Canadian fishermen's incomes and forcing processing plants to close, laying off thousands of workers. Layered one on top of another, these economic battles also have a cumulative force. They establish a cycle of angry rhetoric, suspicion and mistrust that undermines the transatlantic relationship.

Canada's neglect has not been limited to Western Europe. Only late in the game did it recognize the significance of the upheaval in Eastern Europe. By mid-1989, when the most ardent cold warriors were thawing out, External Affairs Minister Joe Clark was delivering frosty speeches on East-West relations. Prime Minister Mulroney's visit to Moscow in late November, 1989, was welcome but a bit behind the pack. Misjudging the magnitude and speed of European change arises from a failure to devise a coherent European policy. That comes from ignorance, indifference and not a little loathing.

Seasoned diplomats on both sides of the Atlantic shake their heads at the state of relations. There would appear to be a firm foundation for a healthy Canada-Europe relationship. The 12 EC member countries together constitute Canada's second biggest trading partner, although a remote second to the United States. The value of two-way trade between Canada and the 12 amounted to about $26 billion in 1989. The 12 countries consume about 8% of Canada's exports, and supply 11% of our imports. The Europeans in 1989 enjoyed a bilateral trade surplus of $3 billion, a legacy of the high values of the Canadian and U.S. dollars during the early 1980s. However, Canada's indifference towards Europe and its growing market has allowed the imbalance to continue.

The 12 countries shipped about $14.5 billion worth of goods to Canada in 1989. Industrial machinery, cars and trucks, and other manufactured goods are big components of this trade. Canada, whose exports to the EC run in the $11 billion range, is a supplier of natural resources, a role that has not changed much since the 19th century. Forest products account for about a third of the total, followed by mineral and metal products, farm products and fish. However, there has been progress — about 60% of exports are goods to which some value is added by manufacturing or processing. It is estimated that 200,000 Canadian jobs are sustained by exports to Europe.

While currency fluctuations have had their effects, Canada's trade gap with Europe is also a corollary of investment trends. Trade usually follows investment, and Canadians have been slow to exploit this opening, except possibly in Great Britain. Europeans in 1988 held $23.1 billion worth of direct investment in Canada, with more than half of that from Britain. Canadian direct investment in the community amounts to about $8.5 billion, with more than 60% of that going to Britain.

While trade underpins the economic relationship, history provides all kinds of emotional links. From the 15th century, when John Cabot and Jacques Cartier sailed to the New World, Europeans have crossed the Atlantic to colonize, conquer and settle Canada. Europe is still the motherland to many millions of Canadians who have fled wars, revolutions and economic upheavals for a new life in a new world.

For some European countries, such as France, the Netherlands and Belgium, the feelings run deeper — Canadians were among the brave liberators from the tyranny of Nazism. You have only to stand amidst the rows of crosses in a well-groomed Canadian military graveyard in Northern France to sense the power and resilience of the bond forged during the Allied march across Europe. Since the war, Canadian forces have maintained a presence on the continent as part of the NATO contingent. And Europeans genuinely like us as tourists and welcome us as business partners; they appreciate our tolerance, good humor and manners. We are viewed as kinder, gentler versions of Americans.

There is certainly no sign of alarm over the state of Canada-EC relations in Ottawa's Lester B. Pearson Building, the red-brick ziggurat overlooking the Ottawa River that is headquarters of the External Affairs department. Officials are not overtly alarmed by the persistent outbreaks of bad feelings. They believe the patient is in fundamental good health. External Affairs downplays the trade irritants, saying they must be viewed in perspective. Any trade relationship valued at $26 billion is bound to have some friction. An External Affairs briefing paper acknowledges that "concurrent with the growth of commercial and financial activity in recent years, there has been a flood of contentious issues . . . They have at times diverted attention from the positive bilateral relations with EC member states. To some extent, such trade issues reflect the complexities of a market with annual global imports in excess of $500 billion."

Even EC diplomats, while expressing frustration in one breath, tend to dismiss the disagreements as "just worries, not problems." Only about 4%-5% of bilateral trade has ever been affected by the disputes. However, diplomats on both sides acknowledge that these tensions hang around far too long, aggravating what should be a mutually satisfying relationship.

The problem, of course, is not with individual Europeans and Canadians. It does not even lie at the diplomatic level. Canada's mission to Brussels and its ambassador are highly regarded by the Berlaymont. The core problem is that Canada, as a government and a nation, has failed to appreciate what has happened in Europe over the past 20 years. It was late in realizing the extent to which the responsibilities of the 12 sovereign states have been transferred to the European Commission. These transferred areas include a number that are of vital interest to Canada, such as European external trade, fisheries policy, environment and agriculture. The EC has assembled cadres of skillful, strong-minded bureaucrats to carve out its territory. Canadians have focused their attention on the national capitals, while the real power in Europe was shifting to a new government in Brussels.

Evidence for this attitude lies in the lack of visits to Brussels by senior cabinet ministers. Trade Minister John Crosbie's whirlwind tour of Europe in early 1989 — in the middle of a fishing crisis — included stops in Switzerland, Italy and Britain, but no visit to the city which justifiably claims the title "Europe's capital." Joe Clark, the external affairs minister, is an infrequent visitor to Brussels. Of course, it takes two to tango, and Ottawa hasn't been exactly swamped with high-level EC delegations. But the Berlaymont bureaucrats are adamant that the neglect is more on the Canadian side. A flurry of Canadian ministerial visits in 1989 suggested this longstanding diffidence was turning into mild interest, but there is considerable ground to be made up.

The infrequency of top-level visits has meant there has been little contact between Canadian cabinet ministers and their counterparts, the European Commissioners. That has limited the pressure on respective civil services to find solutions to festering disputes. Even Canadian officials expressed frustration over this lack of political direction. What has been lacking, they said, is the kind of interchange where a Canadian cabinet minister might say to his top bureaucrat, "Look, when I met with my EC counterpart, I promised to do something about this. Now let's get on with it." That kind of prodding usually yields concrete results.

Canada's approach to the EC has been contrasted with that of the U.S. government whose key cabinet officers meet each year with their Brussels equivalents. U.S.-EC relations have not been smooth, but at least there has been a mechanism to exchange viewpoints. "The most striking thing is that the EC represents one of Canada's biggest economic relationships, but it's the only one that has been left to the management of civil servants," said one Canadian official. He suggested the attitude was a product of Ottawa's mistaken impression that the EC is a bureaucratic entity, and not a real government.

Nicholas Papadopoulos, director of the International Business Study Group at Carleton University, has experienced the same kinds of reaction in surveys of Canadian business leaders and politicians. He has been surprised by their reluctance to recognize the community as one entity, rather than 12 disparate countries. "In many interviews and discussions with Canadian business and government officials over the past five years, it has become clear that most perceive the EC as a vast and unnecessary bureaucracy which can and must be disregarded wherever possible," he writes in his book, *Canada and The European Community: A Troubled Partnership.*

If Canadians need any reminder that the EC is a real, living government, they have only to visit the office building a half a block away from the Berlaymont that houses the community's fisheries directorate. There is nothing in

145

Raymond Simmonet's office to suggest his official function
— no nautical touches, no pictures of fish. But Simmonet,
a courtly Frenchman and director of the fisheries directorate, is a battle-hardened veteran of the fisheries wars.
He is one of the handful of top officials who have master-
minded Europe's tough, unyielding approach to
negotiations with the Canadians.

Nothing has done more to poison the air than the
Canada-EC fisheries dispute, a classic example of a diplomatic battle that has played on too long and too bitterly. It
has also been characterized by an unwavering determination by both sides to hold their ground. "That has been the
main element spoiling our bilateral relationship,"
Simmonet acknowledges. "Each party has good reason to
maintain its own approach, but the problem is that it
refuses to contemplate the other's."

Looking out his office window on the gray Brussels
day, the gray-haired bureaucrat's thoughts are thousands
of miles away, in the rough seas of the North Atlantic, in
"the nose and tail" of the Grand Banks and the nearby
Flemish Cap, just outside Canada's 200-mile economic
zone. That is part of the fishing area administered by the
North Atlantic Fisheries Organization, a 16-member convention to which Canada and the EC belong. It is in these
NAFO waters that Canada and the EC have squared off
over levels of fishing activity. Canada has argued the EC is
overfishing, putting severe pressure on groundfish stock in
the entire area, including within Canada's 200-mile zone.
The community has maintained it is following an alternative — and less rigid — conservation approach.

Each year, NAFO sets recommended quotas for various
species including cod, plaice and redfish. But the EC has
objected to its quota allotments, setting its own quotas as
much as 10 times higher. (The EC's self-imposed quota for
1990 was 50,000 metric tons, three times the NAFO suggested limit.) But the EC's fishing fleets never come close
to harvesting at these levels. In 1989, when the EC's uni-
lateral quota was 160,000 metric tons, its fishermen had
only caught 56,000 tons in the first nine months. Still, the
EC maintains that Canada is pursuing a rigid, narrow
conservation formula, and the other NAFO members toe

the line because they don't want to be denied access to Canadian waters.

Simmonet acknowledged that the EC is in a bind. Its fishing industry is operating at severe overcapacity. Most of its Atlantic fleets come from the northern coastal areas of Spain and Portugal, which suffer depressed economic conditions. By advocating a more liberal conservation approach, the EC wants to buy time to restructure its industry. It would have to reduce the numbers employed in the fishing industry, and funnel regional development funds into the coastal areas. It is significant that the quarrel with Canada over fishing quotas only intensified after Spain and Portugal joined the community in 1986. The community says that after the difficult restructuring is accomplished, it would go along with the tougher conservation policy advocated by Canada.

The Europeans feel Canada should be able to understand their plight because Ottawa is experiencing the same kinds of pressures. Fishermen and fish processing workers in economically deprived Newfoundland are seeing their livelihoods threatened by the sharp reduction of fishing quotas within the 200-mile zone. That only raises the resentment in Atlantic Canada towards Spanish and Portuguese fishermen — and the Brussels officials who allow such high quotas. Further exacerbating matters is the clash of personalities. The EC's fisheries commissioner has been a Spaniard, Manuel Marin. Newfoundland's senior cabinet minister is John Crosbie, who has taken an unabashedly provocative role in the fisheries dispute.

Raymond Simmonet's final comment on the whole imbroglio is "c'est stupide." His administration must share responsibility for that stupidity. Canada has warned that the North Atlantic has suffered an environmental catastrophe because of Western European overfishing. Joe Clark has compared it with a major drought on the prairies, or the burning of the Amazon rainforest. Yet the EC seems impervious to these concerns.

This unyielding response suggests an emerging European-first attitude that distresses some students of international relations. The EC's rising self-assurance has spawned something more unsettling — an inclination to make its own rules, strike its own bargains, then let its trade and economic partners scramble to accommodate to these home-grown rules. This go-it-alone approach can be seen in many aspects of the single market reforms. The EC is movable — it just takes more effort.

Disputes like the fish standoff are inevitable whenever economic interests clash. Canada and the U.S. have quarreled over, among other things, shakes and shingles, softwood lumber, and the Pacific salmon fishery. The search for a mechanism to settle these disputes helped forge the free trade agreement. But Canada's relationship with Europe is in many ways more difficult. There is not the same economic affinity.

Canada in the 20th century has become increasingly estranged from Europe, and integrated into the U.S. economic system. The 1989 launch of the free trade agreement was the culmination of this continental drift. In the mid-1970s under Liberal Prime Minister Pierre Trudeau, the federal government had tried to reverse this pattern. It pursued a "third option" of trade diversification, as an alternative to smothering domination by our big southern neighbor. One tenet of that policy was to pursue more economic links with Europe. The results were mixed, but Trudeau at least kept the idea of diversification alive.

Under the Conservative government of Brian Mulroney, any pretense of a "third option" has been stripped away. The North American relationship clearly matters most. Brian Mulroney was, after all, born in a Quebec "company town" dominated by a U.S. multinational; his corporate career consisted of being a branch-plant president for a U.S. company. His key foreign affairs ministers see Canada's destiny lying more with the U.S. or the Pacific Rim. External Affairs Minister Joe Clark seems particularly indifferent to Europe. Ottawa says its trade development initiative has targeted three areas: North America, the Pacific Rim and Europe. But External Affairs appears divided between officials who feel the European link is in need of careful nurturing, and others who see it as a non-starter.

Canada does maintain close relations with one country in Europe — Great Britain. Warm feelings towards the old

Mother Country have persisted even though the Commonwealth is a shadow of its old self. But Britain is an unreliable guide to what is happening in Europe. In recent years, Britain has been going through its own wrenching identity crisis. Its corporations and business people are being drawn increasingly into Europe and the single market. Yet the government of Margaret Thatcher has seemed intent on ignoring the lessons of history.

Thatcher follows in a not-so-proud tradition. Britain did not join the European Coal and Steel Community in the postwar period, did not send a delegate to the Messina Conference that laid the groundwork for the European common market, and shied away from signing the Treaty of Rome in 1957. When its interest in Europe finally did perk up, Charles de Gaulle blackballed it from the EC club. It finally entered the EC late, and has been an unco-operative member ever since. It continues to play a delaying game as Jacques Delors tries to push towards monetary union and a single currency. Make no mistake — Britain's future lies with Europe. But given its history of misjudging and mistiming, it may move more slowly to this realization than its partners on the continent. The question for Canada is whether or not it should continue to play the British hand so strongly. Recent events suggest that Brussels may be a more suitable partner.

U.S. relations with Europe have also had their share of ups and downs. The air over the Atlantic has been befouled by a barrage of increasingly bitter trade disputes. But beneath the surface, something more fundamental has been going on, a long-term shift in geopolitics. Until 30 years ago, America's presidents were largely from the Northeast states, perched on the "Atlantic lake." Although the U.S. would occasionally lapse into Midwest-style isolationism, her leaders valued the European connection. The two Roosevelts — Teddy and Franklin — the Kennedys, and all those graduates of the Ivy League who dominated the U.S. diplomatic corps had a decidedly Atlanticist outlook. They went to prep schools modeled on British public schools, and to universities that emulated Oxford and Cambridge. They read *Le Monde* and the *Times of London*. They formed their opinions from the *New York Times'*

James Reston, a son of Scotland and confirmed Atlanticist whose hero was Jean Monnet, the father of the European Community.

But since the 1960s, the United States has increasingly turned away from the Atlantic relationship. Shifts in immigration patterns have played a determining role. In the first six decades of the 20th century, the influx of people was largely from Europe — the British Isles, Italy, Germany, Holland and Eastern Europe. In the 1970s and 1980s, the pattern changed, with massive inflows from Latin America and from Asia. More and more people cared less and less about the European links.

As the composition of population changed, so did where they lived. The center of political gravity shifted to the West and Southwest. The presidency of Ronald Reagan confirmed this slide towards the Pacific. Jimmy Carter, Richard Nixon and Lyndon Johnson were sons of the South and West. It didn't help that Europe itself was less inclined to look favorably on the Atlantic relationship. With the rest of the continent absorbed in the quest for internal integration, Margaret Thatcher seemed to be the only Atlanticist left in Europe.

Canadian public life has been much influenced by these trends. Taking our cue from U.S. politicians and businesspeople, Canadians during the 1970s and 1980s awoke to the emerging Pacific Rim as a focus for trade and investment. This recognition has been reinforced by immigration flows from Asia. Canada has also cemented itself more firmly in the Americas. For many years Canada resisted appeals that it join the Organization of American States, the association of more than 30 countries in the Western Hemisphere. It has always clung to its European and Commonwealth relationship. But in late 1989, it changed direction and joined the OAS.

While the West and South have beckoned, Europe, on the other hand, has often appeared decadent, socialist, a home for closet protectionists, and hopelessly gripped in low growth and high unemployment.

But perhaps these attitudes are about to shift, if only because the U.S. viewpoint on Europe is itself in a state of flux. George Bush may be the first Atlanticist president since John Kennedy. Sure, he made his fortune in Texas oil, but he was born of blue-blooded New England stock, a prep-school, Ivy-Leaguer through and through. His vacation home is, in fact, on the Atlantic in Kennebunkport, Maine.

More important, Bush has shown that he is comfortable with the European single market. Of course, hard reality has pushed him towards a more positive endorsement of 1992. The European Community shines as a beacon of security and calm, as events appear to be surging out of control in Eastern Europe. Bush has increasingly come to recognize the EC as an equal partner of the U.S. in economic and political terms. The White House has delicately distanced itself from the anti-Delors mania of the British government. It has called for strengthened institutional and consultative links between the U.S. and the EC. After years of sliding away from the Atlantic, the U.S. may be balancing itself again.

Canada has sometimes seemed out of step with the new U.S. diplomacy towards Western Europe. Perhaps, as a follower, the Mulroney government needed time to absorb the events in Eastern and Western Europe. The Ottawa government has been reactive in its European diplomacy, while showing bold leadership in pushing the North American connection. Canada came late to recognize the new shape of Europe.

It is difficult to gauge how Canada's official stance towards Europe has influenced the attitudes of its business class. Business, after all, should be driven by opportunities and profits. Diplomatic subtleties and foreign policy orientation should not unduly influence export or investment decisions. Yet how can they help but make a difference? Even companies experienced in Europe don't trust what is going on there. Their executives can't help but internalize the news reports, the diplomatic flareups, the rhetoric. Furthermore, governments take a leadership role, alerting private enterprise to new investment opportunities and trading markets. Mature, savvy multinationals rarely need this direction from government, but medium-sized and small businesses do.

If our companies do venture into Europe, they usually

confine their efforts to Britain without braving the unknown waters of the continent. This corporate anglophilia has been a serious limitation, particularly for English Canadian companies. They find it safe and comfortable to do business in an English language milieu, reinforced by old Commonwealth ties. Only a few adventurers — often Quebec-based companies — have looked beyond the English Channel.

Canadian business has little presence, for example, in Brussels itself, a rich source of information and contacts. You don't find many Canadians swapping after-dinner drinks in the bars of the big Brussels hotels. They have not have opened offices or enlisted consultants as listening posts in the Belgium city. Only two Canadian law firms are represented there.

Few businesspeople realize that Canada has a special relationship with the EC that, until now, has not been fully exploited. If used skillfully, it could create a valuable access to the community. It might offer this country the opportunity for a partnership with Europe, instead of the climate of dispute and misunderstanding that has existed.

In 1976, as part of Pierre Trudeau's third option push, Canada negotiated a "framework agreement of cooperation" with the EC. The dream was that this accord would foster an exchange of information and cooperation in industrial matters and in science and technology. Canada is the only non-European industrial country with which the EC has signed such an accord, although similar arrangements exist with Third World nations.

As is typical with the Canada-EC relationship, the agreement has been pretty much a missed opportunity. Even the Trudeau government was unable to do much with it. One problem was its fuzzy objectives — it wasn't always clear what it was supposed to do. Also, outside of a small group of enthusiasts, there was widespread indifference in Ottawa to the whole program. Neither did the EC have an enthusiastic champion of the cause.

The framework has been further neglected under the Mulroney government. A joint cooperation committee, including the EC commissioner of external relations and Canada's minister of external affairs, is supposed to meet every year to discuss avenues of commercial and economic cooperation. There have been only seven meetings in the 13 years the agreement has been in force. After a three-year pause, EC External Relations Commissioner Frans Andriessen finally got together in Brussels with Joe Clark in June, 1989. The conversation ventured into a number of disputed areas such as European beef exports, humane trapping and fisheries. It was just the kind of face-to-face ministerial contact that has been glaringly absent in recent Canada-EC relations.

The fondest hope of the framework agreement's drafters was that it would foster joint ventures between European and Canadian firms to develop new technology. That largely hasn't happened. "It is still a framework without many things inside," admits Jacques Lecomte, the Belgian diplomat who is the EC's ambassador to Canada. "It is hard to introduce the private sector into this framework. Perhaps with 1992 there will be more chances."

Jacques Delors has indicated he wants to "step up the dialogue within the framework agreement" with Canada. That simple phrase could open an important window for Canada to rehabilitate its relationship with the EC. Business could play a particularly vital role by capitalizing on the agreement's provisions for exchanges in research & development.

R&D usually gets treated as one of the footnotes to the single market, but that is severely unplaying its significance. The community is dramatically increasing its funding of R&D programs, with plans to spend close to $10 billion of its own money over the next five years. When matching contributions of industry are added, the total commitment is closer to $20 billion. At least half the money is going towards non-competitive, pre-market research, the kinds of things that Canada would like to plug into. The heftiest funding, over 40% of the budget, is going to vitally important telecommunications, computer and micro-electronics research.

There is already more going within the framework agreement than many Canadians realize. For example, officials in Canada's mission to the European Commission in Brussels have access to workshops in the co-operative

R&D projects. It is much harder, however, to link European companies with their Canadian counterparts for the purposes of developing technology. One executive who has tried to work on such agreements is skeptical: "The framework agreement is not worth anything. How many jobs does it create? Tell me what European company will get on a plane and spend European money in Canada. We just don't have the R&D base here."

Yet there is a prototype for this kind of relationship, up and running now in Europe. Canada, through the Crown corporation Atomic Energy of Canada Ltd., Ontario Hydro and the Ontario government, is participating in Western Europe's thermonuclear fusion project, which is part of a wider venture involving Japan, the Soviet Union and the U.S. A Canadian team has been given the contract expertise for the handling of tritium, a hazardous material that accumulates as a result of the fusion process. Canada has experience in handling tritium in its own Candu nuclear reactors. The project was launched in 1988, and the concrete benefits to Canada can't be gauged yet. But its supporters say the participation exposes Canada to a range of technologies in a crucial field that it otherwise would not be able to tap.

Out of the ruins of trade spats and economic conflicts, a new kind of Canada-Europe relationship may be emerging — a partnership built on the foundations of science and technology. Early indications are promising. In that long overdue June, 1989, meeting between Clark and Andriessen, Canada brought up the idea of a specific framework agreement between Canada and EC on science and technology. The Canadian government believes this area offers so many potential benefits that it merits its own agreement, one that focuses the attention of all players in business and government on the opportunities.

Canada may, after much stumbling, be finally taking a constructive approach to the EC as a real government, a force to be reckoned with in world affairs. It has decided that being present in Asia and being close to the U.S. are important goals, but neither of these precludes a reaffirmation of the oldest partnership we have.

Chapter 10

Being There

It was a discreet dinner of two dozen of the world's top businesspeople, on the eve of crucial Montreal meetings of the world trade body, the General Agreement on Tariffs & Trade, in early December, 1988. The host was David Culver, the handsome, patrician chairman of Montreal-based Alcan Aluminum Ltd., and a kind of roving ambassador for the business elite. Invitations were sent to leading chief executives from Canada, the United States, Europe and Japan. The dinner was an opportunity for a frank exchange of views on the important trade issues dividing their governments, such as farm subsidies and anti-dumping laws.

The Americans, headed by James Robinson III, the high-profile chairman of American Express Co. and John Reed, head of the giant U.S. bank, Citicorp, said they would show up. So would a Japanese group fronted by the influential chairman of Sony Corp., Akio Morita. A Canadian contingent would naturally be there, led by Culver and Trevor Eyton, president of Brascan Ltd. and chairman of the blue-ribbon International Trade Advisory Committee which consults with the federal government on trade matters.

And what about the Europeans? Their response came

back: they couldn't make it. The Roundtable of European Industrialists had too much on its plate with preparations for the European Community's single market of 1992. David Culver's power dinner went ahead without representation from the European corporate community.

In retrospect, European business leaders concede their decision not to attend the Montreal gathering was a faux pas. They regret the meeting was arranged at short notice at such a busy time in Europe. In Canada, however, a different spin is being put on their absence. There are suspicions that the snubbing of this Canadian-arranged event reflects a more fundamental attitude: It is still very difficult for Canadian business to be taken seriously in Europe — or for Canada to be viewed as an important country in its own right, separate from the United States.

This is not a good omen as Canada strives to succeed as a world economic player in the 21st century. Its companies must be taken seriously as traders, competitors and potential business partners. That business is going global is a well-worn cliché, but one that encases a solid core of truth. It isn't enough for companies to show the flag in national markets or even on a continental stage. For Canada to be any more than a second-rate power, business and governments must be prepared to move forward on a multilateral basis — to the U.S., to Europe, to the Pacific Rim and the Third World.

The Europe of 1992 offers the most beguiling opportunities. When Canadian products hurdle that one external tariff wall, they can be sold freely into a frontierless, open space of 355 million people (if you count EC and EFTA countries), compared with 280 million in the U.S. The transfusion of prosperity from economic integration will propel Europe to a new status as the world's biggest, richest economic unit.

Sadly, there is the possibility that Canada won't be a big player in this bustling market. The attitude of European business to Canada — evidenced by the Montreal dinner — stems as much from Canadian apathy as European condescension. As a nation, we are preoccupied with our domestic travails — regional feuding, Meech Lake, language, new taxes — which, however important, distract us from considering our role in the bigger world. We get tangled up in debates over the Canada-U.S. free trade agreement, while ignoring the new Europe.

The free trade agreement is not the only game in town. The integrated North American market should be used as a base to explore other vistas. Selling to the U.S. provides exposure and experience in a foreign but familiar market, before pushing off into the Pacific Rim and Europe.

For all its promise, free trade with the U.S. holds certain risks for Canada. It accentuates an already unhealthy reliance on the increasingly troubled U.S. economy. When Americans quit buying cars, our car industry falters. When they quit building homes, our forestry companies suffer hard times. No country, particularly Canada, can be isolated from the waves rippling out from the world's biggest national economy. When America sneezes, the rest of the world catches cold. But a stronger Canadian relationship with Europe would provide some offset to the ups and downs of the U.S. economy.

Even the common wisdom that a company should approach the close U.S. market first may not be right for everyone. Some businesses might be better off selling to Europe before the U.S. The decision should hinge on the relative strength of markets and potential competition in the two areas. For certain products and companies, Europe may be less risky.

But Canadians will have to approach Europe with a fresh perspective. Traditional import-export relationships may no longer be enough. The dismantling of non-tariff barriers within the community means a shift in the competitive balance between EC-based suppliers and those from the rest of the world. Freed from these barriers, some EC products will win market share from non-EC products.

Furthermore, once shipments get inside the common EC tariff wall — only about 4%-5% on average but steeper for some goods — they could face all kinds of subtle obstacles. The community's liberalization of government procurement will favor EC companies. Technical standards may reflect European priorities. Access to European services markets could be determined by how open Canada's market is judged to be by EC authorities.

The message is clear: Canadians should think about positioning themselves as insiders in Europe. That may mean a sales office, a marketing arm or even production and R&D. And they must move quickly, well in advance of the 1992 deadline for the single market. Their global competitors may have already preempted them.

Building on good feelings

There are intangible factors that Canadian companies could trade on in Europe. Our strongest card is the warm feelings Europeans hold towards us. The French ambassador to Canada suggests that his countrymen take their favorable impression of Canada from the romantic legacy of fur trappers and *coureurs de bois*, and from the stories of Jack London, James Oliver Curwood and Maria Chapdelaine. He says Canadians always rank very high in French opinion polls for lists of "friendly countries." The magazine *L'Express* once published a special issue devoted to "fantasies of the French." The top fantasy was to own a log cabin in Canada.

Europeans, however, have a fuzzy image of Canadian companies, brand names and products. (Although perhaps, we could sell the French some prefab log cabins.) This is reflected in a survey of international consumer attitudes undertaken by Nicolas Papadopolous and Louise Heslop of the International Business Study Group at Carleton University, Ottawa. The survey asked 2,220 consumers, mostly opinion leaders, in six European countries, Canada and the U.S. what they thought of the products and people from five countries: Canada, the U.S., Japan, Sweden and their own country. The survey revealed an abysmal lack of profile for Canadian products, not only in Europe but in the treasured U.S. markets.

Canadian goods ranked low in such key areas as "market presence" and consumer familiarity. The survey confirmed that Canadians are known for commodity-type products such as wheat and forest products, but not for brand-name goods that create a Canadian image. American and Japanese products, on the other hand, scored high on visibility and consumer knowledge, and

Japanese items rated extremely high on quality.

Where Canada truly shines is in foreigners' attitudes towards the people and the country. In every market, Canadians rated highly in trustworthiness and likability. In fact, French respondents gave us higher marks in these two areas than they gave their own countrymen. And Canada was the clear winner when foreigners were asked to rate the nations according to where they would like to see more more investment coming from. The French, for example, gave Canadians the highest rating of any potential investment partners, ahead of the Swedes, the Americans and the Japanese. The Japanese rated relatively low as potential investment sources but high in terms of product knowledge and quality. Canada was the opposite, rating high as welcome investors, but low on products.

The lesson is clear to Papadopolous, a Carleton University marketing professor. Canadian companies, he says, should be pushing their national identities in products they ship to Europe. They should not be hiding their nationality; they should be shouting it out loudly. Our companies could be exploiting this image of personal trustworthiness to lend credibility to their products.

However, doing business in the EC is often more subtle than shipping telephone switches with maple leafs emblazoned on the storage crates. That approach wouldn't necessarily work in an industry where it is important to be an EC insider. In some sectors — such as government procurement or telecom — there may be a premium to being branded as Italian or European, but not Canadian.

But even here, we can build on our nationality. A reputation for trustworthiness and good manners opens doors at European companies for joint ventures, mergers, licensing agreements and technology transfers. That is the case in Britain. "Canadians simply get a thicker welcome mat in Britain than Americans," says Larry Tapp, chief executive of Ontario-based packaging company, the Lawson Mardon Group, which has more than 70% of its assets in Europe. "Canadians aren't as arrogant. That's a big advantage."

This is part of the pitch used by Bernard Esambert, the chairman of La Compagnie de Financière Edmond

Rothschild in Paris, as he tries to attract Canadian clients for his European M&A business. Europeans, he says, see Canadians as more suitable partners than the Japanese or Americans. The French, for example, see the Japanese "not as enemies but not as allies either. We are careful about them. As for the U.S. companies, we know them — their advantages and disadvantages. But Canadian groups have a potential for sympathy in Europe that is enormous. Partly it is the two languages. But we see also Canada as more of a partner than a big brother."

The words are very nice, but they are meaningless unless Canadians have the determination and sophistication to exploit this favorable reception. European business people are often incredulous that so few Canadian businesses take the trouble.

One reason they don't is that a large percentage of our industry is controlled by foreign companies, many of them U.S.-owned. A Canadian subsidiary is usually a supplier to the Canadian market, or part of an integrated North American strategy. It is rare for a foreign-controlled multinational to use Canada as its base to attack the European market. It might happen when the subsidiary has a world product mandate — a brief to produce a particular product for the entire globe. But that kind of role is still infrequent.

Home-grown enterprises offer the most potential for Canadian involvement in Europe. Canada has a handful of global companies that are active in Europe. Alcan, Bombardier Inc., Canadian Pacific Ltd., Moore Corp., Bata Ltd. and John Labatt Ltd. are well-positioned to take advantage of the single market. But we do not have many multinationals with wide horizons. Furthermore, successful global companies are increasingly citizens of the world. They draw their ideas, research and products from anywhere it makes economic sense. Canada, as the home country, may benefit indirectly from these activities, but the rewards are often hard to calculate.

Our small and medium-sized companies are more promising vehicles, but they must find the time, energy and resources. They must be able to lever off their success in Canada — their products, innovation and marketing expertise — to penetrate EC markets. They need good information on Europe — and lots of it.

Tapping into information

That is where government can be useful. Ottawa, for example, hired Business International, the consulting arm of *The Economist* magazine in Britain, to prepare a survey of how European chief executives were preparing for the single market. The result was a rich and detailed 150-page guide to the state of the home team. The government also launched independent studies to assess the effects of 1992 on trade, investment and technology developments in 12 different sectors. Among the fields studied: telecommunications, forest products, consumer goods, auto parts and food. Furthermore, the government is providing an on-line information service on Europe 1992 that will be accessible through the department of External Affairs and through Ottawa's international trade offices across the country.

Public and private sector working groups are probing the 1992 program and advising the government on what action to take. Within the government itself, 15 interdepartmental working groups are looking at the effects of EC legislation in key areas. Individual groups are, for example, examining 1992's economic implications, the technical standards, and the market for defense products (That might turn out to be a fairly short report, given events in Eastern Europe.) Preliminary results are encouraging. A paper issued by the departmental working group on telecommunications was frank and somewhat critical of Canada's lackluster performance in organizing large-scale R&D projects.

These working groups are talking to the International Trade Advisory Committee, the high-powered corporate task force headed by Trevor Eyton. ITAC cut its teeth as a consultative body during the Canada-U.S. free trade negotiations. Now it has set up a task force on Europe 1992, chaired by the ubiquitous David Culver. ITAC itself draws on the work of the sectoral advisory groups on international trade (SAGITs), committees of businesspeople who convey the trade concerns of their particular industries to the government. There are 13 such SAGITS, ranging from fish and fish products to arts and cultural industries.

Any Canadian companies exporting goods or services to Europe — or with any interest in doing so — should be tapping into these government reports, surveys and working group papers on 1992. They should be working with industry associations to raise any concerns about 1992 and its impact on them. They should find out who sits on their industry SAGITs, and contact those people. If they have a particular interest in Europe, they should be talking to the ITAC task force.

There have been concerns that the ITAC-SAGIT network that worked so well in communicating business's views on free trade to the federal government, may be running out of steam now that the Canada-U.S. accord is in force. That would be unfortunate, since the challenge of Europe is just as crucial to the health of Canadian industry.

Ottawa has come to recognize that trade relations are no longer enough to guarantee access to a market. Trade follows on direct investment. A new federal program identifies and assists Canadian companies that would be potential partners with European businesses in joint ventures, technology transfers and industrial cooperation. There are also programs designed to expose exporters to European business practices and marketing. Provincial and federal governments provide assistance for participation in those great European institutions, the industry trade shows. The two levels of government sponsor a constant stream of trade missions to Europe. The departments of external affairs, trade, and industry, along with various provincial ministries, regularly provide information on European business opportunities. Any interested Canadian company should be making use of these services.

They should also be capitalizing on Canada's mission to the EC in Brussels, which gets good reviews as being alert to developments in the EC. The guestbook in the outer office to the EC mission has seemed remarkably uncluttered with signatures, considering the importance of this Brussels post. Quebec maintains a listening post in Brussels, but it stands alone among the provinces in this regard. Ontario, in the country's manufacturing heartland, closed its Brussels office a few years ago.

It is not necessary for a company or an industry association to be physically located in Brussels. Business centers like London, Paris and Frankfurt are good listening posts for European information. A Canadian company may want to be closer to the national market it serves. As a corporate city, Brussels is nothing special — Glasgow, Limerick or Barcelona may look more hospitable as the site of a sales office or production plant. But Brussels does have a central location in Europe, which is why many American multinationals nestled there long before 1992 was hatched. Furthermore, a Brussels location provides instant access to a wealth of contacts in institutions such as NATO and the European Commission.

A company with a future in Europe somehow has to plug into the vast Brussels information database. It must be alert to developments in European standards, to the opportunities to share in the Brussels-funded R&D programs. There is even a small business task force in Brussels aimed at assisting entrepreneurial European companies in benefiting from the single market. And decisions from the European Court of Justice in nearby Luxembourg have implications far beyond Europe's borders.

Tony Brace is a comptroller with Ontario Hydro who spent two years in Brussels attached to the EC mission and coordinating Canada's participation in the European nuclear fusion project. While in Brussels, he observed that the city was not just a government center — it was also the the focus for corporate activity. Major European companies are represented there; high-powered business delegations come and go. He was struck by the number of commercial opportunities that he was exposed to by being in that Belgian city. Brace himself was able to bring four or five possible business ventures to the attention of Canadian companies. He sees the need for a stronger government presence in Brussels — Ontario should have an office there — with a more entrepreneurial approach by embassy officials.

Big European companies maintain offices in Brussels

to lobby the commission and filter information to their head offices. Fiat, for example, is said to have a Brussels staff that is bigger than that of the Italian embassy. Few Canadian firms can afford such luxury. If a company has a British, German or French subsidiary, it can serve as a collector of EC information. A manager with the Amsterdam subsidiary might fly into the Belgian city from time to time to make the rounds.

Canadian companies also have the option of buying the services of one of the many business consultants with Brussels branches. Most big accounting and consulting firms provide databases that can feed 1992 information into the client company's own computers; the EC itself provides this service. The problem is that the information and analyses are rarely tailored to Canadian needs.

Consumers of consultancy services should be alert to what they are buying. A number of instant experts have set up shop in Brussels, peddling information to an infor-mation-hungry business clientele. Some try to get away with spouting vague generalities, the kinds of things that can be gleaned from magazines, brochures and EC publi-cations. A good clipping service would be just as useful. Real insight and an insider's perspective is more elusive — and costs a lot more.

For Canadian companies, one of the highest-stakes games is the development of new Pan-European technical standards. As indicated earlier, Canadian companies can-not join the big European standards organizations, such as CEN or CENELEC. However, a European subsidiary of a Canadian company may have access to these delibera-tions. At least, the subsidiary should join a trade association that has input in setting standards in the industry. Or the European distributor of the Canadian company's products should be a member of the trade association, giving it a role in the standards-setting pro-cess. Officials at the Canadian mission in Brussels say there are many ways for Canadian companies to be part of the action, if they are willing to assert themselves.

Smaller companies may find that membership in a trade or industry association is the best route to becoming informed on Europe. Ethnic businesspeople are often members of associations — such as the Canada-German Chamber of Commerce — that take an active interest in forging Canada-Europe ties. Some associations — forest industry groups, for example — are well-informed on 1992, although none has an office in Europe. American business groups are usually better equipped. The American Chamber of Commerce, which has a Brussels office, is adept in guiding its members through the intricacies of 1992. Canadian companies with U.S. subsidiaries might tap these U.S. sources. Canadian associations should develop a similar expertise.

For companies that need more than information, there is always lobbying. Lobbying at the EC level is fairly new. It has emerged as a big-money business only as the community has assumed expanded powers in the rush to 1992. It is vastly different than the pressure-group tactics employed in the U.S. and Canada. EC power centers are diverse and geographically separate — the commission in Brussels, the parliament in Strasbourg, and various operations in Luxembourg. Furthermore, the European style is subtler and more low-key than in North America. To be successful, any company or pressure group must rely on an experienced operative, someone well versed in the sometimes incomprehensible politics of the community.

One group that sees itself providing influence and information is the legal profession. There has been a stampede of lawyers into Brussels over the past few years. Many are from the EC countries themselves; the growing power of the European Court of Justice and the increase in EC-wide legislation has ignited a boom in Community law. But there are also many Americans who see Brussels as a potential legal gold mine, just as Washington has become. Whether this gold mine will ever materialize is still being debated. Some observers say there is simply not enough business in Brussels for all the new lawyers.

Lucien Lamoureux, the former Speaker of the Canadian House of Commons, represents the firm Fasken, Martineau, Walker, which in early 1990 was one of only two Canadian law firms in the Belgian city. (The Montreal firm Lafleur Brown was the other.) Lamoureux, who has practiced law in Brussels since the mid-1980s, says

Canadian law firms still gravitate to the traditional haunts of London and Paris. This indifference to Brussels, he believes, reflects the lack of recognition by lawyers — and their corporate clients — about what is happening at the EC. He believes that will change as Canadian corporations and law firms recognize the vast volume of European statutes and legal decisions that affect them.

Lamoureux says the European Court will play a central role in defining the single market. The actual treaties setting out the single market — the Treaty of Rome and the Single European Act — are often vague, leaving the court to fill in the details. One of Lamoureux's roles in Brussels is to keep the corporate clients of his Canadian firm informed on this outpouring of legal decisions. He says the demand for this service can only increase.

Law firms, consultants, trade associations — all these are worthwhile sources of information, good starting points for any business that wants to be *au courant* with Europe. But the best information comes from someone who has been there, a company that has already made its mark in Europe. The case-history approach is more effective than flimsy theory.

Unfortunately, the Canadian system provides few opportunities for the kind of networking, in which companies experienced in European exporting and investing can swap stories with the uninitiated. The Canadian corporate world is highly competitive; companies are often unwilling to betray trade secrets. They need to be prodded and nudged. Government has to provide the mechanisms for contact between big companies, experienced in European business, and small- to medium-sized enterprises ready to take the plunge.

The ITAC-SAGIT structure is a good beginning. The myriad conferences on 1992 and Europe provide a worthwhile but infrequent forum for such give and take. The trade fair program is another worthy exercise. But governments should be dreaming up programs whereby savvy players in Europe can take beginners under their wing. Why couldn't Alcan or Bombardier be a kind of international big brother for smaller Canadian companies, perhaps even joint venture partners? Inexperienced companies might be given access to the contacts and expertise of more worldly mentors. A small company could even piggyback its products on the export and distribution system of a more established operator. The French have a program that works that way.

Ottawa should also consider pulling small companies together into consortia or associations, that could set up offices in Brussels or London or sponsor traveling troubleshooters in Western Europe. Two small companies might pool their resources in a joint venture to take on Europe. Government should be looking at ways to facilitate such links. Unfortunately, it is getting late in the game for creative solutions. They should have been developed long ago.

Until such programs are developed, information must be collected and absorbed on a catch-as-catch-can basis. Managers must listen intently to what their fellow Canadian companies are saying about Europe, at conferences, in newspaper and magazine articles and in books like these. First-hand experience is a valuable educator. I hope that the case histories in the following chapters will light some fires.

Chapter 11

The EuroCanadians

Larry Tapp, the stocky, bespectacled president of Canada's Lawson Mardon Group, bounds from his chair and strides across the elegant drawing room of the London townhouse that is his packaging company's European headquarters. "I've got to show you something," he says, pointing from his second-story window across the street to a burned-out shell of what was once another tony Mayfair townhouse.

The charred shell, Tapp explains with the enthusiasm of someone imparting inside information, was recently the branch of a prominent British real estate agent. A few weeks earlier, Welsh nationalists had bombed the building to protest the realtor's prominent success in selling plain, little Welsh cottages at exorbitant prices as weekend homes for wealthy Londoners.

For Tapp, that gutted building is a symbol of the regional differences that will persist long after the single European market is constructed. It is a jarring reminder that even within the borders of a seemingly united Britain, there are resentments and bitter regional differences. These are things, he says, that a Canadian company would not know unless it had a presence in Europe.

"You have to get immersed in the environment and

learn from experience," says the 52-year-old Tapp, his suit jacket off, exposing red suspenders against a rumpled white shirt. "You have to have a base in one of the 12 countries. You can't learn this kind of thing from Bay St. or rue Ste. Catherine. You can't be afraid — you just get in there and do it."

Larry Tapp speaks with the apparent insight of a grizzled transatlantic veteran, a man who feels as much at home talking with investment bankers in The City as assembly line workers in London, Ontario. In fact, the company he heads, Lawson Mardon, is one of the newest Canadian-based multinationals, formed in 1985 and based in Mississauga, Ontario, but with 70% of its assets and sales in Europe.

Lawson Mardon is a global company by accident of birth. Thunder Bay-born Tapp, a veteran manager with experience in several large Canadian companies, was once president of Lawson & Jones, a Canadian packaging company which was 75% owned by a British parent, Mardon Packaging. In the mid-1980s, Mardon's parent, the sprawling British conglomerate BAT Industries, was toying with the idea of selling off its packaging interests in bits and pieces. Tapp led a management group that was seeking to buy out the Canadian piece, Lawson & Jones, from BAT.

But BAT switched strategies, putting all of Mardon Packaging on the block as a single unit. The smaller Canadian buy-out was no longer in the cards. So Tapp and various managers and outside investors, including the late Toronto mining magnate Stephen Roman, expanded their horizons and ended up with the whole thing — a company with production facilities on two continents and more than a billion dollars in sales.

Lawson management had to learn quickly the principles of international business in the late 20th century — be focused, pursue niche markets on a global scale, and achieve economies of scale through joint ventures. They made selective acquisitions in Europe, including a French plastics company. They teamed up with a British firm in a joint venture to produce polyethylene tetrachloride (PET) containers, much used by soft drink companies, for the European market.

Tapp doesn't believe large production runs are suitable for all kinds of packaging. Because of national differences in taste and habit, smaller-scale production often makes more sense. But manufacturing these flexible PET containers is a mass-commodity business, Tapp explains, "and if you're in a commodity business, you have to think big. Putting our resources together positions us to compete very well in that business."

By the early 1990s, Lawson Mardon Group was still grappling with a number of management problems inherited from the previous regime. Tapp believes that operations must be streamlined to compete as a globally. With the bulk of its operations in Europe, Lawson Mardon has been putting more emphasis on boosting its North American — particularly U.S. — operations to achieve a more balanced geographical coverage. Its aim is a neat 50%-50% split of sales between the two continents, rather than the current 70%-30% weight in favor of Europe.

Like any European company, Lawson Mardon is acutely interested in the 1992 project, but refuses to let enthusiasm override basic principles. Tapp acknowledges, "where we can strengthen our core business in Europe, we will do it." But otherwise, he has a jaundiced view of the whole 1992 hoopla: "I try to stay away from the hype." Yes, there will be opportunities to establish European-wide production, distribution and marketing in some products, but regional differences discourage similar integration in other product areas. "If we buy an Italian company, we will assess it as an Italian concern doing business in Italy. There may be some 1992 synergies but that shouldn't be the only criterion in buying the company."

And any time Tapp needs to be reminded of Europe's continuing complexity, he just looks across the road.

Lawson Mardon is one of a core of EuroCanadian companies that are in Europe not because of the 1992 hype, but because they feel any company of a certain size, outlook, ambition and potential has to be there. The single market, with its potential to create a richer, more competitive Europe, only strengthens that commitment.

The EuroCanadian companies can be divided into three

loose categories. There are the old multinationals with historical ties to Europe. Those early connections often involve a founding British parent or a British investment, a legacy of Canada's colonial status. Canadian Pacific Ltd. built Canada's first transcontinental railroad, completed in 1885, using British investors' money. Alcan Aluminum Ltd. has been in Europe for most of its 60-year history. Moore Corp., the Toronto-based business forms company, has its roots in 19th century Britain. Seagram's, a long-time merchandiser of brand names in Europe, has solidified its presence with the 1988 purchase of France's Martell cognac company.

Lawson Mardon falls more into the second category: the new class of striving, expanding global player that has emerged over the past 20 years. The names include Bombardier, Labatt's, Northern Telecom, McCain's Foods, DMR Group, Gandalf Communications, CAE Industries and Power Corp. These companies recognized they could not rely on a small Canadian market that is itself opening up to foreign competition. They believed business is going global and any company that does not respond is doomed. Their European vision is not blinkered by ties to any "mother country." They are comfortable operating in France or Finland, Germany or Spain.

The next category covers the smaller players that have a specialized product or expertise they can sell to the world. These niche players are multinational in vision if not in financial muscle. They are entrepreneurial, often family-owned. The names are not of the household variety — Unitron, the Kitchener hearing aid maker with a strong German sales base; Mold-Masters Ltd., a Georgetown, Ontario, manufacturer of plastics molding systems with a factory in Baden-Baden; Plastique Moderne, a Montreal plastics company with a plant in Lyons, France. There are lots more — but not nearly enough if Canada is to keep pace in the changing world economy.

All three categories of companies would be in Europe with or without the single market. Project 1992 only reinforces their commitment. What they share is a certain fearlessness about the world, a willingness to toss the dice. Their managers are not all urbane sophisticates, but they are creative, persistent and capable of learning. They are excited by the Europe of 1992. But they are also being challenged by the new economic framework, in ways that vary significantly from company to company.

Approaching Europe systematically

It would be hard to find a Canadian businessperson more bullish on his company's prospects in the European single market than Alain Roy, the beefy co-founder and executive vice-president of DMR Group, the Montreal-based management consulting company specializing in information technology. "We have a beautiful business in Europe," he says. "Our margins there are higher than anywhere else."

Roy is a friendly bear of a man, with bushy black hair, thick eyebrows and a gently spreading paunch. He looks more like a well-dressed lumberjack than the stereotypical management consultant. Roy is the "R" in DMR, one of three IBM Canada Ltd. managers in Quebec who deserted Big Blue in 1973 to found DMR and helped guide it to $127 million in sales in 1989. His founding partners were President Jacques Ducros and Serge Meilleure, who left the company in 1984 to establish a successful real estate business, but got bored and returned in 1989.

Roy's role is to keep watch over DMR's large non-North American operations, which contribute more than half of sales. It's a job that keeps him on the road a third of the time. The company is active in three markets — North America, the Pacific Rim (including Australia), and Western Europe. Its European operations are the fastest-growing segment, spurred by a flurry of acquisitions and internal growth. In 1989, 25% of DMR's sales came out Europe; 400 of its 2,000 employees were situated there. European profits were the best in the organization, much better than in the U.S. where DMR has had trouble finding a workable business strategy.

DMR's business is providing solutions to corporate clients who want to use information technology — computers and telecommunications — to become more competitive and productive. The Montreal company has

172

focused with particular intensity on the systems integration side of the business. It has an established expertise in developing value-added networks for financial institutions, retailers and airlines. Among its fortés are multi-bank credit card networks and airline reservation systems.

DMR is the kind of company that Canada needs to nurture. It isn't the classic Canadian resources producer or manufacturer, both of which are valuable in their own right. It exports services and human brainpower. Companies like DMR represent Canada's hope for a balanced trade effort, a deeper economy and a higher recognition abroad.

By the early 1980s, DMR had its feet wet in international business. It had some aid contracts in Algeria, but that wasn't enough on which to build a business. It developed a banking package for an Australian building society. It opened a Boston office. But this activity amounted to a series of adventures, with no overall strategy. DMR realized it would have to follow its customers and support their worldwide activities if it was going to survive and prosper.

Britain was the natural place to start. An important client, Laurentian Group, the Quebec financial services company, had purchased a British insurance company. DMR's big Australian clients were starting to move into Britain, as well. In 1984, DMR set up a British office, which was instantly successful in tapping the financial institutions market. It has, for example, garnered a contract to develop a shared automated teller network for three of Britain's major financial institutions. DMR was also the technical manager for a project to build a national system permitting consumers' store purchases to be debited directly from bank accounts through point-of-sale terminals. The project involves British retailers, major banks and the Bank of England, the central bank.

In a sense, DMR was going against the grain of French Canadian-controlled companies. Many Quebecois businesses have chosen France or even Belgium as their first toeholds in Europe. The shared language is a natural magnet. However, Ducros and Roy have taken easily to the British business style, which they find similar to the North

American model they know.

The British contracts gave DMR a handy expertise in banking systems. With 1992 approaching, management felt the conditions were right for exporting these skills to the continent. The looming deregulation of financial services was spurring the once-torpid European banking sector into action. Banks were trying to defend and build market share, not just in their home countries but right across Europe. Nowhere is that more evident than in Belgium, where sleepy Societé Générale de Belgique, the giant holding company for a network of industrial and financial companies, was shaken awake by a hostile takeover attempt by Italian tycoon Carlo De Benedetti in early 1988. It was eventually rescued by the French white knight, but it had become a more innovative company.

DMR has been able to capitalize on this new dynamism. It has won a dozen contracts within the Societé Générale complex alone. But it quickly learned it could not serve its continental customers from Britain. So a continental presence was established through acquisitions, first in Belgium and later the Netherlands. The Belgian market gave DMR access to some of the big-spending supranational institutions, such as NATO and the European Commission. Roy also believes that small country markets, like Belgium's or Holland's, are often more accessible to outsiders because potential customers can't find all their systems solutions at home. DMR put down roots in these small markets, before going after the big ones. Germany and France would have been much harder nuts to crack first.

DMR has discovered advantages in simply being Canadian. "We are not considered a threat; we are not German or French," Roy says. He is convinced that narrow nationalism will persist despite the integration of the European economy. That is one reason why there will not be a Fortress Europe. Old chauvinistic attitudes will drive some consumers of information services into the arms of unthreatening Canadians. Even Americans, he finds, are viewed more suspiciously than innocuous Canadians. Another factor in DMR's success is that it approaches companies as a consultant only, not as a merchandiser of products. Unlike similar companies in Europe, it does not peddle its own software, thus allaying fears of conflict of interest.

DMR has found that it cannot build operations from scratch in Europe. It is a constant battle to attract top-flight personnel to a company with no track record on the continent. Also, Roy finds that a company has to be of a certain size before the corporate customers — specifically, the managers who make decisions on hiring consultants — start paying attention to it.

That was an important factor behind the acquisition of local consulting companies — the Belgian company, Corfyf Belgium SA, in 1987, and a much bigger Dutch firm, Consulting Associates, in mid-1989. These have provided an instant nucleus of qualified people who know their markets — and, more important, are known by the potential customers. The Canadian company has also opened an office in Frankfurt to sell its expertise in bank and airline systems. A French operation is starting to pull in contracts. However, this heady expansion has necessitated a constant series of management seminars, as Roy and his colleagues try to educate their new managers with the parent company's way of doing things.

DMR has a thin hierarchical structure, which Roy says is vital for any service company that needs to react quickly to its customers' demands. "If there are any more than three management levels in an office, the client loses out somewhere," he believes. But that also puts extreme pressure on top management during a period of expansion. Tom Cullen, the president of its international division, recently moved from Montreal to a Dutch office to assert more hands-on control of this burgeoning business. "I had been spending all my time on airplanes," he sighs.

DMR is one of our international success stories, a company that has proven Canada can export skills in leading edge technology. But like many small- to medium-sized companies, it must make a critical decision. As it expands, it keeps bumping up against much bigger, more diversified competitors, companies like EDS from the U.S., and Gemini, a formidable European firm. If DMR wants to step up to the top rung of information management companies, it needs to match their financial firepower.

Roy concedes that the challenge for the future is that "we need to find some guy with big pockets to compete with these people." He talks about the possibility of an alliance with a big bank or perhaps one of the big international accounting firms which have management consulting arms. It would mean a surrender of independence for Ducros and Roy, two entrepreneurs who fled the safe, stifling world of IBM. However, "we can no longer do it on our own," Roy admits, a touch of sadness in his voice.

Falling in love again with Europe

From in his office perched above London's bustling Trafalgar Square, Harvey Romoff can see beyond the clusters of pigeons and tourists all the way to Paris, Frankfurt, Brussels and Milan. Romoff, a gregarious, bearded economist, is Canadian Pacific Ltd.'s eyes and ears in Europe. He gets excited about 1992 and CP's potential role in its unfolding.

"There is room and scope for a foreign company to get involved here," says Romoff, an urbane man who loves the rush and roar of West End London. "It's a lot more interesting than 10 years ago. It is easier to build a big operation here, to approach Europe as one country instead of 12."

Canadian Pacific through Harvey Romoff is rediscovering Europe all over again. The giant conglomerate, with $12 billion in 1988 sales, is a thick slice of Canadian industry, with interests spanning transportation, waste management, forest products, real estate, energy and manufacturing. But it also has a long tradition in Europe, dating back to its beginnings as Canada's first transcontinental railroad in the 1880s. The railroad's construction was spearheaded by a bunch of Scottish engineers. Much of its early financing came out of Britain. The company still has many British shareholders. For years, CP ran fleets of ships from British seaports to Canada.

But a decade ago, it started pulling back. Like many sprawling holding companies, it decided it was in too many businesses; it lacked that all-important "focus" that was so valued in the 1980s. Furthermore, Europe was not an attractive place to be. CP streamlined its administration there and got out of the shipping business, although it maintains a stake in transatlantic container traffic. Romoff managed CP's disengagement from Europe, but he stayed on to watch how the 1992 would unfold. So far, he has been impressed. He is convinced CP can be a player in the continent again.

Romoff says CP's new activism in Europe will be limited to its core areas — mainly transport, forestry, energy and real estate. But he feels there is lots in the 1992 program that could accommodate it. He gets particularly excited talking about a potential deregulatory "big bang" in transport that will accompany the single market. Transport is in ferment, he says, as the steamroller of reform threatens to sweep through trucking, airlines, rail and shipping.

Britain looks particularly appetizing, because of the Conservative government's zest for private ownership and privatization. CP was, for example, very interested in building and operating the British end of the high-speed rail link with the Channel Tunnel. However, the Canadian company lost out to a public-private consortium that included the state rail company, British Rail, and a couple of big construction companies.

That has hardly diminished Romoff's interest. In late 1989 he talked about the potential for picking up some bits and pieces from the long-promised privatization of British Rail — perhaps some freight operations or certain links, such as the London to Gatwick Airport run. He told *The Financial Post's* Mathew Horsman that, "Generally, we are interested in transportation and comfortable with railways."

That is not the limit to CP's European ambitions. Romoff also keeps an eye open for possible acquisitions by Laidlaw Inc., the fast-growing waste management company which is controlled by CP. Hamilton-based Laidlaw, headed by Michael De Groote, a Belgian-born entrepreneur, is on the prowl for European additions to its empire of service companies. In 1988, it acquired control of Attwoods, a British waste management concern, and a controlling interest in ADT PLC, an international security systems company based in London.

Romoff's mandate may be to find possible European acquisitions, but he would have to do a convincing selling job at CP's head office in Montreal. William Stinson, CP's tough, dour chief executive, is under pressure to improve the company's lackluster earnings. He is not in the mood for risky forays into unfamiliar areas. Stinson makes encouraging noises about Europe, but his interest is fixed on the potential gains from Canada-U.S. free trade. In the pre-Stinson era, CP's business had an east-west orientation; it had a national and, to a lesser extent, Atlantic focus. Now the outlook is north-south and continental. This shift in the most "Canadian" of companies is indicative of what has happened in our business community.

Stinson, a savvy manager with a reputation for keeping his cards close to his vest, can get quite animated talking about the benefits CP should reap from the boost to north-south transport under free trade. The company has been translating that enthusiasm into action. In 1989, it bought out minority shareholders of its Chicago-based midwest railroad, the Soo Line. Earlier in the 1980s, it had tried to sell its interests in the Soo Line.

While the U.S. looks more enticing, Stinson finds it "very difficult to get a hold on Europe. I can't understand those people getting up and saying we should do more in Europe. You just go on over there. They couldn't care less about Canada. Go to France if you think they've got a special relationship with Quebec. They could care less. They're so inward looking."

"The U.S. market is is the only game in town for Canada," Stinson maintains. "The other games are becoming more difficult to play."

But if Harvey Romoff is running into a brick wall at head office in Montreal, he isn't showing it. He remains an unabashed Euro-enthusiast. "There will be growth and change and we are looking at ways to participate."

If it were not for 1992, Romoff says he probably wouldn't be in London. "We decided 'let's keep the toehold in Europe but let's grow with it.' You need an office here. You have to take an hour each day just to read the papers; you have to talk to bankers. You get no flavor of what is happening if you are 4,000 miles away."

Harvey Romoff's enthusiasm seems boundless. Bill Stinson isn't quite so sure. It will be interesting to see how CP works out this dichotomy, as it makes its way back into Europe.

Regrouping for 1992

In 1989, Moore Corp.'s top management held its annual strategy meeting in Brussels, the first time it has been outside Toronto in the company's 107-year history. The selection of drizzly Brussels as the site for this important session was partly practical. Moore's leading executives wanted to get a first-hand look at the Belgian business forms company they had just acquired for $40 million. But the meeting also had symbolic importance. It is the Brussels-based European Commission and its 1992 program that is compelling Moore to overhaul its European strategy.

Moore is the sleeping giant of Canadian industry, the world's biggest business forms supplier with sales of $3 billion a year. Its business is producing endless streams of forms, direct-mail messages, checkbooks, and other mass-printed business communications. Moore is often characterized as a sedate and unexciting company in a mundane business. Despite a sold financial performance over the years, it has been a stock market under-performer and has been rumored as a takeover target. (So much so that management has concocted a "poison pill" to discourage would-be suitors.) But of all Canadian companies, it is also the most active and creative in preparing for the 1992 revolution in Europe — and perhaps the best placed to profit from it.

About the time Samuel Moore, the company's immigrant founder, was establishing a business forms company in Toronto in 1882, he was setting up a parallel operation in his home country, Britain. The two companies operated in relative isolation from each other for years, but gradually drew closer together, finally merging in 1977. One legacy is Moore's strong European presence with 4,500 employees — including 1,800 in France — and more than $400 million in sales there, about 16% of its worldwide turnover.

As Europe languished economically in the early to mid-1980s, so did Moore's operations there. In recent years, profit margins across the Atlantic have been only 5%-6%, about half the levels of North America, where Moore does 70% of its sales. One reason was the sluggish European economy. The business forms industry, whose customers are other companies, is a leading indicator of economic health. But Moore's European operations also suffered from their concentration on low-value-added products, such as paper business forms. In North America, Moore has been more aggressive in the higher margin business of direct mail. Advanced technology allows Moore to take raw data from a customer, electronically manipulate it into a desired format, and run off mass volumes of the message. This adds more value to the direct-mail product than if Moore simply prints the forms.

Another barrier to profits in Europe has been the company's organizational structure. Instead of operating one big Pan-European company, it has maintained stand-alone operating units in each country. Each national company would comprise production, sales and marketing functions. This clumsy organization suited the local buying patterns of Moore's corporate customers, which thought in terms of national economies and national companies. But it prevented Moore from maximizing economies of scale in production or more efficient sales and marketing. Low margins and fragmented organization also inhibited the big investments Moore would need to move into higher-value-added products.

John May, the lanky, congenial American who is Moore's international vice-president for Europe, is painfully aware of the disappointing profit margins. But he sees the dawn of a new age in Europe that offers a glorious opportunity for the giant business forms company to shake its malaise.

As 1992's single market looms, Moore's corporate customers are expanding, allying, merging and acquiring. They are creating larger operations that spill over national boundaries. Moore figures that as customers become Pan-European in their scope and size, their business forms purchasing will be conducted on a European-wide basis. Moore is in an enviable position to take advantage of this trend. It has the widest geographical coverage of any business forms supplier in Europe. But Moore's organization, born out of the old Europe's fragmented markets, have left it ill-equipped to cope with this new Europe's one market.

That will change as Moore embarks on a European reorganization that will shake up the hidebound old company. In 1989, it opened an office of 50 people in Lausanne, Switzerland, that will evolve into a European headquarters in the early 1990s. Through this office, corporate customers will be able to place purchase orders for all of Europe. Instead of May — or his successor — being located in a suburb of Toronto, he will be on the spot in Lausanne. More important, those self-contained national subsidiaries in Europe will be downgraded into purely marketing and sales organizations. European manufacturing plants will be organized into three transnational product groups, each of which will report to product managers based in Lausanne.

The choice of Lausanne as the European head office reflects Moore's assessment of the continent. Switzerland is not a member of the European Community, but Moore foresees an increasingly integrated European market extending beyond the EC's confines, to include not just the EFTA countries but Eastern Europe, as well. Lausanne, with its central location and creature comforts, is as good a place as any.

The 48-year-old May says the new structure will give Moore the flexibility to increase or decrease production in a specific plant or country to allow greater efficiencies. Business forms can then be produced and distributed more economically. The future thrust will be to reduce the number of plants producing traditional business forms, while the company invests more heavily in direct mail technology which generates higher margins.

Moore is determined to take advantage of being the business forms company with the widest presence in Europe. Now that it is thinking European, it wants that coverage to be even wider. It has embarked on a flurry of deals that is unusual for this conservatively run company.

It launched a joint venture with Atel, the biggest Italian forms maker, to combine Moore's printing know-how with Atel's marketing knowledge in Italy. It has opened a sales organization in Germany, and signed a licensing agreement with a Greek company. Then there is the recent purchase of Lithorex, a direct-mail company based in Brussels. There will be more acquisitions to come in countries, such as Spain, where it has little presence. May sees Western Europe as the ideal base to explore the emerging Eastern European markets. He believes the liberalized regimes will privatize state-owned printing companies. The Canadian company would be interested.

May can personally attest to the logic behind Moore's formation of a new European head office in Lausanne. He makes more than a dozen trips to Europe each year to meet with the management groups. That's a lot of wear and tear on a family man, and a lot of wasted hours in the air. Moving his job to Lausanne would cut down on the travel significantly, slicing the number of transatlantic trips about in half.

The changes will be more wrenching for Moore's European managers. The reorganization means breaking up the national companies and forcing the former country managers to think on a European-wide rather than a local basis. It will test the strength of Moore's corporate culture, and its employees' openness to radical change. "For the first time, a French plant manager might have to report to, say, an English product manager in Lausanne. We are moving to become a European-wide company," May says.

He is confident all this will happen, if not exactly painlessly. "The mindset of business people has changed dramatically over the past five years. It is true that people over 40 still see themselves as German or French. But ask a 30-year-old and he will say he is European. That is having a dramatic effect on Moore already. We are doing things that would have been very difficult to achieve 30-40 years ago. But Moore as a European-wide company has such a momentum behind it now, I couldn't change it if I wanted to."

A son of Germany comes home

Jobst Gellert saw the sign in a railroad station in Baden-Baden, West Germany, that read, "Europe — Your Fatherland." The message set off a maelstrom of emotions for the German-Canadian businessman. Born in East Prussia, in a town now part of the Soviet Union, he had left Germany as a 26-year-old plastics mold-maker, determined to find success in the expanding North American workplace. He built a flourishing manufacturing business in a community northwest of Toronto. Now, he was coming home, not as a tourist, but as an investor and direct participant in a European economy that looked just as exciting as Canada did 30 years before.

Gellert is a chubby 59-year-old who looks like a caricature of an absent-minded professor. He has a mischievous smile, whispy white hair and gold-rimmed bifocals that he alternately props on his forehead or perches on the end of the nose. But Gellert is no pussycat. He is a hard-nosed and highly opinionated entrepreneur. His business is designing and manufacturing injection molding systems for the plastics industry. Gellert and his wife Waltraud, a slim businesslike accountant, founded Mold-Masters Ltd., in 1963, after only five years in Canada. Today, the family-owned company employs more than 200 people in a modern Georgetown, Ontario, factory. Mold-Masters' highly technical products are used worldwide in the manufacture of plastic components that end up in everyone's home — in cars, medical packaging, houseware, even toothbrushes.

From the start, Mold-Masters has been export-oriented. There wasn't enough of a Canadian market to sustain the company. Today, more than 90% of production is shipped to foreign markets. Gellert muses that, "I shouldn't be in Canada. To sell a product that does not come from a manufacturing nation is hard. Outsiders think you come from a resource country where there is no added value in a product." Yet he is not about to move. The Georgetown plant is ideally located close to Toronto International Airport.

Gellert has been spending a lot of time in Baden-Baden, an old, elegant city of spas and casinos. In May,

1989, the company opened a new 20,000-square-foot sales and production complex in that city, its first manufacturing facility outside Georgetown. It was a spectacular leap for what is essentially a small business. Mold-Masters is a private company and Jobst Gellert is fiercely protective of his financial figures. But it is probably accurate to say sales are much less than $50 million.

Gellert shows no sign of trepidation. Mold-Masters had been selling in Germany since its creation. It is familiar with the plastics industry there. Gellert has been a constant visitor to his homeland, dealing with agents and distributors, and manning a booth in the giant plastics industry trade show in Dusseldorf. But what clinched the decision to build in Germany were reports of the economic integration of Western Europe, followed by the dramatic changes in Eastern Europe.

"If you read the newspapers you knew it was bound to happen — there would be a united Europe," Gellert says. He also observed "a kind of scariness about Fortress Europe" in North America. He decided "it is better to have something in Europe before it closes down. Also, I wanted to be there before the Eastern European market starts. When that market opens up, it will be too late."

Even Gellert couldn't have predicted the speed with which the walls around the Communist bloc came tumbling down. But he knew the pressures were building. Months before the Berlin Wall was breached, he was saying "I feel the cold war is over." Gellert had gone to Leipzig in East Germany a couple of years earlier. He visited family members who were deprived of soap, perfume, things we take for granted. "I saw what was going on. They need us and they need us badly." He also observed an industrial machinery that was still able to turn out high-quality products. He was saddened, frustrated and encouraged at the same time. Like many Western entrepreneurs, he does not believe the Eastern European market will provide instant returns. But he wants to be close by in Baden-Baden for the day that happens.

The German beachhold makes sense in another way. Gellert believes it is very hard to build a business by merely exporting to a country. In Mold-Masters' early years in the U.S. and in Germany, it relied on independent agents. It had unhappy experiences with its representation. Gellert felt his company was learning very little about the market, and was having its secrets poached by the opposition. Mold-Masters quarreled with its agents.

Gellert eventually put its own sales and service organization into Europe. He warns other Canadian companies: "You must be there and listen." He says some agents take information they learn in the market and use it for their own purposes. "You don't work with agents if you want to continually improve. Or if you do have an agent, you must work out a good contract that is enforceable." He counsels that any Canadian company should never engage a partner that is much larger. The bigger the partner, the more the potential that it will exploit the relationship for its own good. After an unhappy history with hired guns, Gellert's investment in his own sales-manufacturing operation doesn't seem so risky.

The choice of Baden-Baden as a factory site was one of those wonderful, fluky things that makes business so much more than graphs and management principles. In fall, 1987, the economics minister of the German state of Baden-Wurttemberg was visiting Toronto. Baden-Wurtemberg is highly aggressive in attracting investment, particularly in high-technology industries. The minister wanted to see a successful business run by a German-Canadian. Someone came up with the name Mold-Masters.

Gellert remembers the high-powered delegation that turned up on his door in Georgetown — a couple of Ontario cabinet ministers and a posse of German businesspeople accompanying the minister. The group was very impressed with Gellert's operation. At the end of the visit, the German minister observed how sad it was to see this German talent at work in other countries. What about bringing some of it back home in the form of a branch plant?

Gellert was receptive. He had been reading those stories about 1992. He visited Germany looking at possible factory sites. He was able to enlist a qualified and trusted German relative as a consultant. Baden-Wurttemberg was able to arrange financing at half the prime rate. Eventually, the Gellerts settled on a location in Baden-Baden, which is Waltraud Gellert's home town.

The choice of a manager to run a foreign venture is always difficult, especially for a small company. But Gellert found it easier than most. His daughter Petra, 28, like her mother an accountant, had just married Jonathon Fischer, 27, a skilled machine maker who had apprenticed in Germany. Gellert convinced the young couple to head off for Baden-Baden to run the family operation.

He finds no little irony in the fact that, just as he and his wife embarked on an adventure in a new country 30 years earlier, his Petra and her husband were about to do the same. The new frontier for his daughter and son-in-law is the country he had left behind. In setting up Mold-Masters Europa, Gellert gave the young couple the mandate to produce one of Mold-Master's specialized products for the world market. "They can sell it to any country, including us," Gellert says. "I told them, 'You must complement our needs. Don't duplicate what we do here.' "

He says proudly, "My son-in-law is a practical man; he went to Germany to apprentice to become a machine maker. With their mix of skills, it gives them a good chance to assume leadership of the company some day."

The Baden-Baden plant is still in its infancy. It is far too early to determine if Mold-Masters' bold push into European production will be successful. Around the Georgetown plant, it has been a bit of a novelty. Posters with pasted-on snapshots of the new building are scattered around the shop floor, as if to say, "Hey, look what we're doing!"

But Mold-Masters is already caught up in the remarkable transformation of Europe. After only a few months in operation, the plant had already employed 35 people. Five of them were skilled tradesmen newly arrived from East Germany in the first wave of migration. Jobst Gellert was excited about the prospects."They are willing to work overtime," he exclaimed.

Sticking to what you know
Tom Wacker is drawing little blocks in red ink on a

sheet of scrap paper. The senior vice-president of international financial services for Toronto-based Royal Trust is charting the structure of his organization, based in London, England. His diagram has turned into a jumble of rectangles, arrows and lines. There are lines to companies on the Channel island of Jersey. Two blocks represent private banks in Zurich and Vienna catering to wealthy individuals. Another line zips down to Royal Trust's recently acquired 25% interest in a Berlin-based private bank. The silver-haired Wacker, a 46-year-old Indiana native, has drawn about two dozen blocks and he isn't done yet.

By the mid-1990s, Tom Wacker's messy diagram will look even more cluttered. Royal Trust, one of Canada's biggest trust companies, is on the move as an international acquisitor. Michael Cornelissen, its ambitious, impatient South African-born president, has stated that the company will have 50% of its assets outside Canada by the mid-1990s, up from 25% in 1989. Hence, his company is the most aggressive Canadian financial institution pushing into foreign markets. It has targeted the United States, where it is picking up bargain acquisitions in the troubled savings & loan industry, and Europe, where it hopes to capitalize on the single integrated market. It is also building a business in the Far East, but its plans are nowhere near as ambitious yet.

Ironically, Royal Trust is expanding in Europe just as Canada's big banks are paring back. Although this pull-back has been going on for years, it was underscored in the late 1980s as Royal Bank, Canada's largest financial institution, engineered a reorganization in Europe. Royal Bank had been a lender to corporate clients in several European countries. It had moved into the wild and woolly London-based Eurobond markets. But the returns never justified the investments. The bank got out of Eurobonds in the mid-1980s, as a number of North American-based financial institutions did. In 1989, it closed down a number of its small national banking units. From now on, the bank said, it would concentrate mainly on serving its North American corporate clients, and its trimmed-back

European operations would reflect that. Canadian banks are very interested in the single market, but, having been burned by European expansion before, they have been taking a wait-and-see approach.

So what makes Royal Trust think it can succeed where others could not? For one thing, it has sworn off the all-things-to-all-people approach of its big-bank rivals. The trust company believes it can build on its Canadian successes in specialized banking areas. These include private banking for the affluent individual; asset management for private portfolios and mutual funds; home mortgage lending; and specialized services for business, such as foreign exchange, money markets and selected lending. "We can add value in these areas because we are good at them," Wacker maintains.

Royal Trust aims to create a mirror image of the company that has been successful at home. That explains the interest in U.S. savings & loan companies. They handle the same deposit/mortgage business as Canadian trust companies. Royal is also scouting around for a British building society, a deposit institution that lends residential mortgages. Building societies were once required to be mutual institutions, owned by depositors. However, new laws allowed the societies to be shareholder-owned. Some have "demutualized" to become publicly traded companies. Royal Trust would like to capitalize on this trend.

Wacker's aspirations for his London-based Royal Trust International don't stop at the English Channel. He and his colleagues like the looks of private banking on the continent. Rich people in Europe have traditionally done their banking at specialized institutions that provide thick carpets, attentive service, tailor-made products and investment advice. Royal Trust provides a comparable service to well-heeled clients in Canada, so it knows the business. The company already owns private banking interests in Germany, Austria and Switzerland. It would like to add some in France and expand its operations further in affluent Germany. Italy, Spain and Portugal aren't quite as interesting markets.

Ironically, the 1992 project makes it tougher for Royal Trust to carry out its European game plan. The Canadian company is finding it harder to acquire attractive targets as prices are driven up by the single market hype. This has slowed expansion in France, particularly. Fortunately, Royal Trust kicked off its European expansion in 1985 before values really got out of hand.

Despite the steep prices, Wacker is enthusiastic about 1992. As boundaries fall, markets for financial products should become more efficient and competitive in Europe. That should reduce consumer prices for all kinds of financial services. Margins in banking have been healthier in Europe than elsewhere; well-run institutions should continue to pull down good profits. It will be easier to do business across borders; countries like France, where financial services markets have been largely reserved for domestic companies, will open up. Royal Trust should benefit from the higher standards of living in Europe through its network of private banks. The Austrian and Switzerland banks are particularly well-placed, because they sit outside the EC's tax net.

Wacker believes Canadian institutions have little to fear from protectionism in the 1992 program. The first draft of the banking directive caused some nervousness by propounding a vague doctrine of reciprocity. However, reciprocity was given a more benign twist in the second draft of the directive, and fears have abated somewhat.

Royal Trust feels it can exploit synergies among its far-flung international subsidiaries, particularly in private banking and asset management. Affluent people are, after all, mobile; they need banking services in Hong Kong and Vancouver, Zurich and Toronto. Wacker also sees the potential for S&L branches in the Western U.S. to identify real estate investments for European clients.

Royal Trust belongs to the family of companies controlled by Peter and Edward Bronfman, the Toronto branch of the Bronfman family. All these companies see themselves as operating in an entrepreneurial culture. Corporate hierarchy is relatively flat, and decision-making is decentralized. Managers get low salaries by big-business standards, but are rewarded with company shares whose value is more closely tied to performance. Managers are expected to act like the company belongs to them.

The international operations are no different. Each subsidiary has a managing director with personal performance goals. Besides running their companies, the managing directors are on the lookout for acquisitions that will strengthen Royal Trust. "Every one of these managers is a shareholder in Royal Trust," Wacker says. "In every deal I know my money is on the table. Therefore, acquisitions are not just done to get bigger."

In this climate, corporate culture gets a lot of attention when Royal Trust sizes up an acquisition candidate. "We get people who buy in on our culture," says one Royal Trust manager. "Wherever we have a problem, it is because the cultures don't mix."

Wacker sees the 1989 purchase of 25% of Gries & Heissel, a Berlin private bank, as a model relationship. Like the Canadian company, G&H is highly entrepreneurial, non-bureaucratic, and risk averse. It needed the international network of a Royal Trust, and the Canadian company wanted a piece of a valuable German banking license, a valuable commodity in a market that has been fairly closed to foreigners. Wacker would like to duplicate this happy chemistry right across Europe.

These EuroCanadians are a mixed bag of Canadian business — small, privately owned and entrepreneurial to big, publicly traded and bureaucratic. For some, like Mold-Masters and DMR, Europe 1992 is a new adventure. For Canadian Pacific and Moore Corp., it is a challenge to rethink old strategies and to regroup for a new market.

All these companies share one characteristic: They have all carved out a presence in the European market. They have recognized it is not enough to ship products or people blindly into the common market. They have decided it is crucially important to have someone there who is protecting and advancing their interests. Not all these companies will be successful in their endeavors. Their strategies will be continually shaped and adjusted as time goes on. But they have leaped over the first hurdle. They are now inside the market and running full-speed towards the next obstacle — and opportunity.

Chapter 12

The McCain's Way

Harrison McCain, the high-energy force behind the world's largest frozen french fry producer, is momentarily lost in quiet thought as he gazes out the window at the wide and rambling St. John River. It is a frigid late November day, and the river is dotted with chunks of floating ice. Across the river, the land rises sharply to the top of the valley, where tidy white frame farmhouses are scattered along the horizon. "Have you ever seen anything that looks better than that?" the chairman of McCain Foods Ltd. asks.

The view from Harrison McCain's desk is a metaphor for the business that he and his brother Wallace run — a global and sophisticated company, but one with roots deep in New Brunswick soil. This mix of worldly and rustic is reflected in the art in McCain's office. Behind his desk hangs an oil painting of an old New Brunswick farm scene, showing plainly dressed men and women digging up potatoes. The opposite wall sports a still life of red berries tumbling out of an overturned bowl, framed by the window of a Paris apartment. A four-foot-high world globe stands in the corner.

The brothers' affection for the St. John Valley is the overriding reason why McCain Foods, despite its world-

191

wide reach, keeps its home office in tiny Florenceville, a pretty hamlet of 700 people, 90 kilometers up the river from Fredericton. Harrison's and Wallace's spacious offices sit atop McCain's three-story red-brick headquarters, just off the Trans-Canada Highway and part of a sprawling complex that employs 1,000 people and turns out frozen french fries, frozen vegetables and desserts.

Florenceville is thousands of miles from Paris, London and Rome, but that has never got in the way of the brothers' ambitions. The company they founded 30 years ago is probably the most successful Canadian-owned business operating in Europe (with the possible exception of shoemaker Bata Ltd.). It may in fact be the most adept Canadian company selling to the global marketplace. Many other companies have greater overall sales, slicker public relations and higher-profile chief executives. But none have been more skilled in pushing its products and its brand.

The brothers have built a great Canadian success story, a company with $2.1 billion in sales in 1989, more than 40 factories and 12,500 employees. They have managed to keep the company private and independent, even though big American food companies, such as H.J. Heinz Co., have approached them to sell. McCain's worldwide operations turn out half a million pounds of potato products a day. Its french fries are a staple ingredient in the diets of millions of Canadians, in homes, restaurants and public institutions. The name McCain is a ubiquitous presence on Canadian television, promoting frozen dinners, desserts, vegetables, pizzas, and microwave burgers and fries.

The McCain's processing plants are an important market for primary farm production right across the country. But in New Brunswick's potato industry, they are the overwhelmingly dominant player. The brothers' relationship with the 600 local growers is something akin to that of feudal lords. Each year, they take 50% to 60% of the province's annual potato crop of 600,000 metric tons, all under a fixed-price contract negotiated in advance. Despite this power over many peoples' lives, they are respected, if not always loved. It is accepted that they have brought a good living to the valley.

But McCain Foods in Canada is small potatoes compared with McCain's in the rest of the world. Only about 25% of its worldwide sales are in its home country market. Another 20% comes from the U.S., where it processes french fries, pizzas and concentrated juice. McCain's is one of Australia's major food companies; its per capita sales Down Under have been the highest in its worldwide empire. It has gained a solid toehold in Japan, selling fries and vegetables. However, the strongest market by far is Europe, where in 1988 it rang up sales of close to $900 million, about 45% of its worldwide turnover. Sales in Europe more than tripled over the 1985-1989 period through organic growth and acquisitions. McCain's as a private company does not release its results, but company insiders say its European operations are highly profitable. In fact, Europe chalks up the best financial results of any region where McCain's does business.

The New Brunswick company is by far the largest producer of frozen french fries in Europe, a troublesome competitor to the food giants Unilever and Nestlé. It controls a commanding 60% of the frozen french fry market in Britain. Even in France, arguably the home of the french fry, it leads its competitors by a country kilometer. Its sales are expanding quickly in Italy, the powerful bastion of pasta eating. It has made inroads into Spain. It is the most recognizable Canadian brand name in Europe, although few people would know it as Canadian. That stylized "McCain" logo with a dazzling yellow star dotting the i, is the calling card for Canada's only true global brand — "now or at any time in the past," Harrison McCain declares.

All this has been achieved with a family partnership that is rare in big business. Here are two brothers who can seemingly work together without apparent jealousy or conflict. Each seems at ease with his role in the company. On a typical working day in Florenceville, they putter around the office in casual V-neck sweaters, slacks and open-neck shirts. They slip in and out of each other's offices for consultation.

At 62, Harrison is the older of the brothers, a charismatic manager with a ruddy skier's tan and a shiny bald head. He is round-faced and fit-looking except for the small hint of belly edging over his gray flannel slacks. His ruddy face and rounded features lend him a cherubic look — a cherubic dynamo: He sends off enough energy to light up the St. John Valley. Harrison has a firm handshake, a direct way of speaking. He never sits still; he is notoriously impatient, at times brusque. "He can light up a room; he has this aura about him," marvels a former McCain's manager. "My wife could tell when I had just come from a meeting with him. His dynamism is contagious."

Wallace, 58, offers a sharp contrast in physical presence and personality. A weekend tennis player, he is taller, slimmer, more angular with sharper features than his brother. He is also much less outgoing. Wallace speaks more slowly and softly and with a rural New Brunswick twang. In interviews with journalists, he is prone to giving one-word answers, until he hears something that engages his interest. Then he speaks forcefully and at length.

Company insiders say Harrison is the visionary and the financial man; Wallace is the nuts-and-bolts detail man. Harrison is chairman, and Wallace president; they share the chief executive's position. They have carved up responsibilities for the world, with Wallace taking Australia, the United States and parts of Canada, and Harrison getting Europe and the remainder of Canada. The company is owned by the two brothers and their families, although Charles McCarthy, the loyal longtime managing director of McCain's British subsidiary, is believed to hold a small minority interest.

McCain's has the enviable facility for becoming a corporate citizen of whatever country it is operating in. It never denies its Canadian parentage but never pushes it either. It would never slap maple leafs on its packaging. The raw potatoes that get sliced into golden fries are rarely shipped from Canada; they are not processed in Canada. The only thing Canadian is the name on the box.

To drive home this point, Harrison tells the story of the Prince of Wales, who on a state trip to the province several years ago, was told by the agriculture minister that McCain Foods, a giant french fry producer in Britain, was actually a local New Brunswick company. Prince Charles firmly informed the minister that he knew McCain's and they were not a New Brunswick company — they were quite clearly a British company.

The local politician stuck to his guns, and the argument went back and forth for an embarrassingly sustained length of time. The prince finally consulted his advisers, who informed him that, yes, McCain's is a Canadian company based in Florenceville, New Brunswick.

Harrison McCain is clearly on Prince Charles's side in this debate over his company's nationality. "My God, we aren't a Canadian company in England," he says in his rapid-fire manner. "My God, we've got six factories in England, we employ 1,500 people there. It's a British company as far as the British are concerned, and as far as Prince Charles is concerned. So that's that."

He swivels around in his chair, facing his interviewer to drive home his point. "Those french fries we are selling in England are made in England. The french fries we sell in France are made in France. What we want is the brand McCain on it. We are selling a global brand."

The McCain brothers like to say they have nothing to teach other Canadian companies. They went to Europe at a different time, under different circumstances than are faced by companies today. Wallace, talking slowly and softly, says, "Taking a food company and label and taking it global today? Nothing's impossible, but I wouldn't try it for all the money in Canada combined." But then he adds: "Unless you had a good product." Not every Canadian company aspires to be a McCain's, but many have good products. The McCain's story is inspirational to any manager whose vision of markets to conquer extends beyond Buffalo or Seattle.

Long before the 1992 project, in the early days of its company's existence, Harrison and Wallace McCain saw the potential in the fragmented, often difficult market in Europe. They were not blinded by the close and familiar attractions of the United States. They recognized that their particular products and circumstances were best suited to markets across the Atlantic. Although country boys, they were hardly rustic in their ambition or outlook. They were not hung up by the "foreignness" — the cultural and language differences. The McCains were never "ethnocentric" managers, people who thought that North American practices were, by definition, superior to those elsewhere.

As outsiders, the brothers were able to see the big picture, a perspective that escaped their local European competitors, who were still burdened by national and local strategies. Yet the McCains also saw the need to approach Europe as an insider, with a real tangible presence in the market, and not just an export relationship. They recognized that the economics of the french fry business made local production imperative. The brothers were able to capitalize on the immense goodwill that Europeans in all countries feel towards Canadians. They approached Europe with a prudent, conservative expansion strategy, but they were willing to gamble with big bucks when they saw the opportunity for a breakthrough. The McCain boys won that gamble in spades.

Establishing the beachhead

The rolling fields that reach back from the St. John River would appear to be unpromising terrain in which to plant and nurture a multinational company. There have been McCains in the Florenceville area since the 1830s, when the firm immigrated to Canada from County Down, Ireland. Even back then, potatoes were, quite naturally, in the family blood. Harrison and Wallace grew up in a farm family; they were used to getting up early and doing the chores. Their father Andrew was a quiet, hard-working man who made a good living. His business was shipping and selling seed potatoes all over the world. In fact, Andrew McCain died of a heart attack in the early 1950s, just as he was about to take his first trip abroad to one of his prime markets, South America.

After graduating with arts degrees from good Maritime universities — Harrison from Acadia and Wallace from Mount Allison — the two boys worked for the New Brunswick timber and petroleum baron K.C. Irving. Harrison had a good job in the Irving oil business; Wallace was on the hardware side. Still in their 20s, they were too

196

ambitious to contemplate a lifetime of employee status. In the late 1950s, they decided to strike out on their own. They had grown up in the large and well-established potato-growing industry; two other brothers still ran the family potato export operation. They saw opportunities in the fledgling frozen food sector of the business. They would establish a new processing plant to buy locally grown potatoes, as well as green vegetables such as peas and beans.

The french fries started pouring out of the small Florenceville factory in January, 1957. In that first year, 30 employees turned out 1,500 pounds of frozen fries an hour. (Today, McCain's plants around the world process 500,000 pounds an hour.) Gross sales the first year — $152,678 — showed it was still a small-fry operation.

Harrison and Wallace McCain say their father's export business gave them an international outlook that has stayed with them all their lives. They were comfortable doing business abroad. They thought no more about sending a load of french fries around the world, than about trucking them down the road to Toronto.

The brothers had no sooner started up the business when they made their first international sales — frozen peas — into Britain. The timing was right: The British government had just lifted import controls, which had been imposed after the Second World War for austerity purposes. Within a few years, the McCains had built up a healthy transatlantic trade in frozen vegetables and french fries. The fries were becoming big sellers, serving Britain's food-service market in hospitals, schools and restaurants. But they were not sold as "McCain's" products, or any brand at all. They were just a commodity poured almost anonymously into the British market. That did not sit comfortably with Harrison McCain, who as early as the 1960s had dreams of building a major international brand. Right from the beginning, the brothers had put their family name on their products in Canada. They had built up their own sales force, bypassing the food brokers who slap private brands on the food boxes. They wanted to do the same thing in Britain.

However, to build up a brand, the McCains needed a

local presence and a local sales force. They needed someone who knew the market intimately, who approached it
as an insider. Soon after he started selling to Britain,
Harrison McCain struck up a friendship with a production
manager and buyer for a British frozen food company.
Charles (Mac) McCarthy was a handsome, charming man,
knowledgeable about the industry, a natural salesman.
The brothers hired him away in 1965 to run their British
operations. That was a turning point for McCain's in
Europe. They began the evolution from being a supplier of
other people's french fries to a purveyor of their own brand
name, with their own sales force. The concept of branded
frozen french fries was new to Britain. British companies,
such as the big Unilever group, had tried to build brand
names, but Harrison today dismisses these efforts as
"mickey mouse." Powered by Mac McCarthy — and the
acquisition of a British catering supplier — McCain's business took off.

It was inevitable that the brothers would move from
export sales to production in Britain, but the timing was
dictated by events. Canadian imports to Britain enjoyed
favorable access and preferential tariffs because of the old
Commonwealth ties. Britain had not yet joined the
European Common Market, but the McCains realized its
entry was probably inevitable. (It actually happened in
1973.) That would shut out the Canadian french fries,
because tariffs in Europe were prohibitively high for outsiders.

Harrison McCain remembers the night in the mid-
1960s he was sitting in a British hotel room when a BBC
news announcer reported that the pound was being devalued by more than 14%. The Canadian businessman
realized that was the end of McCain's export business to
Britain; the devalued currency gave local competitors an
insurmountable advantage in their home market. For the
boys from Florenceville, it was either get out of Britain or
become a local processor. The McCains never hesitated.
They set about building a factory in Scarborough in
Northern England, a plant that would be supplied by
British growers. It opened in 1969, the biggest and most
efficient french fry processing factory in the world. The fac-

tory lent a very powerful impetus to McCain's already well established strategy — to become a branded french fry producer in Britain. From that base, it has never looked back, and even today, dominates that subsector of the British potato market.

Crossing the channel

By 1970, McCain's was a $40 million company, with almost half of those sales coming out of the British operation. It was an amazing track record for a 13-year-old Canadian company. It had yet to penetrate the markets of Western Canada, but was already a significant player offshore. But Harrison McCain was, typically, not satisfied. His vision of a global brand name was pushing the company in other directions. He and Wallace would have to make a decision on where to push that brand next. The United States was close and familiar. However, potato processors there had already moved into the frozen food market. The established companies, with their big potato-growing acreage in Washington and Idaho to draw from, would be hard to overtake. Continental Europe was at a much earlier stage in market development. McCains's was already sending some shipments into the continent from its Scarborough plant. The McCains had never found geographical remoteness much of an obstacle. The decision, in the end, was fairly easy. "We chose Europe and it was a wonderful blessing for us," recalls one McCain's executive.

The big question was: Who would take McCain's across the English Channel? Mac McCarthy was busy enough in Britain. Besides, the channel was a much wider body of water than it is today. British businesspeople in those days just did not understand other Europeans — and vice versa. Harrison, going with his instincts, selected an outsider, a new recruit who brought a quite different combination of skills to the highly entrepreneurial management team. George McClure came to the company from the federal government, where he had been an economic policy official in the departments of regional economic expansion and forestry. He had a Ph.D. in economics, had been an economics professor at Royal Military college, and a private management consultant in transportation, land use and economics. Like most people, he was captivated by the can-do personality of Harrison McCain.

McClure still remembers Harrison, with typical bumptious enthusiasm, walking up to him and saying, "George, I wish you would go to Europe, put your hands in your pockets and walk around for awhile." In the winter of 1971, George McClure spent a couple of months doing just that. He talked to everybody he could reach in the potato industry, in Holland, Germany, France and Belgium. He gathered statistics and analyzed them. He came back to Florenceville and told Harrison he saw an opportunity there. There was no mass-volume french fry processing in Europe. Holland was the most efficient producer of potatoes — the best place for a processing plant. From there, they could ship into the biggest potential market, Germany.

That report confirmed to the McCains that Europe was the way to go. Harrison sent McClure back to Holland to set up a local company. That began a long, lonely period for the economist. He tried to drum up some french fry business — no one would bite. He scouted around for processing operations to buy; no one wanted to talk to unknown Canadians. McCain's even shipped a million pounds of fries from England to sell in the continental market. No one would touch them. The Dutch and Germans like a creamy yellow-fleshed potato called *bintje*; McCain's British potatoes are Prince Edward type which have a white flesh. It took a year to sell the shipment.

Then in the summer of 1972, McClure's persistence paid off — he got a break. The continent was having a bad potato crop, while Britain was swimming in spuds. McClure cranked up the shipments of french fries from Scarborough. "We were the first people to sell a frozen french fry to the food service markets in Holland and Belgium," McClure recalls. Suddenly, the small processors in the Benelux countries paid attention. Local processors suffering from the poor potato crop approached McClure about selling their plants. McCain's bought its first factory in the Netherlands in 1973, and added another the following year. The beachhead was established.

With the entry into Britain and the launch of this first continental venture, McCain's established a strategic approach that was to be repeated over and over again around the world. It was conservative yet devastatingly effective in one market after another. First, McCain's would use exports of french fries to develop a target market. Then it would establish its own marketing operations and sales force to push the McCain's brand and build up volumes. The next step was to construct or acquire a modern factory with advanced processing methods. With those facilities in place, McCain's would become by far the dominant producer in the national market. Country after country fell to this beachhead approach — Holland, Belgium, Germany, France, Spain and Italy.

Right from the beginning, McCain's had a Europe-wide vision. There was none of this local-production-for-local-market syndrome. The brothers never hesitated to establish production facilities where they made good economic sense. From Holland, for example, they could ship into the rich and close German market, or into neighboring Belgium or France. It is true that McCain's 16 European factories are spread over a number of countries. But location decisions are driven more by the peculiar economics of french fries. Fries are a relatively low value, high-weight commodity. It is simply uneconomic to ship large volumes for long distances over an extended period of time. Once export sales reach a certain volume, the company starts looking at production closer to the market, with shorter transport distances.

However, the brothers insisted right from the beginning on having marketing and sales people located in the distinct national markets, close to the customers they had to know and sell to.

French fries, McCain's primary product, are usually the first thing it sells into any market it wants to develop. In most European countries, it has pioneered mass-produced frozen french fries. Once the McCain fries establish a firm hold, the company looks at growth through product diversification. After fries come frozen green vegetables, frozen pizzas, frozen entrees, frozen deserts, and on and on. This diversification is most advanced in North America,

Australia and Britain, where McCain's has been established the longest time. But in new markets, the french fry tends to dominate the product mix.

French fries are a large-volume commodity. North Americans eat an average of 10 kilograms a year; Europeans from four to nine kilograms, depending on the country. On any day, McCain's has a squadron of 20-ton refrigerated containers on the roads between Amsterdam and Italy, piled to the rafters with cardboard boxes full of fries. There is usually, however, a little room on the top to wedge in a few crates of a low-volume product — say, frozen pizzas, desserts or TV dinners — that the company is trying to establish in the destination market. The idea is to piggyback new products on to its high-volume french fries, providing a low-cost means of shipping.

As McCain's has expanded into more and more countries, marketing people would suggest the company change the name on the package to something in the local language. "We went to Germany with our product and were told you can't sell a product there with the name McCain on it," George McClure recalls. "They said, 'you can't pronounce it.' But I felt if you can sell something called Blaupunkt in Canada, you can sell McCain in Germany." Besides, the brothers were adamant — the name had to stay. The decision was probably driven by ego to some extent, but also by the brothers' insistence on reinforcing that brand name in every market they served. They were right, of course. The McCain name has never stood in their way.

Harrison finds the whole issue amusing today: "We've been told people with other languages can't pronounce that name McCain — well, they can't. We've been told people can't spell that name — and they can't. Nobody in France can spell McCain. In France it is always spelled Maccain, except on our packages. They just can't put the M and the C together. It's just not right. They still can't spell or pronounce it. But you don't care what they say; you just want to keep on selling that brand. We're not going to lose our focus."

Assault on Europe's kitchens

By the late 1970s, McCain's had a very nice business going in Europe. But an important piece was still missing in Harrison McCain's global jigsaw puzzle. The company was still selling its french fries primarily to a food-service market. It had still not reached into the homes of Britain, Holland or Germany. The fish-and-chips lovers of Britain preferred to buy from local "chippies," not in the frozen food departments of supermarkets. On the continent — where eating was a deadly serious matter — the idea of frozen food was totally foreign and usually abhorrent.

The British retail market was further restrained by the fact that the distribution system was controlled by McCain's competitors. Traditionally, food processors moved their products directly to the stores; these processors owned vast fleets of trucks to serve thousands of shops and supermarkets. But by the 1970s, the expanding supermarket chains had moved to central warehousing; a company like McCain's only had to ship its products to a single warehouse, not a hundred stores. The chain would look after the distribution to its own outlets. That made life a lot easier.

One more thing was needed, though — a product that would make a big retail impact. McCain's was able to take advantage of a fortuitous set of circumstances — the right product at the right time. By the late 1970s, Europe was experiencing the revolution in social values and family life that had already taken hold in North America. Women were flooding into the workforce. They had less time to prepare elaborate meals. Families didn't have time to sit down for long dinners at night. They desperately needed convenience, efficiency, and time-saving devices. This was also the time when a new labor-saving appliance — the deep freeze — started making inroads in northern Europe.

McCain's had already introduced a product in Canada that was geared to this new convenience market — a french fry that could be cooked in an oven, instead of in a deep fryer or frying pan. It was fast, clean and tasty. But would it work in Europe? Companies there had looked at the oven-cooked fry before, but never thought that discriminating European families would ever accept it. McCain's market testing showed promising results. Perhaps the timing was right for this radically new product. Harrison agreed, and McCain's launched the oven-cooked fry, called "1-2-3" on the continent, and "Oven Chips" in Britain.

Consumer acceptance was overwhelming. "It was a magic period, when we revolutionized the food market in Europe," recalls one former McCain's manager in Europe. McCain's was the pioneer in a new wave of cook-in-oven products that have captured a wide market. Sales keep rising as the social revolution extends deeper into the southern areas of the continent. With the drive to convenience, the microwave oven has found a place on the counters of kitchens from Amsterdam to Madrid. Europe has been a bit behind North America in microwave use, but the market is expanding rapidly.

The former McCain's manager attributes the oven-fry breakthrough to Harrison McCain's gutsy call. "Harrison is willing to roll the dice. He will take a risk. He is highly opinionated but he is willing to let his people run. Once the market testing came in, he kept feeding the money. It was a very sophisticated, high-spending marketing approach."

One would think that the least likely market to fall to McCain's quick-cooking fries would be France itself. Yet even here, in the sacred ground of good cooking, working wives and busy families are turning to quick and easy solutions. The French market has been vigorous enough for McCain's to justify acquiring processing facilities there. However, pure economics isn't the only logic behind the company's presence in this market. McCain's has learned that any company doing business in Europe has to be alert to the political undercurrents. France has been an important learning experience. It has taught the brothers the need to be sensitive to the political culture of the countries where it does business.

Relying on its tried-and-true strategy, McCain's started out by shipping potatoes into France from its highly efficient Dutch operations. That didn't sit well with the French potato growers, who complained bitterly to the government. France had a large potato crop, but very little processing activity. The French potatoes, which were not of high quality, were going to the fresh table market. McCain's began to notice that the trucks carrying its fries into France were being searched with particular thoroughness by French customs officials. The officers would demand to inspect boxes stored near the front of the trucks. Whole truckloads had to be pulled apart to get to the desired box. The delays were long and costly. McCain's was beginning to get the picture. The company was also aware that it would have to add processing capacity somewhere in Europe to meet the demand. This would be difficult in Holland where the crop was already spoken for. A decision was made to open a processing plant in France.

The Canadians then learned their second lesson about French politics. The Paris government believes in industrial strategy, in guiding the development of the country's industry. Since food is a strategic industry, the government insisted on having a majority French partner for McCain's venture. Joint ventures are not the McCain's style, and the brothers refused. Meanwhile, they began canvassing the local potato industry, including the growers, for support. A strong lobby developed in favor of a McCain's plant. The government relented and said it would allow McCain's to come in as a majority owner. The brothers again refused the offer — it was 100% or nothing. There followed more negotiations, more lobbying. Finally, Paris allowed 100% ownership by McCain's of a new processing plant, which was completed in 1981. Another plant was purchased in 1986, and the original operation has doubled in size.

France has developed nicely; it is now McCain's fastest growing french fry market. Sales are also moving up in Spain and Italy. The company sees this "southern tier of Europe" as the most underdeveloped and, therefore, most promising potential market for frozen food. The changes in families and lifestyles that transformed dinner time in Britain, Germany and the Benelux countries are taking hold around the Mediterranean Sea. Meanwhile, the countries of northern Europe are becoming mature markets. But Harrison McCain warns that growth will not be as spectacular in these southern countries because potato consumption is not nearly as high. It will be hard for french fries to dislodge spaghetti, fettucini or ravioli in the affections of Italian diners. Pasta is too firmly entrenched as way of life. Will the little mass-produced frozen pizzas that roll off McCain's conveyor belts supplant the custom-made home-grown varieties? Hardly. Even Harrison McCain realizes that the Europe of the 1990s will remain a collection of cultures and eating habits. He will be happy with his small but growing niche in each of these cultures.

Family ties

Harrison and Wallace McCain live in big, white houses on Florenceville's River View Drive, a paved road that runs along the top of the valley, across the river from the company head office and french fry plant. Some years ago, they had a landing strip constructed in the fields behind the houses. As the company has expanded, the McCains have kept upgrading the airplanes they own. Today, two small jets — a seven-passenger Westwind and a nine-passenger Falcon — sit on the tarmac, poised to carry their owners to McCain's operations around the world.

Harrison can climb into his plane in Florenceville and, 5 1/4 hours later, disembark at Britain's Luton airport, just northeast of London. From there, it is only a four-hour car ride up to the British head office in Scarborough — or a 50-minute hop into the City of London. It is a trip that he makes at least six times a year; Harrison has estimated he spends up to 150 days a year on the road. He travels to Europe every two months, visiting subsidiaries and attending the management committee meetings. The brothers have devised a loose sort of system. When one is away, the other one tries to be at home, looking after matters at the head office. But there are many days when both are in the air at the same time.

The jets are absolutely necessary for a global company that keeps its headquarters in a remote place like Florenceville. It is difficult to reach this small, rural village from, say, Amsterdam or Paris. A Dutch manager would have to fly to Montreal or Toronto, and catch another flight to Fredricton. Then it's two hours by car up the St. John to world headquarters. The brothers decided long ago that it was easier for them to travel to their managers, than for their managers to travel to them.

For many years, McCain's had a reputation as a two-man show. The brothers, particularly Wallace, liked to be hands-on, directly involved in the decisions of every subsidiary. That discouraged many a promising, independent-minded manager from joining the company. However, the brothers have learned that they have to pull back, to decentralize their operations. As McCain's widened its global net, managers found that the farther they get away from Florenceville, the more latitude and independence they were given. Nowadays, Harrison tends to fly in, review plans, then fly out again. He realizes a $2.1 billion company can't be run by a couple of guys with some fast airplanes. However, Wallace is believed to exercise the old top-down, hands-on approach in the company's Canadian operations. Perhaps it's simply a matter of proximity and familiarity.

There is nothing fancy about the way the McCains structure their international empire. They tend to have strong regional managing directors who report directly to the brothers. In Europe, they have two chief executive officers: Mac McCarthy runs Britain and Spain; Paul van der Wel, a Dutch-born, Canadian-trained manager, is the CEO for continental Europe, based in the Netherlands. The McCain companies in Germany, France, Italy and the Benelux countries report to van der Wel; each has its own managing director and management committee.

Wallace McCain likes to say that the company simply doesn't have a corporate structure. The worldwide corporate staff at Florenceville, he says, consists of himself and Harrison. There are a few people in engineering, the only function of the global company that is located at head office, but that's all. Everything else is done at the local-company level. There are other managers in Florenceville, but they are attached to the Canadian operations.

The McCains like to recruit managers from the country in which they will be managing. French nationals run their two French subsidiaries; Dutch nationals head their operations in the Netherlands. This is a textbook approach for any consumer products company. When you are selling food, clothing or cars, you have to have some affinity with your customer. The assumption is that local people know local markets best. Still, McCain's does not hesitate to move a Canadian into a foreign subsidiary if it has a particular problem it wants addressed.

Like any multinational, McCain's tries to inject its own corporate culture — the culture it developed in Florenceville — into its far-flung subsidiaries. For this reason, it wants to have a Canadian somewhere in the middle of each subsidiary's management. He might be a deputy managing director, perhaps the head of marketing. He probably wouldn't be the managing director. What is important is that the individual know the McCain method of operations, and be known and trusted by the brothers. Whenever the subsidiary strays a bit from the McCain way of doing things, the Canadian manager is there to remind his colleagues of how things would be done in Florenceville. He wouldn't be a corporate spy, Harrison says, just a spreader of the culture.

And what is the McCain's culture? Harrison describes it as "an aggressive sales posture; we want to be in position to achieve profitable growth. We won't expand for the sake of expanding; and we are not in the business for all the profit we can milk out of it. Everything we do, we do ethically and thoroughly."

Beyond 1992

For a Canadian company to move beyond its home market into the global arena, it must have a champion of expansion, a key executive who is devoted to the goal of exploring foreign markets. At McCain Foods, that champion is the chairman himself, Harrison McCain. His enthusiasm for international business, and particularly business in Europe, is deep-seated and contagious. He travels widely in Europe; he talks to people, gets to know Europeans. A passionate skier, he is no stranger to the Swiss Alps. It is Harrison's enthusiasm, as much as anything else, that explains McCain's expansion to continental

Europe more than 20 years ago and its success since then.

The McCains came to Europe as objective outsiders, just as Ford and IBM did. They were never confined by parochial views; they never saw Europe as 12 national markets. Very early, they established a Pan-European organization. They became the first frozen food company to ship processed products across national boundaries. McCain's today is able to exploit its transnational structure. It is able to move french fries around the continent in the most economically effective way. If potatoes are more expensive in Britain than in France, it can ship frozen fries from France across the channel. Or it can go the other way.

Hence, Europe 1992 is more of a non-event for McCain Foods than for many other companies. The dismantling of non-tariff barriers will not change the way McCain's does business. It simply makes things a little easier, a little more efficient, a little less costly. The program to create European product standards will mean some changes in the food additive laws and labeling. McCain's will be able to recruit and move people more easily across national borders. French fries shipped from one country to another will be inspected only once, by officials of the receiving country, instead of by both the exporting and importing countries. McCain's encounters few delays already in shipping its products across borders, so the gains from streamlined border checks are minimal. The single market is, says Harrison, not an earth-shaking event. He gets more excited talking about the new spirit of the people he meets, the growing sense of being European, rather than French, German, British or Spanish.

The McCains also sense, as many businesspeople do, that Eastern Europe has emerged as the most commercially exciting part of the continent. It will take time to realize that potential but McCain's is establishing a presence there. The region holds particular interest for a potato processor. The Warsaw Pact countries are prodigious spud growers. Poland itself harvests 40 million tons of potatoes a year, which is more than the production of the entire European Community. At the moment, much of that production is being directed to cattle feed and vodka production. Growers in Western Europe are afraid that some of that low-cost production will start moving into European Community markets. The governments of Western Europe are, after all, committed to coming to the aid of these regimes. Opening the doors to massive potato sales would be one way of doing it.

Harrison McCain believes there is potential in processing potatoes in Eastern Europe. However, for some time yet, it will be the citizens of those very countries who will be wanting that food. McCain hears reports of severe shortages of food in the stores of the Communist bloc countries. Someone has to process potatoes and other food products to meet these needs. Yes, he says, McCain's is interested in Eastern Europe, but it will take time to make a breakthrough. In 1989, McCain moved two people to Moscow to help McDonald's Restaurants of Canada set up a potato growing and french fry processing operation for their pioneering outlets in the Soviet capital. They have been scouting for business opportunities, as well.

By the time McCain Foods becomes a power in the Soviet Union's — or Poland's — food processing industry, Harrison and Wallace McCain may not be leading the corporation they founded. Both men are determined that the company in the 21st century will be headed by a new generation of McCains. Harrison has two sons in the business, Wallace has two. At least two of them are in positions of major responsibility. A nephew is the deputy managing director of the British subsidiary. However, the next generation will face some large challenges. It will be more difficult to justify keeping the head office in Florenceville. And McCain Foods, for all its fast growth over the past two decades, remains a small company by world standards, a niche player in the frozen food side of the global industry. The food sector is rationalizing worldwide. Big dollars are being paid for high-profile brand names. It will be hard to remain independent.

Furthermore, the departure of Harrison and Wallace McCain from the scene will create an unfillable void. Both men, and particularly Harrison, have been rare kinds of entrepreneurs — questing, restless, blessed with an insatiable curiosity about how the world lives and eats. So far, the children appear to be competent professional managers, but not necessarily the people who can guide McCain's to the big leagues of world companies. Yet whatever happens to the company, the legacy of its founders will not be erased. They have showed what it takes to build a successful global company, which just happens to be based in Canada.

Chapter 13

Getting Started

A bleary-eyed David Buddle is sipping a Coors Light in a sandwich bar in Terminal One of Toronto's Pearson International Airport. He is waiting for the boarding call for the Canadian Airlines flight to Amsterdam. Buddle, the Brussels-based European managing director for STM Systems Corp., a Canadian computer services company, has just wound up a few days of marathon meetings with his head office managers in downtown Toronto. This schedule has become a way of life for the bearded, 48-year-old manager — five weeks in his office in Brussels, then a week conferring with colleagues in Toronto.

Buddle's schedule is actually more humane now than it was before he had moved to Brussels a year earlier. As an international marketing director, he had lived in a state of permanent jet lag, shuttling among Toronto, Brussels, Madrid and New York. What's more, Buddle, who was responsible for marketing stock and bond trading systems to the financial services industry, was losing sales as a result of STM's airborne strategy.

"We just needed to be there in Europe," Buddle says. "We tried to get business long-distance, but we lost two situations in England and another in New York to local companies. You have to learn the culture of the country you're selling in. And it is also a question of responsiveness. Long-distance selling is simply asking too much of a customer."

STM Systems is part of a fast-growing constellation of international companies controlled by International Semi-Tech Microelectronics Inc., of Markham, Ontario, and its chief executive James Ting. In 1988, Ting, who has been acquiring companies at a frantic — some say alarming — speed, bought two large computer services companies, Canada Systems Group and Datacrown, and combined them to form STM Systems. One of the group's most successful products has been electronic messaging software that gives stockbrokers fast communication with traders on Canada's stock exchanges. Buddle's job was to find an international market for this and other systems.

A former bond trader who drifted into computer services, Buddle first considered New York to be more fertile ground than Europe. Europe, with its protected, undynamic financial institutions and antiquated markets (save for London's), hardly seemed a ripe target. However, the Wall Street players were skeptical of what Canadians could teach them about stock trading technology. Markets in Europe were preparing for a technological overhaul, and were receptive to Canadian products.

Buddle shifted his attention to Europe, and with surprising results. Brokers on the Madrid Stock Exchange bought the messaging system. He landed a contract for online deposit trading in the Italian inter-bank market of 1,200 institutions. The 850-branch Belgian bank, Kredietbank, acquired a computerized securities-handling system. When it became clear STM could not manage all this business by remote control, Buddle and a colleague moved to Europe. They chose Brussels because of its central location and the potential for more Belgian business.

Buddle doesn't make a tidy connection between 1992 and his presence in Europe. But all around him, he sees evidence of modernization and deregulation, some of it 1992-inspired, but a lot arising from market forces and rising consumer demand. Europe's strong economic performance in the late 1980s has increased the size of an affluent middle class in countries like Spain, Belgium and Italy. Buddle believes 1992 will only reinforce that trend. This monieed class is demanding efficient capital markets with the immediate access to information that Canadians take for granted. A European investor no longer wants to wait three days to discover the price he paid for a stock — the traditional waiting period with old systems that relied on bicycle messengers. STM's electronic solution reduces the wait to 15 seconds.

STM is one of the lucky companies. It has been able to respond quickly to an emerging demand for its products in Europe. It has benefited from having an internationally-oriented parent. Other companies are coming later and more painfully to decisions about Europe. They are reading about how it will be the economic superpower of the 1990s. The breakout of democracy in Eastern Europe and the unification of Germany only feeds this interest. But they don't know where to start.

Preparing for the new Europe demands more than a few technical adjustments, a couple of appointments, and an expenditure of cash. Companies that aspire to be successful across the Atlantic must look at the fundamental nature of their organizations at home. They must ask themselves what kind of companies they are. Are they responsive and flexible enough to meet the challenge? Do they have the right stuff in terms of personnel, products and marketing channels? The barriers to success in Europe often lie at the heart of the organization, in the company's culture. Qualities that make companies better in Europe will make them more effective everywhere they operate, including in Canada. The European companies they will be encountering in France or Italy are going to be more effective adversaries in Canada, as well.

The first step for companies that have never made a European sale is familiarization. That entails information collecting, conferences, discussions with knowledgeable government and private specialists, and trade missions to Europe — the kind of information described in Chapter 10. During that learning phase, it might then make preliminary contacts with agents and distributors.

The next big step would probably be participation in one of Europe's trade fairs — there are fairs for practically everything, for plastics, chemicals, consumer goods, food and so on. At a fair, the company's managers might collect indications of interest from potential customers. Some established European hands can fill 50% of their order books from trade fairs, not just from European customers, but from Japanese and Pacific Rim visitors. The trade show is a valuable stepping stone towards a global business presence.

If the trade show response is encouraging, a company might be in position to build up a healthy export business through a carefully chosen agent/distributor. As business increases, it might establish its own sales and marketing operation to push its product and brand name more aggressively. A highly technical product requires after-sales servicing support. Later, a bigger decision looms — should the company do some production in the foreign market, and perhaps even research & development?

Any organization facing these kinds of decisions has to move carefully but quickly. It must deal methodically with the 11 key points in doing business in Europe: The company should know its business thoroughly; it must have the right people on the ground. It should decide on how deep its involvement in Europe will be, and then stick to what it does best. An alertness to consumer trends is vital. The company must decide whether to start big or small. Should it build from scratch or acquire? Is a joint venture the way to go, or are there other options for strategic alliances? Many operations must grapple with whether to seek new ownership with deeper pockets. Then, there is the challenge of choosing a location. The following pages expand on these themes:

Know yourself

A company considering global expansion must first embark on a thorough examination of its products and markets, customers and supplies, strengths and weakness, threats and opportunities. Management consultants call this "a strategic audit." If Europe looks intriguing, the business must understand the market — or more accurately, 12 markets — the 1992 process, and how the single market would affect its prospects. It should be familiar with its potential European competitors, their strengths and weaknesses.

It may be necessary, for example, to change a product to conform with European technical standards. Transportation and distribution channels will be affected by the lowering of border barriers. It may be possible to develop Pan-European marketing strategies. David Culver, the former chairman of Alcan Aluminum, believes any business that has targeted Europe should spend a spare week every quarter working on its strategy. It doesn't sound like much, but that is a hefty commitment for small outfits.

Although earlier chapters have emphasized the risks of ignoring Europe, this self-examination may conclude it is wiser to concentrate on the closer, more familiar U.S. market before looking abroad. One company taking this route is Mercury Graphics, a Saskatoon printing company which has scored some success supplying tickets for European sports and arts events. Mercury is clearly interested in the 1992 Olympics in Barcelona and the World's Fair in Seville. But President Douglas Vaughan says its European involvement will be on a job-to-job basis. He sees a more pressing challenge in building the brand name in its Canadian and U.S. backyard. He views the U.S. as a more immediate target than Europe because it is virtually part of Mercury's national business.

Vaughan says it would not make a lot of sense to plunge into Europe when the company has a long way to go in establishing itself at home. "Maybe we're looking at Europe for 1995, not in 1990 or even 1992," Vaughan says. There is the risk, of course, that 1995 is too late, that competitors will have already seized some major opportunities. But the risks are greater that a small company might blow itself up by trying too much, too soon.

Get the right people

One of a chief executive's first steps should be to make

a critical assessment of managerial personnel. Does the company possess people with the right blend of linguistic skills, familiarity and openness towards foreign cultures, and just pure enthusiasm about the project? If it doesn't, it might have to recruit them.

The issue of who to put in charge of European expansion is crucial, management consultant and academic Joseph d'Cruz maintains. Companies that put their best people on any foreign expansion project make the biggest impact. However, by designating a full time champion for international expansion, an organization is taking one of its top people off everyday operations. That presents risks to ongoing performance, particularly for companies with a lean and tightly stretched management.

Canadian companies are fortunate to have a valuable source of managerial firepower to throw into European ventures. Thanks to the country's cultural mosaic, almost every company of any size has ethnic managers who speak European languages and are familiar with the cultures of parents or grandparents. These men and women are usually the most enthusiastic champions for a bold push into Europe. They often get their way because they are the owners of the company. Recent immigrants and their children have been the most fertile ground for entre-preneurialism in Canada.

Every company that pushes into a foreign market has to overcome the psychological distance between Canada and this unfamiliar culture. Some companies fail miserably because they assume that whatever worked in Canada will work in Europe. Others take years to overcome that yawning distance in attitudes and tastes. Ethnic managers bridge this gap very quickly. Their knowledge and enthusiasm creates big opportunities for companies that encourage them. The danger, of course, is that this enthusiasm, if not properly channeled, could lead the company into unwise ventures.

Enthusiasm and adaptability can sometimes compensate for a lack of familiarity with culture or language. David Buddle, STM's man in Europe, does not speak a second language, and French would come in handy in partly francophone Belgium. But Buddle has a good grasp of technology, marketing and financial services, a disarming openness to ideas and experience, and a zeal for the project at hand. Furthermore, he, his wife, and their teenage son are eagerly immersed in French lessons.

Another attribute to look for in a European champion: He or she should not display the chronic North American smug superiority towards "the Old World." Buddle, for example, admires ways in which European application of high technology is running ahead of Canada and the U.S. He rarely has to write a check for household bills. Almost everything, including grocery bills, is automatically debited from his bank account. When he orders food in the old Falstaff bistro, across the street from Brussels' stock exchange, he marvels as waiters transmit the order information by cellular telephone to the kitchen. This open-mindedness is a valuable trait. Europeans tire quickly of North American know-it-alls.

Decide depth of involvement

Deciding how to penetrate the European market is perhaps the toughest decision. No two companies can approach the issue exactly the same way. It is particularly wrenching for firms that already have good trading links with Europe. Trade ties may no longer suffice in the post-1992 era. Physical presence — whether a sales/service office or a full-blown production facility — may be the only avenue to exploit the single market. To benefit fully, a firm may have to guarantee that its products are largely European in origin.

There are other big incentives to grabbing a spot in Europe. The EC has dramatically boosted its financial commitment to R&D programs. The aim is to sharpen the technological skills of European firms, so they can better exploit their single market. Most of these R&D programs require that participants be located in the community. For a Canadian company to participate, it may have to perform part of its R&D in Europe. A number of Canadian companies are already involved in the Eureka program, which joins European companies in collaborative technology development.

Furthermore, companies find it increasingly difficult to maintain a trade relationship unless they are willing to make a direct investment in the foreign market. Investment feeds trade; trade paves the way to investment. Companies that invest in a market gain a deeper knowledge of it. They are better placed to protect their market share against domestic competitors. Ambitious Canadian companies should, in fact, pursue a three-pronged global strategy involving trade, investment, and, increasingly, research & development.

R&D may be the price paid to do business in a European country. Des Hudson, the president of Northern Telecom World Trade, the division covering the telecommunications giant's non-North American operations, believes that "to truly serve your market well, you have to be close to customers with your R&D. Your design engineers, for example, need to know the requirements of the market. The D function in R&D should be particularly close to the marketplace."

All this means that a Canadian company will end up creating some wealth and jobs in a foreign country, rather than in Canada. But the alternative might be an inability to compete globally, with the cost of many more jobs at home. One thing is certain: A company that puts money and jobs into Europe — or any foreign destination — should expect to get close scrutiny of its activities back home in Canada.

The decision to put an office, factory and people in Europe can't be taken lightly, even by large firms. Major European cities are expensive places to maintain offices and personnel. The challenge is particularly daunting for small- to medium-sized companies — those with annual sales of up to $150 million — whose resources are already stretched thin by the demands of the North American market under the Canada-U.S. free trade pact.

After a critical self-analysis, a business's managers may decide it should not establish a heightened physical presence in Europe. It may not feel quite ready at this stage. A more traditional export relationship might still be the right approach. This will depend on the product, the product's strength in the market, and the vigor of the

European competition. If a Canadian company is successfully exporting a high-value, specialized product into Europe, it may continue this relationship successfully after 1992.

Unitron, a hearing aid manufacturer in Kitchener, Ontario, sees no need to alter its successful exporting approach. Founded 25 years ago by a family of German immigrants, its managers realized very early that they couldn't live on Canadian markets alone. In 1969 — five years after its formation — Unitron opened a sales office in Bremen, Germany. Today, 30% of its sales are in Europe.

President and founder Fred Stork says its hearing aids are already sold in a relatively unrestricted worldwide market. There are no North American tariffs; the European duty is only about 3%-4%, and non-tariff barriers are not imposing. Unitron has a good business in Europe, although it has made few inroads in the home markets of its tough Scandinavian competitors. Transport is no problem with Unitron's lightweight, high-technology products. "We can really ship our merchandise worldwide without restriction," Stork says. Therefore, Stork says, there is little premium in Unitron changing its approach to Europe after 1992.

Even companies that haven't got to the exporting stage might decide to stick to Canada for now. "It is not your national duty to export," a French speaker said at a 1992 conference. Not all companies are ready for it. Alain Roy, the savvy co-founder of DMR Group, the Montreal consultancy group, says unless it has a truly unique product, a small business that is not yet exporting should prove itself first in Canada. "Establishing yourself in foreign markets is very expensive and you must reach a certain critical mass in order to support export activities."

However, Roy adds if small companies feel comfortable exporting and have products that set themselves apart from the competition, "they should not hesitate because Europe is a fantastic market."

Stick to your knitting

It is standard advice that any company contemplating

European expansion should stick to what it does best. Europe is not the place to go off on a diversification tangent. After its little exercise in soul-searching a business should have a pretty good idea of its strengths and weaknesses. Small operations can become global by establishing a competitive advantage in one narrow area, and taking it worldwide.

Some European sectors offer more promise than others. Telecommunications is an obvious candidate, both because Canada has some strong expertise here, and Europe is determined to catch up in this area. But telecom is tricky because some national governments are reluctant liberalizers. Transportation also looks interesting as a result of promised deregulation, privatization (particularly in Britain) and some big ticket projects, like the exorbitantly expensive Channel Tunnel. Montreal-based Bombardier Inc. has mined this territory successfully, with its Belgian mass transit subsidiary picking up railway-car contracts for the high-speed Channel Tunnel express. Canadian Pacific has been looking for opportunities.

Financial services look intriguing, because of 1992's program to open up once-protected national markets. For example, Canadian life insurance companies, already established in Britain, see opportunities on the continent, not only for insurance but for mutual funds, mortgages and investment management.

But Canadian companies will find that retail financial services will retain their national character for some time yet. There is a cultural bias against buying financial products from foreign companies. And it would cost a bundle to set up branch networks to rival established institutions. Canadian institutions might consider joint ventures or alliances with local firms.

Watch consumer trends

The consumer goods industry also offers exciting opportunities. The food and beverage industry looks particularly attractive. McCain's has demonstrated the potential for establishing brand names in undeveloped product areas, like frozen food. John Labatt Ltd. is targeting the convenience food market, and has built a British base for supplying pizza and pizza ingredients for grocery stores. Elsewhere in Europe, it is building on its Canadian strengths in starch production and beer-brewing.

Both McCain's and Labatt's are reacting as much to Europe's changing social conditions and consumer tastes as to the reforms of the single market. More and more women are working, widening the market for easy-to-prepare food. Microwave ovens are becoming more prevalent. These trends are spreading slowly southward in Europe, into countries like France, Spain and Italy. The single market is not the only factor in consumption trends in Europe.

Labatt's believes that to survive as an international brewer, it has to have a presence inside Europe. But its tactical approach reflects the changing tastes for alcoholic beverages. In Britain, demand is growing for lager beer, which is cutting into ale's dominance. Labatt's, a lager producer, is brewing and selling its Blue product through a network of regional brewers. Meanwhile, the Canadian company has observed rising beer consumption among the younger generation in those wine-drinking bastions of Spain and Italy, so Labatt's is becoming active in those markets as well.

Starting big versus small

Once a company has settled on its products for Europe, it must determine the proper scale of its first maneuver — a small raiding party or a full-scale invasion. The think-small approach seems less risky — the punier the initial investment, the less there is to lose if the whole thing flops. The traditional Canadian approach is to plant a seed and nurture it slowly. But the track record for gradual growth is not unblemished. Companies sometimes find they are continually pouring in capital, and end up paying more in the long run. It may be better to take a little longer planning, then hitting the market with a big impact. That way, a company benefits earlier from the efficiencies of a large organization.

Buying vs. building

The ultimate success of a transatlantic venture may hinge on one tough call: whether to establish a greenfield operation from scratch or acquire an existing business. The answer, predictably, depends on all those familiar factors — the product, the market and the competition. A company with a strong, world-beating product or a highly advanced technology might dare to go it alone in a new market. The same may be true if the Canadian product commands an overwhelming cost advantage over the European competition. Otherwise, acquiring a European partner may be the better route.

If a company already has a solid core of export sales in the market, moving to local production on its own might be relatively painless. McCain's has demonstrated in many European venues that an outsider can build local production on top of heavy export sales. But most startups can be expected to lose money over the first few years; the parent had better have the strength to absorb these losses.

An acquisition, on the other hand, provides an instant management and labor force that knows the home mark and can make those key contacts in European government and business. That kind of thinking is what animates Bombardier in its takeover activities. Again, the nature of the industry and product dictates the approach. Selling consumer goods, for example, requires a knowledge that can only come from established local marketers. Similarly, retailing requires a familiarity with regional customs and tastes. That is why so many Canadian store chains have fallen on their faces in attempted U.S. expansion. Europe would be even more difficult.

A company that rejects the greenfield approach to expansion must then focus its collective mind on how it wants to buy its way into a market — on its own or with a partner. The straight acquisition has the advantage of giving the buyer complete control, the ability to call all the shots. There is not the messy ambiguity that plagues partnership arrangements. One complicating factor is the Europe has become very expensive for acquisitions in the run-up to 1992. Any good company in a sector that will flourish in the single market commands a steep price.

Another problem with acquisitions is the task of melding the corporate culture of the acquiring company with that of its new subsidiary. Any company that undertakes an acquisition should determine whether or not the business styles are compatible — or can be made compatible through efforts on both sides. This is probably the facet of takeovers that requires the most work, but is most often ignored.

The joint venture decision

Joint ventures are much loved by seminar-givers, consultants and government officials, who laud these arrangements as the most painless and effective way to penetrate foreign markets. The idea has a beguiling attraction: Two or more companies share ownership of an affiliate, in which they pool assets for attacking a market. These tie-ups often combine the interests of a foreign company entering the market and an established local business. They are quite common in Europe, where the tradition of industrial cooperation is deep-rooted.

The advantages of such alliances to Canadian companies are many and varied. They provide a way to enter markets where national governments restrict foreign ownership. A venture partner provides instant management and important contacts in an unfamiliar area. The two partners working together may be able generate technological capabilities that each company could not develop on its own. By combining operations in a narrow field of activity, companies can achieve economies of scale that lower their unit costs. They can also turn out the revenues to support expensive research & development.

The joint venture is much admired by federal government officials who argue that small and medium-sized companies with little experience in Europe urgently need savvy local friends. According to one official with the External Affairs Department, "there are only so many desirable partners around and the dance cards are going to get filled up."

However, advocates of joint ventures sometimes forget

to talk about the downside. These marriages have a higher divorce rate than Zsa Zsa Gabor. Recent studies show that as many as two-thirds — and some suggest 80% — of joint ventures eventually break up.

Joint ventures can entail huge costs of money and management time if entered at the wrong time and with the wrong partner. There is always the danger of unseemly battles over who actually controls the joint operation. Furthermore, a company may be inadvertently creating a new competitor by sharing its technological knowledge with a foreign partner. Canadian companies have often found this is a hazard in dealing with foreign agents and distributors.

Canadian companies have to be sure their potential partners have the right stuff. Do they have the physical plant and labor force to meet the venture's production requirements? Do they have access to the necessary distribution channels? Are they Pan-European enough in their thinking to attack the entire single market? And are they plugged into the key decision-making bodies in government and business? It is crucially important that a European ally is in tune with public opinion in its markets. A Canadian pulp and paper company would want a European ally that is alert to environmental concerns. A partner might be efficient and well-managed, but the venture could still be bust if it ignores social, cultural and environmental issues.

Management consultant d'Cruz is one who is skeptical of the value of joint ventures with foreign companies. They are, he says, an unsatisfactory compromise, particularly for small companies. For one thing, they inhibit the learning process a company must experience in a new market. "You leave to your partner all those aspects of the business you don't know already, but that works against ever learning these things." He also believes joint ventures require a lot of work, negotiation and compromise to be successful. The question must be addressed: If you are putting all that that effort into the venture anyway, why not go it alone?

Joint ventures work best where partners have complementary, not overlapping capabilities. But it is also important that the two partners share the same overall goals for their combined venture.

Joint ventures usually fail for two reasons: they should never have happened in the first place, usually because the partners were wrong for each other; or industry conditions change so that the partnership is no longer useful. This suggests there is a natural cycle for such ventures — they are created, they work for awhile, then they become obsolete as conditions change. This underlines the requirement that contracts be carefully worked out in advance. When the marriage breaks up, the Canadian company should be able to walk away with its product, its technology and its pride intact.

Alliances with European companies offer intriguing possibilities at this stage in history. Both Europe and North America are undergoing internal trade liberalization, converting national markets into huge continental ones. European companies are looking at Canada as a site from which to attack all of North America. Canadian businesses similarly look at a Europe target, such as Britain or Holland, as an entry point to a market of 324 million. There is a potential for reciprocal arrangements, whereby a European company uses its Canadian connection for access into the big North American space, while the Canadian partner uses its European connection to sell throughout the EC. This might be done through the classic joint venture or some less binding marriage of convenience.

Other alliance options

If a merger is the equivalent of marriage, a joint venture is living together. But there are other looser forms of cohabitation between Canadian companies and European partners. One popular, and reasonably clear-cut, arrangement is the co-marketing agreement whereby each partner markets the other's products in its market in exchange for a commission or royalty. This avoids messy arguments about who will control or manage the combined operation. However, it may provide little in the way of learning about a new market.

A licensing agreement is a bit more complicated. A

European company might acquire a license to manufacture, assemble and distribute a Canadian company's product, with the right to the item's patent and trade name. Similarly, a Canadian company might do the same for the European company in North America. The licensee pays the product owner a licensing fee plus an annual royalty based on sales.

But like joint ventures, these deals require a lot of trust on each side. Some companies that try licensing grow restive because of the lack of control they have over how their technology is being applied. They may feel the license is being underused, and their product is not reaching full potential. The choice of partner is just as crucial as in a joint venture.

There are other forms of strategic alliances. For example, a company might combine a licensing agreement or joint venture with the purchase of a minority stake in the European company. This shareholding offers a way to gain knowledge of a market, particularly if it involves a seat on the board. This can be used as the first familiarization stage, working towards a deeper relationship. Northern Telecom has taken that route in Britain with the purchase of 28% of STC PLC, a computer and telecommunications equipment manufacturer. The link has opened access to British Telecom. However, Northern is not wed to one specific format of partnership. In France, it has established a production facility as a joint venture with local companies.

Labatt's also operates in Europe under a variety of arrangements. Its guiding principle is that when it makes an acquisition in a foreign market, it takes a local partner. Often, it encourages the previous owner to remain a part of the business. In Italy, where it has has purchased 70% of the Birra Moretti brewery (which in turn bought out another rival brewer), the patriarch, Luigi Moretti, retains a minority ownership and stays on as chairman.

Ed Stewart, vice-president, corporate affairs, says Labatt's can bring marketing experience, production efficiencies and financial muscle to Moretti, which is the number-three Italian brewer. But Luigi Moretti contributes that vital familiarity with the Italian market. Stewart says Labatt's is convinced it has to be physically close to the market it is trying to serve. "And you need to have people in your organization who have been a part of the market. We wouldn't have gone in there unless Moretti had stayed around."

Coming up against such established operators as Peroni, the major Italian brewer, and Heineken from Holland, a Canadian interloper couldn't have hoped to succeed on its own. "You just don't come in and steal big chunks of market from seasoned competitors like them," Stewart says.

Labatt's has also been seeking brewing partners in Spain. In France, Labatt's has joined local partners in the ownership of a manufacturer of starch and gluten in Bordeaux. However, it is taking a somewhat different tack in the British beer market. British brewers have traditionally controlled retail sales through their extensive pub holdings. Any newcomer has to work through their networks. Labatt's found that the major brewers already had lager brands, so it went after regional brewers that were still looking. Labatt's now has arrangements with 10 brewers, whereby it rents their brewing and bottling facilities, produces lager under the direction of its own brewmasters, then sells it to the brewers. The strategy has been generally successful except in London, where the big national brewers dominate the pub market.

Looking for a big brother

Labatt's, controlled by the Toronto Bronfman family, can pour considerable resources into its international planning. Its decision to expand in the European beer market arose from a study of international brewing commissioned from British consultants. Labatt's has people in its British and Canadian offices who do nothing but look at possible acquisitions. Now that it has made some purchases, people are flocking to it with possible deals.

But for smaller businesses, time, energy and capital are scarcer commodities. At some point every small player has to ask if it can advance any farther on its own without a rich benefactor. Unitron's Fred Stork worries about this: "We have had temptations to find a big brother. But we feel we can stay in the the business on our own if we're on the ball with our products. We are 12th or 13th in the world in hearing aids, and we're shooting for the top 10."

As they move into Europe and other global markets, companies in the $10 million to $300 million sales bracket may have to sell their independence for a shot at bigger vistas. A federal government report on telecommunications prospects in 1992 suggests that "a firm, however small, with a specialized good or service that fills a niche, has something more than a product to sell. It is literally in a position to sell itself to a larger acquisition-minded firm." Although not all entrepreneurs like this idea, a sell-out would reward them with capital gains. Moreover, the report says, "the process creates an incentive to new entry by entrepreneurs with an idea worth developing — and if successful, a firm which in its turn is profitable to sell."

Location, location, location

The question of how to tackle Europe can't be answered in isolation from *where* to tackle Europe. Where does a company locate its sales, distribution or production facilities? The location decision is just as crucial for a company that is comfortably established in Europe as for one getting started. The single market would allow a company to move goods and services from one location to a number of country markets with a minimum of fuss and red tape. The promised harmonization of taxes will remove a large incentive to operate a subsidiary in every country. Decisions are less likely to be driven by the old factors of national borders and national rules.

Andrew Brown, a management consultant in Ernst & Young's Brussels office, told a *Financial Times* of London conference recently that the single market was turning location theory on its head. Companies already in Europe should be grouping their operations in new geographic patterns. He suggested that they should start thinking in terms of units serving several countries instead of one — Britain, Ireland and Denmark as one grouping; West Germany and the Benelux countries as another; Italy and

Greece together; and France, Spain and Portugal.

For many Canadian firms, particularly from English Canada, the easy choice for a European base was Britain. The appeal was a shared language and a familiarity with customs and conventions. Economic ties forged during Empire and Commonwealth were never entirely broken. These days, the British government vigorously courts Canadian investment by extolling its productive economy, a free-enterprise mentality, and the improved labor relations of the 1980s.

Clearly, Britain has its attractions. It is a comfortable starting place from which to launch an assault on Europe. But a Canadian company should not view it as an end in itself. There are much more prosperous venues on the continent. Also, Canadian companies find it hard to serve the continent from Britain, because British managers do not always understand continental markets. It is usually better to set up a continental beachhead that is quite separate from Britain.

Building on a British base has another troubling aspect. The strained relationship between Margaret Thatcher and Jacques Delors suggests that Britain will move more slowly in integrating itself in a united Europe than the other 11 countries — or for that matter, than the EFTA nations and many of the Eastern European states. Britain will delay the lowering of border barriers; it will drag its feet on monetary and economic union. A Canadian company that uses Britain as a European base may find that the borders barriers remain a little steeper than on the continent. Conversion and hedging between the pound and continental currencies will persist longer than it may like. That may cause some companies to hedge their bets with a strong base on the continent.

For location, Belgium or Holland are hard to beat. These countries reserve a soft spot for Canadians, a holdover from the world wars. A large number of our companies are using the Benelux nations as their continental launching pads. Indeed, the whole "golden triangle" defined by London, Paris and Frankfurt has the advantage of central location, good transport links with all of Europe — which will improve with enhanced high-speed rail networks — a very rich consumer market, and a skilled workforce. The downside is that it can be very expensive to run a business in this affluent, high-cost and congested central area of Europe.

As national borders become less important, companies will pay more attention to regional clusters of population that can be serviced from a single warehouse, factory or sales office. These regions cut across borders but share similar income, lifestyle and demographic characteristics. The lifting of borders may actually stimulate their economic development. A consumer goods company could develop a uniform marketing and sales plan that blurs the old boundaries. For example, the northeast French province of Lorraine, Luxembourg and the German Saarland zone could be approached as a single unit. France's southwest Languedoc region and Spanish Catalonia might be approached as one region. France's Rhône-Alpes and Italy's Piedmont areas share more with each other than with other part of their own countries. The closely integrated Benelux states will become more intimate. Companies will find ways to exploit these synergies.

Within the golden triangle, there are pockets of old industrial centers that have fallen on hard times. The northeast of France, for example, is a traditional steel manufacturing center that suffered some de-industrialization in the early-1980s recession. Governments are offering incentives to companies that locate in high-unemployment areas. One of these is the city of Calais, which offers tax-free enterprise zones to offset the closure of huge shipyards. Nearby Lille is enthusiastically courting outside investment. Both these cities are on the high-speed rail links connecting the Channel Tunnel to Paris. Canadian companies should be alert to these kinds of opportunities.

But the really hot areas of Europe are Spain and Portugal, which are getting a lot of attention from foreign investors. The big reason is a skilled and relatively low-paid workforce. And it doesn't hurt to have a sunny climate that relocating foreign managers find attractive. Some enthusiasts call Iberia the "California of Europe." Spain is particularly popular because of "the Spanish miracle," the dramatic upsurge in economic growth through the 1980s. It has become Europe's fastest growing car-producing and car-buying area.

Ireland, perched on the northwest edge of Europe, is concerned about losing industry to the prosperous center and the warmer, sunnier Iberian Peninsula. It too offers attractive incentives, such as its duty-free zone in the Shannon airport corridor. The Irish have persuaded the European Community to allow these temporary exceptions to the EC's otherwise hard line on national subsidies and tax incentives. The Irish have managed to retain a 10% corporate tax rate vs. the 35% rate in nearby Britain. Ireland can also offer companies a well-educated, young and relatively low-paid workforce. The government is making the most of the longstanding barriers to obtaining birth control devices in Catholic Ireland. Industrial development officials point out that about 50% of the population is under the age of 28 — a striking statistic in an otherwise aging Europe.

Ireland or Portugal may become more inviting as the EC spends more regional development funds in enhancing the infrastructure in have-not regions. Areas like Portugal's fishing communities, Sicily and Western Ireland should benefit. Also, remote regions of Spain, Portugal and Ireland should creep closer to the centre of Europe as the EC gets its act together on the deregulation of transport. Trucking costs would fall as a result of the long-promised lifting of the ban on cabotage. Massive projects to expand high-speed rail networks should lower the cost of transport and quicken the pace of moving people and goods around the continent. Spain's prospects would look even better if it follows through on the long-promised adjustment of its rail gauge to conform with the rest of Europe.

Canadian companies should not restrict their sights to EC countries. The single market is evolving into the European Economic Space, a configuration that covers not only the inner 12, but the outer six countries of EFTA — and, now, Eastern Europe. Trade will flow unimpeded from the Algarve to the Elbe, from Lapland to Sicily. A company in Graz, Austria, will be able to serve customers in northern Italy; a Danish branch office might look after Sweden, Poland and Northern Germany.

Corporate decision makers will soon realize that the center of Europe is not London or even Brussels, but Warsaw or Prague. Companies are already thinking in terms of how to serve both Western and Eastern Europe from a single base. Mitsubishi Bank, for example, in early 1990 was considering moving its European headquarters from London to Frankfurt to keep closer tabs on developments in Eastern Europe. And don't forget Berlin, which after the unification of West and East Germany, will again be an important industrial and head office city.

Big and small, savvy veterans and pink-cheeked neophytes — all kinds of companies must make fundamental decisions about how to attack Europe. Consultant Joseph d'Cruz says the successful ones will share a fundamental characteristic. They will be learning companies, organizations that are capable of absorbing information about the new market, and building strategies from that knowledge.

Too many managers embark on foreign ventures believing they know it all. They have been successful in Canada; they assume they cannot fail in the rest of the world. These companies invariably fall flat on their faces. They were incapable of learning.

The ability to learn arises out of corporate culture. Hierarchical organizations are relative dunces. Top grades go to companies with relatively flat management structures, where information passes quickly up and decisions quickly down. Middle managers hand in their strategic recommendations, then sit around and talk about them with the top guns. If your company isn't working this way, it may be time for a makeover. Whether your market is Madrid or Medicine Hat, it will help.

Chapter 14

The 1992 Manager

When Northern Telecom Ltd. invaded France in the late 1980s, it rolled out the heavy artillery. The manufacturer of telecommunications equipment built a factory in Verdun in eastern France to assemble its SL1 office telephone exchanges. It set up a facility for research & development just south of Paris, and offices in the city. The $60 million investment, Northern said, was an acceptable price to pay for the right to sell its private branch exchanges (PBXs) inside the sheltered French market.

In retrospect, that price may have been unnecessarily high. A few months after the Verdun plant started turning out PBXs in early 1989, Des Hudson, president of Northern Telecom World Trade, the division encompassing operations outside North America, was musing that if the company had to do it again, it might not have made such a heavy commitment of money and resources to France.

Hudson, a gray-haired, cerebral engineer, manages Northern's World Trade division out of an office building in Etobicoke, a western suburb of Toronto. But he spends 85% of his time on the road in Asia, Canada and Europe. Hudson's mandate is to build a truly global presence for the Canadian company. Northern's $6.5 billion in 1988 sales were drawn from 70 countries, but more than 90% of that total came from its North American base of Canada and the U.S.

In recent years, foreign competitors — companies like Sweden's Ericsson, Germany's Siemens and France's Alcatel — have been nibbling at these home markets. Meanwhile, Northern's corporate customers are going global, and are demanding a more international communications service. If Northern is to survive, it must build its presence outside North America. It cannot expand everywhere at once, so it has targeted major markets in the Pacific Rim, and core countries of Europe, including Britain, France and Germany.

With Europe 1992 looming on the horizon, the Canadian manufacturer was uncertain about what form this expanded market would take. From the protectionist rhetoric being tossed about, Northern began to worry about a Fortress Europe that would be closed to companies from outside the EC. France seemed to be the stoutest bastion of this Fortress mentality. A top priority of French public policy has traditionally been to protect its own strategic industries.

The twin fears of Fortress Europe and a *dirigiste* France spurred Northern into negotiating a trade-off. The company would put production and R&D facilities into France. In return, it would be able to sell its PBXs. "The French understood that we would bring some added value in terms of technology and R&D capability. There was a net gain to them and a net gain to us," Hudson says.   It all seemed to make sense.

Yet here was Hudson suggesting that, while the extensive French investment was a good move in the mid-1980s, "probably over time, we would have made a different decision." Why the new perspective on France? For one thing, fears of Fortress Europe were not as intense as they were a few years earlier. And the European Community, led by the bureaucrats in Brussels, had been fairly effective in guiding member states away from protectionism.

Northern Telecom's experiences encapsulate the challenges facing big international companies the 1990s. It underlines the difficulty of managing across frontiers. Big corporations learned long ago that they could not flourish by sticking to a circumscribed national market. They felt the hot breath of foreign competition in their own backyards. Since the Second World War, trade barriers have been steadily falling and imports have been rising worldwide. Advanced computer and communications technologies bind the globe together. Any company of any size talks about "global strategy."

But as Northern Telecom has discovered, companies must still respond to local conditions and political pressures that are always changing. Strategies must be wide and flexible enough to accommodate diversity and regionalism. Companies must develop managers with the strategic bifocals to see big and small at the same time.

"The task of organizing an international company remains one of the toughest in business," *The Economist* concludes. Dezso Horvath, dean of administrative studies at York University in Toronto, says the organization of the modern multinational corporation has become so complex that organization itself has become a competitive advantage, just like R&D and marketing. Companies that do it well are perceived to have an edge.

Towards the transnational company

Europe 1992 only heightens the imperative of thinking global. The single market will generate more trade, within the EC and between EC and non-EC countries. It will result in more muscular European companies. Old assumptions about an ossified and fragmented EuroMess no longer hold up. Even mature, sophisticated multinationals can be caught off-guard by the speed of change. Yet, old national ideas will take time to die. Despite Des Hudson's second thoughts, Northern's factory in Verdun may yet look like a prudent hedge bet.

The previous chapter dealt with the teething pains ahead for a company that wants to get started in Europe. However, those challenges are, in some ways, less daunting than for established European operators that have to learn new ways.

At first glance, that sounds absurd. A more integrated European economy looks like a win-win situation for companies established in the common market. Goods and services will move smoothly across national boundaries. Players can become more efficient in production, distribution and marketing. Greater competition in financial services should make corporate financing less expensive. Competitive financial markets — along with lower interest rates — should help Canadian companies, as well as European firms.

These pluses, however, are tempered by the transitional adjustments for managers who have become set in their ways. They will have to discard the old ideas and start looking at Europe afresh. This acclimatization is similar to what North American managers must undergo to prepare for Canada-U.S. free trade. Europe's giant multinationals, like Holland's Philips, Germany's Siemens, and the French food group BSN, are going through this wrenching process. Having lived with, even profited from, the rigidities of the old Europe, they are adapting to the flexibility of the new Europe. Their managers are, often reluctantly, being forced to adopt the "European mindset" — the perception that Europe is greater than the sum of its parts.

Mature companies preparing for 1992 must examine the entire business environment in which they work, including marketing, supplies, distribution, purchasing and the competitive climate. A more integrated continent will have implications for all these relationships. Purchasing of supplies, for example, can now be carried out on a European-wide basis. Negotiations on prices can be centralized, while deliveries, support services and credit arrangements could be left to the national subsidiaries. And distribution channels will change. But managers have to be careful not to fall in love with bigness and rationalization. Europe's tastes will remain diverse, and small production runs will still be needed for many products. Management consultants say there is a different optimum scale for each aspect of a company's operations — R&D, production, distribution, marketing and sales. In one industry, costly R&D might work better on a large European scale, while sales and marketing are done well by smaller local teams.

Alcan Aluminum is one company immersed in this kind of decision-making. Alcan considers itself as a seasoned insider in Europe; its presence goes back to 1930s, shortly after the Montreal-based company was formed as a spinoff of America's giant Alcoa. Now Alcan is one of Europe's — and the world's — biggest aluminum companies. According to *EuroBusiness* magazine, Alcan in Europe constitutes the 309th biggest European company in terms of 1988 sales. Its European operations racked up $2.8 billion of sales in 1988, generating 32% of Alcan's worldwide revenues.

Alcan was very early in looking at the European Community as one entity, instead of 12. It has had an integrated European strategy for some time. This perspective allows it to ship its aluminum from a British plant to Europe's largest rolling mill in Dusseldorf, then send the rolled product back to Britain. But within that continent-wide strategy, some refinements have been necessary.

At one time, Alcan emphasized a superregional management, with decision-making on a wide European scale. Then in the early 1980s, it became fashionable to think local. The company moved decisions closer to the field, giving more authority to its single-country subsidiaries. Managing directors of these national companies would meet to co-ordinate a European approach, but there was nothing approaching a European head office.

Now with 1992 emerging, Alcan has gone back to the drawing board, and is looking again at European-wide strategies. Jacques Bougie, its trim 40-year-old president, says, "Borders no longer interfere with management. We have national companies, but we are currently looking at one market, and rationalizing plants and focusing our operations . . . Our plants are being focused on one product with a mandate [for distribution] throughout Europe."

These preparations are forcing Alcan to review its various businesses. Some operations have a global orientation. Therefore, it makes sense to move to Europe-wide production and distribution. But many of the things Alcan produces — such as products for the building industry — serve a national market. For these businesses, the management focus will remain intensely local.

Alcan seems to have the facility to shift its perspective. The aluminum company can be local, European or global in its decision-making, depending on the problems being addressed. This is a tough balancing act. It is, indeed, the multinational's challenge worldwide.

Running a multinational company never used to be so difficult. In the early decades of the 20th century, an Alcan might have developed its products and technology at home, then exported them through branch plants. Operating behind national tariff walls, these subsidiaries were usually mini-versions of the parent company. They enjoyed decentralized management and were essentially self-sufficient.

In time, a different kind of international company emerged, with more central control and with a worldwide strategy directed by head office. These companies don't want a collection of clones of themselves. They want an integrated organization that transcended boundaries.

Some companies impose this global vision by rigid centralization. Many American corporations use matrix systems, whereby managers in a European subsidiary might report to a regional manager for, say Europe, but also to a product manager in head office. A local manager might report to several bosses at once — one for product (say, widgets), one for geography (the Italian managing director), and one for function (say, marketing or production). It makes for a complex, highly centralized structure. Every decision is made with the global strategy in mind; there is minimal dilution of the company's overall effort and corporate culture.

Both the multinational and matrix models have been found lacking by two academics, Christopher Bartlett of Harvard Business School and Sumantra Ghoshal of Insead in France. In their book, *Managing Across Borders: The Transnational Solution*, they argue that today's global business requires a different kind of organization that allows companies to be both global and local at the same time. Their model would be a "transnational," a company with a worldwide vision and identity, but with the flexibility to take decisions at whatever level makes sense in terms of the company's goals. Some initiatives will be taken locally, some globally. It all depends on what works. The people at Alcan would subscribe to this pragmatic school.

Canada's big global companies don't usually talk in such abstract terms. Still, the successful ones seems to contain a lot of those transnational virtues. With few exceptions, they eschew the extreme centralization of many American companies. If anything, the trend in Canada is to keep the head office personnel fairly light, and devolve responsibilities to the subsidiaries. Hierarchy is flat and uncomplicated. There is a great premium put on entrepreneurialism within the company.

But such organizations also promote a shared mission and a common corporate culture. This blend of decentralization with core principles puts pressure on chief executives or international managers who are on the road almost constantly. People like Harrison McCain of McCain Foods, Alain Roy of DMR Group and Des Hudson of Northern are the keepers of the global strategy and the spreaders of the culture. They are in constant contact with overseas managers. Canadian companies can operate this way because most of them aren't that big — yet. As they grow, they may have to develop new approaches to that constant challenge of thinking global while acting local.

Overcoming culture shock

Heard the jokes about the business oxymorons? "Corporate culture" is one of the biggies. Laugh all you want, but culture is one of the things that management consultants talk about incessantly. This is a fuzzy concept — a company's way of doing things, its style, ethos and philosophy. But anyone who has been involved in a takeover, merger or joint venture knows the meshing of cultures is the most difficult thing. It is never painless. That is true when two Canadian companies are joining. Think what happens when a Canadian company tries to absorb European nationals into its worldwide operation.

Europe is still an unfamiliar place to do business. Europe 1992 will break down some of the internal barriers, but there are still widely dissimilar management traditions, labor relations, work habits. That will not change after 1992.

For many Canadian businesses, the British style seems most familiar. But crossing that English Channel can make a world of difference. Businesspeople in Germany, France and Spain speak English more and more, but that is where the similarities end.

For starters, continental countries generally accept a more intrusive state presence in the economy than Margaret Thatcher's Britain. National governments often have industrial policies, which involve stimulating sectors and companies and putting strict conditions on foreign investment. Canadian companies find they must play an alert political lobbying game. These practices remain particularly resilient in France, as the experiences of McCain's and Northern Telecom attest.

Large European companies are more likely to be family companies, tightly controlled with smaller public share floats than in North America. They may be less accessible to the media and to representations from other companies. Personal contacts are important to doing business anywhere in the world, but crucial in the EC. Success comes to those who display politeness, who work through channels, and who get introduced to the right people.

Alain Roy, of the DMR Group, points out that a persistent Canadian can make contact with a middle-manager in a British company, and expect eventually to gain access to a higher-level person. On the continent, unless you are introduced at the top, you might be forever frozen at a lower level.

Although European managers often seem like status freaks, labor relations in continental Europe emphasizes worker participation and consultation on management issues. The social dimension of 1992 should strengthen these practices. A Canadian company has to be able to bend with the winds of corporatism. Most experienced companies find it is no big deal; in fact, some find it easier to relate to their workforces. Our history of strong labor unions and social welfare makes it easier for us to adjust to Europe's workplace than Americans, who cling to free-enterprise myths and anti-union prejudices.

No Canadian company is more experienced in merging its corporate culture with that of European companies than Bombardier Inc., the little Quebec snowmobile company that has emerged as an international manufacturer of mass transit systems and commuter airplanes. In 1988, 80% of Bombardier's sales of $1.5 billion were outside Canada. Bombardier has been on an acquisition binge in Europe over the past few years — it bought Short Bros., a troubled Irish commuter airplane manufacturer in 1989; it has acquired rail car manufacturing operations in Belgium and France. Its roots in Europe go back 20 years, to the acquisition of an Austrian producer of engines for its Canadian snowmobiles. But it was only in 1985 that it actually developed a European strategy.

Raymond Royer, its razor-sharp president and COO, says the company has developed three basic principles in approaching Europe: First, it controls its technology in all its contracts. Second, it pursues certain selected markets. These are areas where Bombardier believes it can play a global leadership role — mass transit, certain leisure vehicles (like snowmobiles), and aerospace (Canadair and Short Bros.) being the most prominent.

Last, but not least, it seeks to implant its management philosophy in all its worldwide operations. The key elements are: an emphasis on quality products; a decentralized, entrepreneurial management; and the customer as the focus of the company's efforts. These seem almost tritely self-evident principles, but Bombardier believes they are often forgotten.

It does not spread this culture through transplanted Canadian managers. Subsidiaries are run by local people. "Being Canadians, we understand what foreign ownership means in terms of management, and we are very sensitive to local management's aspirations," Royer explains.

Royer and his team have to work hard on the culture-sharing process. It takes time to identify managers in a newly acquired company who can share and spread the Canadian company's culture. In the case of BN Constructions Ferroviaires et Metalliques, the Belgian railroad car builder acquired in 1985, "our biggest challenge was to gain their trust and make them understand that they were responsible for their own future and that Bombardier was really there to support them. It took us two years to establish good communications and to be able to share our values and objectives with them."

As soon as Bombardier acquired BN, Royer sat down with the Belgian company's 75 union leaders to talk about company philosophy. It initiated a program for BN managers to spend time in other parts of the Bombardier organization. They were shown how to motivate people in the Bombardier style.

Royer emphasizes the role of Bombardier's decentralized management structure in fostering initiative in its subsidiaries. The company is divided into industrial groups — mass transit, aerospace, defence, consumer products and financial services — each headed by a vice-president. Corporate head office consists of only 50 people, whose role is essentially to support the divisions and groups in their financing. "We decentralize and force the decision-making at the group and division level. It is left with management teams of groups and divisions to come up with solutions."

Royer believes the Bombardier approach has contributed to the success of its European operations. BN, for example, has provided a way into Europe's mass transit market, where local presence and well-placed contacts make a big difference. It is part of a consortium building locomotives and cars for the Channel Tunnel train. It is involved in the consortium developing a high-speed train network connecting major cities in Western Europe. This high profile has helped Bombardier snare the North American rights to the French high-speed TGV (*train à grande vitesse*) railroad technology.

Not all Canadian companies have had unalloyed success in adapting to Europe's business culture. Cascades Inc., a paper manufacturer based in Kingsey Falls, Quebec, has a different story to tell. Cascades was successful in the early 1980s turning around troubled Canadian paper mills. Then the three Lemaire brothers who run Cascades decided they might duplicate their success in France. In one of its first ventures, it formed a 1987 joint venture with Groupe Pinault SA, a French company, to manage and then to buy bankrupt Chapelle Darblay SA, the country's leading newsprint producer. But almost as soon as the two companies took over Chapelle Darblay, they bickered about who was in control.

Cascades' dark-haired, bearded chief executive, Bernard Lemaire, spent most of 1988 trying to salvage the joint venture. The control issue ended up before a French commercial tribunal which ordered Cascades to sell its share to its estranged partner. Cascades was able to recoup a small return on its short-term investment.

Bernard Lemaire says a major complication was the involvement of the French government, which had invested large sums of money in the ailing paper mill. He sensed a reluctance in public circles to see an outsider take a major stake in this important French company. Then, when the two companies began running the mills, they found they had different perspectives.

Cascades was undaunted by the failure of this foray. It has expanded its presence in France (where its 1989 sales reached about $300 million), and has added mills in Sweden and Belgium. Lemaire seems content with his company's choice of France as its entry point to Europe. He also believes that politics in France are shifting away from protected industries and state interference.

However, Lemaire's challenges have extended beyond high-level politics. Although Cascades speaks the same language as its French managers and employees, it has encountered a wide gulf in attitude. Cascades' Quebec managers had always emphasized free and open communications with rank-and-file employees. They spread the idea that "we're all in this together." That is harder to do in French companies. "Levels of management are important in Europe," Lemaire says. "They don't talk very much to workers. As soon as someone switches into management, they change their attitude. We still insist we are all together."

Cascades has tried to spread the idea that everyone is dedicated to a common purpose. "It is working," says Lemaire, "but maybe not 100% in all cases." Taking a different approach than Bombardier, Cascades has felt compelled to move a number of Canadian managers into

France. The goal is to reduce gradually that Canadian presence over time.

Lemaire feels that the European approach is quite different in another context. There is not the emphasis on controlling costs that he sees in North American companies. "They tend to stress quality ahead of costs. But sometimes to be perfect, it costs a lot of money. Sometimes, you have to say it's enough. The price has to be right."

Managers of the future

When football coaches draw their Xs and Os on the dressing room blackboard, everything works. Pass receivers run perfect patterns, runners glide effortlessly through holes in the line. But when their teams run the plays on the field, things get complicated. Those diagrammed plays break down, passes are overthrown, runners can't find holes. The problem is personnel — the opposition is simply better.

So it goes with corporations. It is all very nice to draw diagrams of complex matrix organizations, of people and functions moving together toward a common global purpose. But companies need their Joe Montanas to make it all work. The challenge in the corporate game is finding good managers.

That is the plight facing Canadian companies, both big and small, as they move into Europe: How to recruit a certain quality of manager who commands a broad perspective — "European" or "global" — but is sensitive to local markets, customs, and labor relations. They need managers who can take a good marketing idea from the parent company, discard what won't work in the local market, and adapt what is left over. They must feel comfortable in managing diversity — they should be able to communicate effectively with a Spanish personnel manager or a French marketing specialist. It helps to have a facility in two or more languages, a willingness to travel and lots of patience.

For all its ability to plan strategically for the single market, even Alcan admits it is having trouble finding the personnel to execute its neatly diagramed Xs and Os. President Jacques Bougie says the company has been trying to convert its old national managers to think more in terms of an integrated European market. Its national operations have been managed by Europeans, often natives of the country. However, these organizations will have to become more European-oriented as Alcan rationalizes operations. National managers must be turned into European managers. That is a key challenge facing all companies.

Some old-line managers can make the switch, but not all. As their employers try to change, the country managers become obstacles to necessary change. Many European businesses are eliminating or downgrading the status of their local managers. The option is often to relegate them to a paper-shuffling role or relieve them of their duties. A similar trend seems to be be at work in North America, as Canadian managers in U.S.-based multinationals find their roles reduced under the free trade agreement.

To replace the hidebound old guard, companies are looking to recruit a new generation of European-minded managers, either from the ranks of other companies or from university business schools. This recruitment has spawned intense competition for a scarce commodity. "We are all looking for these managers in competition with others," Alcan's Bougie sighs. "We all need to find and develop them." The supply-demand squeeze has raised managerial salaries. Some consultants say that the once-wide compensation gap between North America and Europe may be about to narrow.

Canadian companies face certain handicaps in recruiting top people in Europe. Native Europeans are often reluctant to leave bigger, well-established companies for a relative newcomer. As suggested earlier, status and perks matter a lot to managers. A Canadian computer executive complains that Europeans prefer to work for big national companies or American multinationals, like IBM, Honeywell or Hewlett-Packard. "Our biggest task in Europe is to find managers who are nationals but attuned to the global high-tech industry," the executive says.

Canadian multinationals usually prefer to recruit local nationals to run their European subsidiaries. There may be a few Canadians sprinkled throughout the organization, but not as managing directors or presidents.

There is a view that the ideal European manager shouldn't be a local national, or a national of the home country of the parent company. The most adaptable managers seem to come from third countries — for example, a Briton working in Italy, or a Dutchman in Spain — with experience in various international postings. The ideal management team is probably a generous mix of local and non-local personnel.

Stereotypes are dangerous, but Canadian companies find that certain countries tend to turn out successful Euromanagers. The Dutch, who come from a small central European nation with an open, trading economy, flourish in international companies. The Scandinavians also play the international game well. Belgians seem to be highly adaptable. British managers are coming on, although they are handicapped by their traditional disinclination to learn foreign languages. The French, despite the fine international business school, INSEAD, are a mixed bag.

One clear sign of encroaching globalization is the emergence of foreign nationals as heads of some of Europe's biggest multinationals. German Helmut Maucher runs the Swiss food giant Nestlé; a Welshman runs French cosmetics company L'Oreal. Philips, the Dutch electronics company, is making a concerted effort to promote foreign nationals in the parent company. The practice is spreading to North America. Apple Computer's president is a German citizen. The true test of a Canadian company's global aspirations will be its willingness to promote a European or Asian national to the CEO job. Which will be the first? Northern Telecom's last two CEOs have been American, reflecting the 60% of its sales that come from the U.S.

A headhunter, interviewed in *EuroBusiness* magazine, suggests the top European executive of the future will likely be a native of a small European country; have parents of different nationalities; attend an internationally oriented business school; possess a flexible mind and brilliant social skills; and have a background in banking and marketing with a multinational company. "How many brilliant Danes with an Insead MBA and an Italian mother can there be?" *EuroBusiness* jests. The headhunter may have been exaggerating, but just a little bit.

Canada, like Holland and the Scandinavian countries, has been a small country with a trading tradition. However, we have been slow to produce this quality of adaptable manager who will thrive in Europe. The lack of aptitude for international management seems to be a North American failing. The most comfortable practitioners of global management are the Europeans and Pacific Rim nationals, from Hong Kong or Singapore.

One reason Canada has been slow to produce internationally oriented managers is that it never had to. We have been international traders because we have mineral, forest and farm commodities that the rest of the world needs. There was never any reason to fight for markets. High tariff barriers made us soft and insular. Even when we looked to a foreign market, it was an easy one. Doing business in Buffalo and Spokane, or even Houston or New Orleans, has rarely required a second language or much cultural adaptability.

The state of Canada's business education reflects this ingrained parochialism. Business schools have only recently started emphasizing international management education, a staple of the quality European schools for many years. One of the pioneers is the administrative studies school at York University, the first in Canada to give an MBA specializing in international management. The three-year program offers enriched language training and more in-depth coverage of global management, and requires its students to work abroad for a period.

The York program reflects the mindset of the business school's dean, Dezso Horvath, a slight, bespectacled 47-year-old who is a kind of walking, talking role model of the international manager. Born in Hungary, raised in Sweden, he speaks several languages. Horvath sees global management as his school's strength in the competitive world of business education, where cash-starved universities scramble for the best students and faculty.

The York initiative, and others like it, are a promising

start. But they come late in the game. This country desperately needs managers who can function in Europe, Asia or the Third World, but it must wait awhile for the influx of students from the new international business programs. Inadequate management training may be the biggest obstacle for Canadian firms trying to penetrate international markets. "Despite its emphasis on trade, this country is one of the poorest in the world in terms of knowledge of international marketplace. In MBA programs, the international training is quite dreadful," Joseph d'Cruz argues.

When these programs become established and their graduates pervade Canadian companies, Canada will finally have a pool of international managerial talent. But education isn't the only crying need. There must be a fundamental change in attitude, as well. The business community, and Canadians generally, must discard their narrow perspectives. Says Horvath: "One of the most difficult things to do in Canada is to change the cultural outlook, for companies to get the idea that they should have a global perspective. This has to happen to both big and small companies."

There are no neat and easy ways to change the culture of a people. But we do not have the luxury of time, because the challenge is here now. Our companies and their managers have to hit the ground running, gaining experience and knowledge as they move. It is not just culture change; it is culture shock.

Chapter 15

Looking East

For François Mitterrand, the summit meeting with Helmut Kohl in early November of 1989 was a chance to clear the air. The French President was eager to show that he understood the changing face of Central and Eastern Europe. He wanted to assure Germany that France was open to a gradual reunification of the two Germanies.

"I should be surprised if the next 10 years should pass without us having to face up to a new structure in Europe," Mitterrand acknowledged at a joint press conference in Bonn with his West German counterpart.

Three days later, his statement looked absurdly out of step with events. The East German government, powerless to stop the flood of its citizens to the West, opened the despised Berlin Wall. Hundreds of thousands of East Berliners streamed past Checkpoint Charlie, strolled down the wide avenues of West Berlin, and gawked at the well-stocked store windows. The talk was no longer of unification in 10 years or five years. The Germans, divided since the defeat of the Nazi armies in the Second World War, were thinking in terms of a year or a few months.

The French president should be forgiven for not anticipating the pace of change. Most experts were left red-faced by the events of late 1989. Through the 1980s, there had been a growing realization that the political balance was being altered. The Communist bloc was disintegrating. The Germanies might unite. The European Community would embrace these newly liberalized economies. But the assumption was it would not happen soon.

But the dominos of Marxist-Leninism fell with accelerating speed. France's ambassador to Canada, François Bujon de l'Estang, recalls seeing a placard waved by a Prague demonstrator: "It took 10 years in Poland, 10 months in Hungary, 10 weeks in East Germany, 10 days in Czechoslovakia." And, he added, it happened even more abruptly in Romania.

The upheaval captured the rapt attention of the North American public, to a far greater extent than the 1992 process in Western Europe. Although the cumulative impact of the EC's single market is powerful and far-reaching, its regulatory changes and wrenching compromises often seem as exciting as paint drying. By contrast, the collapse of the Iron Curtain unleashed a non-stop sequence of gripping symbolic events. Television captured scenes of the Berlin Wall broken up in pieces; exultant crowds greeting 1968 Czechoslovakian reformer Alexander Dubcek in Prague's Wenceslas Square; the swift overthrow and execution of Romanian dictator Nicolai Ceausescu; the opening of a McDonald's restaurant — that icon of capitalism — in downtown Moscow.

These were events that people could see and understand. By contrast, the EC's reforms seemed technical and bureaucratic. One Toronto manager of mutual funds says his company's new Europe fund, first introduced to capitalize on the 1992 phenomena, was "a yawn" until the Berlin Wall was breached in early November of 1989. Only then did investors start to buy, because they saw the Western European companies as vehicles for investments in Eastern European factories and properties.

The investors, of course, were quite right. Western European economies and companies will be direct beneficiaries from the opening of Eastern Europe. It is fallacious to look at the two movements — 1992 and perestroika — in isolation from each other. Soviet President Mikhail

Gorbachev's reforms were aimed at rebuilding the Soviet Union's economy and, indirectly, those of its satellites. He wanted the former Comecon states to move closer to prosperous Western Europe. Eastern European countries want to participate in that big, bustling marketplace, and in the growth spurred by the integration of the 12 EC members. As the Communist hierarchies dissolved, the new regimes have obtained special trading relationships with the community. Poland, Czechoslovakia and Hungary are taking up corners of that vast European economic space already occupied by the EC 12 and the EFTA six.

How does Western Europe benefit from these ties? At first, there will be some costs as it pours aid and investment money into these ravaged economies. But over the long term, the West's private sector gains access to a rich source of skilled workers and potentially growing markets. The early birds, like Finland, Italy, Austria and particularly West Germany, have an instant advantage; their companies have been doing business behind the Iron Curtain for years. But they have been joined by a flood of outsiders. Spend a day in the bustling lobby of the Intourist Hotel near Moscow's Red Square, and you will meet British shoe manufacturers, French high-tech salespeople, Austrian import-export specialists, squads of Japanese businesspeople — not to mention a mission of Western Canadians trying to sell the Soviets agricultural equipment.

The potential synergies between Eastern and Western Europe are apparent in the auto industry, a key sector in any industrial economy. Western Europe's automakers have already been looking ahead to a booming 1990s. The penetration of their potential market is far lower than in North America. More than 13 million cars were sold in 1989, up from an average of 10 million in the 1980-84 period. General Motors in Europe is calling for sales levels of 14.5 million to 15 million units by 1995.

But the opening of Eastern Europe could make those numbers look conservative. In East Germany alone, 6.5 million car orders are waiting to be filled — in a country with fewer than 17 million people. Car buyers in some East European countries face waiting periods of up to eight years. These frustrated would-be owners will no longer be satisfied with functional tin cans. They will want Volkswagen Golfs and Ford Escorts. Even the beloved Trabants, the smoky workhorses that carried the first exodus of East Germans into the West, are in danger of obsolescence.

The Eastern bloc should emerge as a carmaking center, as well. The big car manufacturers are scrambling to set up joint ventures. Fiat with its long history of business relations with Eastern Europe is planning to produce 300,000 cars a year, starting in 1993, from a plant southeast of Moscow. Volkswagen and Daimler-Benz are laying the groundwork for East German manufacturing. General Motors is planning a joint venture in Hungary. A recent consultant's study on 1992 and the auto industry estimates that Eastern bloc producers will produce 4.5 million autos a year by the end of the century, about double the production in 1989. And this is just the auto industry; other sectors are gearing up with equal intensity.

These plans are proceeding even though the prospects of selling Western goods in Eastern Europe are still uncertain. The biggest obstacle is the non-convertibility of most Eastern currencies into hard Western currency. Ambitious automakers — and other industrialists — will have to work at finding ways to repatriate their future profits.

When he came to power, Mikhail Gorbachev talked of "a common European home," a Europe loosely bound by trade, investment, and a shared vision of a peaceful future. At first, that sounded pie-in-the-sky. The Cold War looked like it would last awhile. NATO and the Warsaw Pact seemed unlikely to disappear overnight. The state-run economies and communist dictatorships of the Eastern bloc would have trouble blending with the market economies and democratic regimes of the West. One of the EC's iron-clad conditions is that its members are democracies — and not so-called "people's democracies."

No one any longer dismisses Gorbachev's vision as an impossible dream. A single market from the Bay of Biscay to the Pacific, including what has been the Soviet Union, would comprise more than 800 million people and a combined gross domestic product of more than US$7.5 trillion (compared with 324 million people and a US$5.5 trillion

GDP in the EC.) The emergence of such a colossus would remove any doubts about Europe's claim to be the world's most powerful economic bloc.

Strains in the EC

Two weeks after the Berlin Wall came tumbling down, *The Economist* magazine ran a cover that captured the alarming pace of change, and the dilemmas it posed for the European Community. It was a cartoon drawing of the EC's leaders — Thatcher, Kohl, Mitterrand et al. — enjoying a rich and elegant dinner in a stately mansion. But standing in the doorway was an uninvited rude and noisy rabble, wearing peasant clothing, sporting Cossack beards, and holding out their crude bottles to be filled with wine. The title was "Gatecrashers' Europe?" The commentary on the editorial page said the EC's 12 leaders "sense the end of an affair — of the timeless dinner that leads to an undefined but 'ever closer' union."

The changes in the East caught the EC flatfooted. Until the 1980s, it had been mainly a trading relationship, a customs union with pretensions to being much more. But with 1992 on track, it was moving in an orderly fashion towards a closer union. Member states had been ceding to Brussels the right to establish policy in environment, product standards, mergers and even social affairs. Jacques Delors hoped to push the community towards economic and monetary union. His ultimate goal was a federal union, a United States of Europe.

But the opening of the East seemed to leave Delors' game plan in limbo. The need to deal with these new players, and their insistent demands, added pressures to the already strained relations among the 12. The prospect of German unification in particular threatened to divert the EC from its task of integration. The momentum of reform was in danger of slowing. It all played neatly into the hands of Margaret Thatcher, the one head of state opposed to a more intimate union.

The trade-related reforms of Project 1992 seemed fairly safe from these diversions. Enough had been approved that there was no danger of turning back. But Delors' program beyond 1992 was likely to be delayed, perhaps derailed. The challenge of uniting the two Germanies' monetary systems was daunting enough. Tackling European monetary union seemed out of the question.

Delors and his fellow EC leaders were also unprepared for the role into which the EC has been thrust by perestroika. The community has no common foreign policy or defense policy, only a loose form of "political cooperation," which amounts to periodic consultation among the 12 foreign ministers. The events in Eastern Europe — and their implications for defense, foreign relations, aid, investment, even possible expansion of the EC itself — exposed a vacuum of political institutions to deal with cascading change.

The shock of events strained the once happy union of 12. However attractive Eastern European markets looked to Western companies, there was also the fear that investment money intended for the EC might be diverted eastward. Some Japanese companies were moving new plant investments to Eastern Europe. Analysts talked of Hungary, Poland and Czechoslovakia as the emerging "European tigers," with potential for high growth built on low production costs and skilled, low-wage labor.

This caused concern in the EC's southern tier, which has been enjoying an influx of investment to take advantage of low-cost production. Spain, Portugal, Greece and Ireland might continue to benefit from 1992, but the rewards would not be as rich as they would be if the Berlin Wall were still firm. The effects threatened to spill over into the 1992 program. The southern countries will swallow 1992's more difficult reforms — such as the freeing up of capital controls — as long as there is a payoff in investment and prosperity. Could this appetite for reform abate, as investment and job growth gets siphoned off into the Eastern economies?

Even the EC's leadership role in providing aid to Eastern Europe has caused bruised feelings. The East Bloc countries were buried under crushing debt and faced massive costs in repairing a tattered infrastructure. The G-7 industrial nations, including Canada and the U.S., agreed that the EC should be the coordinating body for the West's aid efforts. But the community's traditional aid beneficiaries in the Third World, already worried about Fortress Europe, have been agitated that their sources of assistance might dry up. There were only so many ECUs to throw around.

But these ripples were nothing like the rough waters stirred up by the unification of Germany. Few of Europe's leaders doubted that the two Germanies would probably reunite some day. But East Germany's hard-line Communist leadership collapsed with unexpected suddenness. The country was in danger of dissolving, as the westward exodus of its best people continued. These events pushed the unification issue to the front. But Western leaders — and the alarmed Soviet Union — had the sick feeling that events had slipped out of their control. There was no framework to deal with the important questions of unification: Would a united Germany belong to NATO? Could it be neutral? Would Soviet troops remain in East Germany? Who would negotiate the terms of unification? What would happen to borders with Poland? Would a united Germany be a confederation or a more closely linked federal state? How could currency union between two such unequal economies be carried out? The Germanies, their neighbors and allies had to move quickly to knit together a unification process.

Even before the dramatic events of 1989-90, there had been fears that the Bonn government would begin to look eastward, and away from its Western partners. France was most concerned. The French had worked hard to make the Franco-German alliance the solid core of the EC, the relationship that made everything else work. They were fearful of a distracted, isolated, and perhaps neutral Germany, a country no longer anchored to the Western alliance. These fears strengthened the French leadership's resolve to push quickly towards economic and monetary union in the European Community.

Throughout Europe, there lingered bitter memories of two world wars, when German armies overran the continent. The Second World War ushered in a particularly unhappy chapter in French history, with the Nazis and their French collaborators pitted against the Resistance. The EC's founding father, Jean Monnet, believed that the continent could be safe from war only if it was integrated, politically and economically. His dream was a Europe so entangled with itself that conflict was out of the question. Many Europeans worried that Monnet's dream was being endangered by Germany's lapse into a preoccupied, self-obsession. (One country in Europe that has not been invaded in this century is Britain. Perhaps that explains the British lack of enthusiasm for European integration. The horrors of war were considerable in Britain, but it was never occupied by another power.)

And yet it seems extremely unlikely that a united Germany would turn away from the West and the European Community. West Germany on its own has been tightly tied into the single market and the NATO alliance. It would be a major beneficiary of 1992, whether united or apart from East Germany. Bonn has clearly cast its lot with Western Europe; a united Germany would not alter that relationship.

Unification would strengthen Germany's unassailable position as the EC's dominant economy. Its population would climb close to 80 million, up from 62 million for West Germany alone; its gross domestic product would be about a third the size of the total GDP of the community. Germany's leadership in manufacturing would be particularly striking — its manufacturing sector in the late 1980s was already about 70% of the size of France's, Italy's and Britain's put together. It is estimated that this percentage would rise to 85% after unification. Furthermore, a combined Germany would rival Japan as the world's most successful trading nation.

The idea of a dominant Germany has caught the imagination of international investors. The Germany Fund, a closed end investment fund which holds German securities, was one of the best-performing stocks on the New York Stock Exchange in 1989. As the Berlin Wall was crumbling in late 1989, it was trading at a staggering 100% premium over the value of the securities it held. That premium reflected investors' bullish outlook on Germany's economic future. Typical is the view of Barton Biggs, head of equity research with the Morgan Stanley investment bank in New York. He told *Barron's* magazine in early 1990 that "This is going to be the decade of Europe, just as the 1980s was the decade of East Asia and particularly of Japan. The Nineties will be the decade of Europe and particularly of Germany. Germany will be the strongest currency in the world. Its stock market will also be dominant."

Much has been made of the potential tensions arising from Germany's enhanced power in the EC. The French already chafe under Bonn's command of economic decision-making. The German central bank effectively runs the European Monetary System of linked currencies. After unification, Bonn, more than ever, would call the tune. However, this shouldn't be exaggerated. Britain, France and Italy are strong economies. In some sectors, such as fast-growing services, they more than hold their own. But the French would no doubt like the stand-offish Britain to take a little more interest in EC matters, thus providing a Franco-British balance to the German power.

So there are problems, but they hardly add up to a collapse or even a weakening of the European Community. If anything, the unification of Germany and the liberalization of Eastern Europe strengthens the community as an economic unit. Admittedly, the political challenge is more daunting, but it is no less brimming with potential payoffs.

It is clear now that the community is the only firm ground amid Europe's shifting sands. All the old certainties have evaporated. NATO is shifting from a military to a quasi-political alliance. The Soviet Empire is crumbling. The U.S. will still have a voice in Europe, but it will no longer be the "chairman of the board," just an influential outside director. The community is the glue that binds the continent together. At a time when old wartime fears are being revived, it is a reminder that once-hostile nations can forge a peaceful, prosperous union. But having dealt with German unification, the EC must quickly recapture its momentum of reform. It must move towards a true federation of Europe.

Jacques Delors has talked of the need for a stronger institutional framework at the EC. The system of Parliament, Commission and the Council of Ministers looks jerry-built and fragile. The community's executive branch, the Commission, lacks democratic legitimacy. In early 1990, Delors was calling for a new EC constitution with a stronger Parliament. The EC's external role was also in need of an upgrade. Its new mission of in coordinating aid for Eastern Europe was part of that thrust. Add to this a rising interest in building a distinct "European pillar" within the NATO alliance — at least, for as long as NATO remains relevant. If the EC is to be the framework around which the Europe of the 21st century will be built, it must have credible institutions.

All this demands leadership of a rare skill and foresight. Delors and his successors as European Commission president will have to juggle conflicting demands. Success also depends on the care and maintenance of the crucial Franco-German *entente*. Unification of Germany is bound to stir up emotions and some misunderstanding. But the Bonn-Paris relationship must work if Europe is to work.

Delors would like to have seen a deeper EC — a completed single market, a more integrated union, the first steps to federation — before having to deal with a wider EC with new members. It now appears the deepening and widening must proceed together. The single market and economic/monetary union must be forged if Europe is to realize its economic potential. But the gatecrashers will have to be let into the banquet — and not just Eastern Europe, but Austria, Norway and the members of the European Free Trade Association. This cannot be avoided if the community is to provide the framework of the democratic, free and peaceful Europe.

Ronald McDonald meets Karl Marx

As McDonald's Restaurants was opening its first Moscow restaurant in early 1990, a truckload of onions was sitting in war-torn Baku, Azerbaijan, waiting for the fast-food company to pick it up. McDonald's Moscow joint venture had lined up the supply the previous summer. A Russian employee of the Moscow McDonald's joint venture had traveled to the southern Soviet republic in December to hand pick the onions. But as the racial tension in Azerbaijan broke into a bloody civil war, no trucker was willing to brave the bullets and haul the onions up to Moscow. "They kill people down there," one road-hauler complained.

In the end, Muscovites did not have to do without onions on their "Big Maks." The joint venture was able to find an alternate supply. However, the onion incident highlights the enormous pains McDonald's took to ensure supply of food ingredients for its Moscow venture. The company quickly discovered that Russian agriculture and food processing were not up to its exacting standards. By the time the restaurant opened, it was able to source 80% of its food locally, but it wasn't easy. McDonald's had to built its own vertically integrated food production, processing and distribution system.

The hub of this system is a rambling, two-story US$40 million processing center in a southeast Moscow suburb, about a 40-minute drive from Red Square. This center, set among high-rise apartment buildings, is like no McDonald's operation in the 51 other countries where the fast-food chain operates. In most of these markets, McDonald's receives mainly finished products, such as buns, patties and desserts, from local processors. In Moscow, it takes the raw products from the farms and does the processing itself. The 100,000-square-foot processing center contains a bakery, dairy, meat production center, french fry processing line, apple pie factory and various food-testing laboratories.

For George Cohon, the president of McDonald's Restaurants of Canada Ltd., the potential of the Soviet market more than makes up for the costs. The Moscow opening was the culmination of a 14-year struggle for this 52-year-old Chicago-born lawyer, who came to Canada in 1968 as owner of the Eastern Canadian franchise for McDonald's and quickly built it into one of the gems of the worldwide system. It was Cohon who decided McDonald's had a future in the USSR, and he convinced management of the parent company, McDonald's Corp. of Oak Brook, Illinois, to support his efforts.

The appeal of the USSR lies in certain indisputable facts, Cohon says. "There were 291 million people there — that's a great potential market. There are people who like

260

eating meat, bread, potatoes and milk — and that's what we serve. Going into a market like that, God knows where, 30 years from now, that will lead us as a corporation. We have 11,000 restaurants in 50 countries, but 7,500 of them are in the U.S. The U.S. population is 220 million and you have 291 million here. God, what's the potential of that market? Thousands and thousands of restaurants."

This bubbling enthusiasm is typical of companies that are the pioneers, the leading edge of the Western invasion of Eastern Europe. These early birds see millions of people, with a cultural background similar to North Americans, and with a buying power that has been pent up for decades. They see a skilled labor force that, given additional tools and incentives, could be the source of low-cost manufactured goods.

But not every company can call on the vast resources of a McDonald's — or the "patient money" to wait an indefinite period before the investment pays off. McDonald's Canada could rely on the muscle of its U.S. parent's worldwide organization. The project drew on the expertise of Swedes, Finns, Germans, Brits, Americans, Dutch and Yugoslavs. It is the product of a global organization with more than US$16 billion in worldwide sales in 1988.

This massive effort underlines the challenges of doing business anywhere in Eastern Europe. Decision-making is slow and bureaucratic. Production and service standards are still shoddy. Workers, deprived of any reason to work hard, are reluctant to give the necessary effort. The black market remains a stubbornly durable parallel economy. There is the huge challenge of dealing with nonconvertible currencies. It will take time before things change — if they ever do. But the pioneers go ahead, believing the complications can be overcome with imagination and hard work.

A number of Canadians have been in the vanguard of Western businesses active in the Communist Bloc. Among this contingent are many immigrant entrepreneurs who fled from East-Central Europe to find a better life in Canada. Or in some cases, it is the sons and daughters of these immigrants. George Cohon's father was born in the same Russian city as former Soviet leader Leonid

Brezhnev. Cohon likes to joke about the possible shape of history if his father had stayed at home and Brezhnev's had emigrated to North America. Two Hungarian-born businessmen, Toronto investor Andrew Sarlos and property developer Albert Reichmann, are kingpins in an investment fund for Hungary. Thomas Bata returns to Czechoslovakia with plans to produce shoes in a country he fled 50 years before. And there are many others.

For these people, the emotional ties have been a powerful catalyst. Sarlos had left Hungary during the bloody 1956 uprising when the Soviets crushed an abortive revolution. He says his involvement in Hungarian investment was inspired first by "80% sentiment and 20% hard-headedness. I wanted to create an opportunity for Hungary and that is what motivated me. I am putting in more time and effort than the return justifies."

Sarlos also sees potential for entrepreneurs motivated by profit alone. But economic prospects vary greatly from country to country. Reform is not happening at a uniform pace — it may lurch ahead in one country, and stumble clumsily in another. Hungary looks like the best bet now, having started the liberalization process as early as 1968. It is more attuned to individual initiative and choice than later converts to capitalism. Privatization is already well advanced, although the national debt remains a staggering burden.

In Poland, the Solidarity-led government has a strong commitment to liberalization, but the economy is in horrible shape. Solidarity's overnight deregulation of prices has triggered considerable hardship. The Poles are receiving huge dollops of Western aid — and there are all those Polish expatriates in the West helping the efforts.

Czechoslovakia is making dramatic strides after a late start. It has been able to emerge from Soviet domination as a relatively prosperous country, and could become an industrial power fairly quickly. But everyone's choice as the East's most promising market is East Germany. Its economy has been the strongest in the Comecon bloc. Its industry and infrastructure are in the best shape. It contains a number of state-run companies that could become competitive in world markets with a little help. Of course, the West Germans are already there, and are seizing many of the better opportunities.

Four countries in southeast Europe face more uncertain prospects. Romania, under its late dictator Nicolai Ceausescu, slid backward into a dark and repressed condition, where people were deprived of a decent living and self-esteem. Now freed from that yoke, Romanians have much to do before the country is an attractive investment target. Events are moving quickly in Bulgaria, but it too has far to go. Yugoslavia, although progressive economically, is torn by ethnic divisions and crippled by Latin American-style inflation. At the time this book was written, Albania remained the last hard-rock holdout of unregenerated Stalinist rule in the Eastern bloc. But in time, it too will be open for business.

The most fascinating and, at the same time, frustrating market is the Soviet Union itself. Population alone makes it an intriguing target — 291 million people, compared with only 113 million in the rest of Eastern Europe combined. But perestroika seems to have made the fewest gains in its own homeland. The old *nomenklatura*, the top Communist officials, are entrenched. Economic liberalization has been accompanied by severe economic conditions — food shortages and long lineups — that make perestroika a difficult sell. Many people resent the new free enterprise co-operatives which are free to pay — and charge — market prices for scarce commodities, while state stores do without. Soviet society seems to be splitting into a cruel class system, consisting of those few with hard currency who can buy things, and those with worthless rubles who do without. Because liberalization seems more dynamic in the satellite countries, many Western businesses prefer to start there.

There is also corruption, evident in all Eastern European countries but most prevalent in the USSR. This is the unavoidable outcome of total economic collapse and degradation of the national currency. People grasp constantly for hard dollars or marks; bribery is a way of life. It is difficult to get things done without under-the-table payments. On landing in Moscow, the visitor is immediately confronted with the basic reality of Soviet life. The taxi driver wants to make a black-market currency transaction, or demands payment in a pack of cigarettes or in U.S. dollars. There are stories of food warehouses stripped of almost all their contents by insiders selling on the black market, while ordinary people must wait in line for tidbits. The Soviet leadership must somehow restore confidence in its debased economy and worthless currency.

But the boundless potential keeps drawing Westerners. One American lawyer in Moscow calls the Soviet Union "the last great frontier for capitalism." And the Soviets need everything — capital goods, consumer goods and services. Personal computers, commonplace in the West, are in short supply here. Convenience and consumer choice are foreign concepts in Moscow. Street vendors outside the big GUM department store in Moscow sell large quantities of ice-cream cones. But the only flavor is vanilla. A Canadian businessman notes that eggs are packaged in plastic bags and the breakage is enormous. So he comes home convinced there is a market for paper egg cartons.

Soviet-watchers say Canadian companies must be hard-headed about doing business in the USSR. "The euphoria gets cooled quickly," says Basil Kalymon, a management professor at the University of Toronto and an advisor to Canadian companies involved in joint ventures. "You immediately have to face the crudeness of the infrastructure. The structure of the economy is so ruined. The centralization makes doing anything so difficult. The hard reality quickly sets in." He says the country desperately needs currency reform, price reform, and greater incentives to work and ownership.

But liberalization spawns its own set of problems. Decision-making, once centralized in Moscow, has devolved to the republics, municipalities and even local state enterprises. People in crucial positions don't know how to do their jobs. Western businesses that have been active in Eastern Europe find the whole perestroika thing disruptive. A West German importer who has been traveling to Moscow for 20 years say he finds it difficult to do business in this new, more decentralized structure. He once dealt with a small group of state officials who always knew the score. Now he has to contend with all kinds of different people, many of them inexperienced in the ticklish style of East-West commerce. He bemoans that these new decision-makers don't know how to set prices the way the old bureaucrats did.

The joint venture way

Joint venture is the flavor of the month in international business. Any company that dreams of global expansion ponders strategic alliances with foreign companies. And nowhere is the joint venture more crucial than in Eastern Europe. The only way for a Western company to establish businesses in most East bloc countries is through a partnership with a local enterprise, usually state-run. Countless numbers of these have been signed — in the Soviet Union, in the first three years of joint venture legislation, more than 1,400 were set up. Unfortunately, fewer than 50 of these were believed to be actually producing anything by that time. Early enthusiasm is often tempered by the practical problems of doing business in Eastern Europe.

In these couplings, the Western partner usually comes to the table with a certain expertise, technology, or production methods. It also has access to that all-important Western financing in hard currency. The Eastern partner contributes manpower, real estate, essential services, such as power and construction, and knowledge of the right bureaucratic buttons to push to get things done. This last factor is crucial. In the Soviet Union, for example, it has been possible for Western companies to link up with the new private-enterprise co-operatives. Co-operatives are usually run by the kind of risk-taking, free-thinking entrepreneurs that Canadian companies might like as allies in their new ventures. However, they should usually be avoided as partners. Co-operatives usually lack the necessary capital base, the land and resources, and the important state contacts needed to get established.

Rules on ownership vary widely from country to country. Majority ownership by the local partner has usually been required, but that is changing. The Soviets, for example, first demanded at least 51% Soviet ownership, but recent rules allow up to 99% ownership by the Western partner. Hungary and Poland have moved towards a privatization of state-run industry, with ownership by outsiders. The U.S. General Electric has made the most dramatic plunge with its $150 million acquisition of 50% of Hungarian electric goods supplier Tungsram — plus an option to buy 20% more if the company's exports can double. General Electric sees it as a risky, but necessary entry into a region where rivals Siemens of Germany and Philips of the Netherlands are already established.

As joint ventures become a fact of life, foreign ownership restrictions should be further relaxed. This will allow Western partners to exercise more control over the projects, and to repatriate more of any profits that may eventually be earned — assuming they can solve the currency convertibility nightmare.

Then there is taxation, and the rules range all over the map. In Czechoslovakia, joint venture profits are taxed at an onerous 40% rate; also, half of the venture's wage bill must be contributed to a special social security fund. In the USSR, profits are taxed at 30%, although a venture enjoys a holiday of two years after earning its profits before paying taxes on them. When profits are repatriated by a Western company, there is an additional 20% tax.

Many companies view profits as a remote consideration anyway. Their profit horizon is long-term, at least 10 to 20 years. Their goal is to get a toehold in a market that may, at some time, contribute to bottom line. But that does not mean it is impossible to make money right off the bat. It depends on the kind of business being done. Ventures that sell goods or services to foreign customers for hard currency may be able to make a buck immediately.

The first rule to remember is doing business in Eastern Europe has little in common with North American or even Western European practice. Companies find themselves performing bizarre gymnastics in trading, accounting and financing. It is instructive to look at two such businesses operating in Moscow — with two very different approaches.

The McDonald's restaurant on Pushkin Square is the first of 20 the company plans to establish in the Soviet capital, under its joint venture with Moscow City Council's

Food Administration. As this restaurant was opening in early 1990, George Cohon wouldn't be pinned down on when the business would be profitable. "We have no master plan of five or 10 years. We think customers will like it so much, they will want us to expand rapidly. But we will have to take our time and crawl before we run. When it all falls into place, we will make money."

The first restaurant took payment in rubles only — it was designed for the Muscovite customer who is forbidden to hold foreign currency. The second would be a hard-currency outlet for foreign tourists and businesspeople. Cohon talked about putting drive-through outlets on the ring road around downtown Moscow, and of expanding outside the capital, into Leningrad, for example. Then there is Eastern Europe. The company already has ventures in Budapest and Belgrade.

The trick is how to earn hard currency from a country with a nonconvertible currency. If a venture generates sales in rubles, the ideal is to become self-sufficient, sourcing everything in rubles as well. But McDonald's travails shows the difficulty of sourcing everything you need in the USSR. At some point, the venture will have to pay some expenses in hard money.

If the venture does start to make profits in rubles, the Western partner would have to consider barter or some other form of countertrade. Pepsi-Cola, for example, has been selling soft drinks in the USSR for 18 years, and converting its rubles into vodka, which it distributes for hard cash in the West.

That is not of immediate concern to McDonald's. Its joint venture with Moscow city council won't make profits for awhile. When it does, these will be reinvested into the continuing development of restaurants. Furthermore, McDonald's will be opening restaurants that take payment in both rubles and hard currency; therefore, profits could be earned in both kinds of currency.

But McDonald's is planning other ways to make real money besides the hard-currency restaurants. The Canadian company gets a hard currency royalty on all restaurant sales. It has also built extra capacity into its food processing plant, so that it can supply food to outside customers — perhaps even in Western Europe — for hard currency. The meat line, for example, could be adjusted to turn out steaks instead of patties. French fries could be cut a different way to suit an outside client. Large hotel chains appear to be interested. McDonald's also plans to put an office building on top of one of its restaurants, and lease the space to foreigners for hard currency.

Across Pushkin Square from McDonald's, an elegant seven-story office building stands out among the dingier, unimproved buildings on the street. The restoration of this pre-revolutionary building is the work of the appropriately named Perestroika Joint Venture. It was the first joint venture to report a hard currency profit — US$1.6 million from sales of US$13 million — and after only its first year of operation. Worsham Group, an Atlanta real estate firm, is working with the Moscow city council to renovate old buildings into modern offices. Worsham's stake in the joint venture is 40%, with the Moscow council holding 60% through various departments.

Unlike McDonald's, Perestroika tries to stay out of the messy job of earning rubles. Its business is to lease space to foreign corporations that pay rents in hard currency. The fact that there is a shortage of office space in downtown Moscow boosts the money-making potential. Foreign companies are willing to pay mid-town Manhattan rents for quality space. The Pushkin Square building houses, among others, the Germany chemical giant BASF, the Japanese industrial power Mitsubishi, and the American law firm Baker & Mackenzie.

Another factor generating quick profits is that Perestroika asked many of its tenants to pay rents in advance, for periods up to six years. That gave the venture a fat cash flow in the first year to help finance its renovations. The up-front cash also allows it to report a "profit" after only one year. Perestroika's partners say they have several similar projects in the works, which, presumably, will also pay rents in advance.

The real estate project earns its revenues in hard currency, but it still faces currency complications. It has to pay out expenses to workers and suppliers in rubles. Dollars of income often can't be converted at a satisfactory exchange rate into rubles for expenses, so the venture has found separate sources of ruble income. It operates a number of ruble-earning businesses on the side. Many joint ventures must maintain complicated separate accounts, with hard currency income and expenses on one side of the ledger, and local currency income and expenses on the other.

The clash of systems

These two joint ventures take different roads to profitability, but they share some characteristics. Each has a joint venture partner that has shown it can get things done. Many ventures have languished because either the Western or Eastern partners were found to be deficient. Worsham, a big private developer in Atlanta, brought expertise and organization in managing office restorations. Its major partner is Mosinzhstroi, the Moscow department responsible for the city's infrastructure construction, such as streets and sewers. General director of Mosinzhnstoi is the sleek, well-dressed Andrei Stroyev, who is also chairman of the joint venture. The English-speaking Stroyev is known to be a shrewd, U.S.-style deal-maker, described by Western observers as "the Donald Trump of Moscow."

Financing can also be a challenge for joint ventures. Some Western banks are lending money for Eastern European business, but they are taking an extremely cautious approach. They are still feeling the hangover from the Third World and Eastern European debt problems of the 1970s. McDonald's, for example, got financing from both Soviet and Western banks. But Cohon says Western financing would have been difficult without the covenant of a major corporation like McDonald's.

What makes financing even tougher is that the Soviet deal-makers cannot guarantee that the Kremlin will bail out their joint ventures if the projects threaten to go under. Before perestroika, when foreigners would sign contracts with the Foreign Trade Ministry, they had some assurance that the venture was backed by the Soviet government. In the more decentralized economy of today, that guarantee no longer stands.

Many of the joint ventures' biggest headaches relate to people. It is possible to find highly skilled workers, and many Western companies are gravitating to countries with high education standards. That is why East Germany and Hungary attract so much interest. But managerial skills are a problem. Eastern Europeans have little understanding of Western managerial techniques, employee motivation, quality control and organization. It is difficult to get local managers to think in terms of profits and market measures of performance, rather than simple quantity of output or planned measures of performance.

A number of companies send their best local people to North America for management training. McDonald's selected four crack managers (from 1,000 applicants) for a nine-month training program in North America. Perestroika dispatched 40 Soviet managers to the United States for immersion training, including experience with a number of American construction companies. Building up these skills is a heavy investment, but ultimately necessary. It also carries acute risks. This expensive expertise could easily walk out the door, lured by new joint ventures that will pay heavily for instant managerial talent.

One promising longer-term development is the emergence of Western-style business schools in centers like Riga, Moscow, Kiev and Budapest. These schools are usually funded by Western entrepreneurs and guided by Western business schools. The first priority is to prepare local managers for joint ventures, but they will eventually evolve into full-blown business schools.

A more fundamental problem is the lack of Western-style work ethic. Years of mismanagement and lack of work incentives have bred bad habits. Some companies, like McDonald's, try to change this through performance-related bonuses for workers and managers. But the old ways are ingrained. A manager with the German car maker Porsche in Munich told a Canadian businessman that he had hired four skilled mold makers who were refugees from East Germany. He was very pleased, for such tradesmen are in short supply. But after only a few days working in the Munich factory, they quit. The problem: They couldn't stand the stress.

270

There are other obstacles, too many to mention here. Working in a system of central planning means deadlines are rarely kept. Achieving quality is a constant battle. The pricing of products sold in local markets is difficult, because there are no reliable yardsticks. The state-imposed prices are artificially low; hardly anything is available at those prices anyway. Accounting standards are not well developed, although they are slowly improving. It may be some time before a venture can report a profit-loss statement using accounting standards that would make sense in the West. Finally, companies have no mechanism for selling their stakes in joint ventures. Only Hungary among East bloc countries has a stock market.

Yet if Canadians are serious about being in the global game, they have to be there, just as they have to be in Western Europe, Japan and the United States. On the surface, Eastern Europe may actually seem easier — and therefore less urgent — because it appears to be uncultivated soil. Don't believe it. The West Germans have been there for years; the Austrians, Finns, Italians and French were close behind; and the Japanese and Americans are moving in quickly.

There are good little companies in the Eastern bloc that could be turned into strong competitive partners. There are managers who are forceful and dynamic. But these are in short supply, and are being gobbled up. Canadians have to move quickly. They should start with small investments and manageable risks — don't bet the store on a Hungary or Poland, at least for now. Once inside, they have to be extremely patient. North American companies, with their short-term focus, have trouble waiting for the long-term payoffs that Eastern Europe is likely to deliver.

Any company considering business east of Berlin should examine how this strategy fits with its approach to Western Europe. The best path might be through a joint venture with a Western European company that has strong commercial ties east of the Elbe River. A Canadian auto parts company that is subcontracting to Bosch, the big German parts company, may lever this contact into access to East Germany. The relationships can work the other way: A joint venture in the East bloc could provide a

Canadian firm with entry to the big Western European market. The continued blurring of East and West will offer opportunities. The important thing is not to be narrow and blinkered in vision. This is the time for creative solution

Eastern Europe is still an unpredictable place. No one could have predicted five years ago the shape of the region today. The next five years may provide less striking images for television, but no less important changes. There may be setbacks in individual countries. The German question could flare into bitter debate. But the revolution of rising expectations will continue. Companies and countries that recognize this will have an advantage.

Chapter 16

Conclusion

The 1992 single market, and the opening of the East bloc, point towards the emergence of an economic powerhouse, anchored by the European Community and a united Germany. Japan and the United States won't be easily dislodged from the top of the economic leagues, but they will have to make room for Europe.

Material rebirth is being matched by the emotional revival. The spirit of Europe, broken by the oil price shocks and economic stagnation of 1970s, has been aggressively reborn, and has led to sense of identity that is European, and not just British, Italian or Spanish.

Canada must become an insider in Europe. Being present in this vigorous marketplace would be a transfusion to the Canadian economy and its corporate life. Being absent would consign us to second-rate status as a trading, investing and innovating nation.

A business doesn't have to be the size of McCain Foods or Northern Telecom to have an international outlook and ambitions. Small and medium-sized companies can make it in Europe. And they don't have to be located in big cities or in Central Canada. McCain's has demonstrated that. Our future as a trading nation is being determined in industrial parks in Trois Rivières and strip plazas in Lethbridge.

These companies have to move very quickly. The Japanese, the Americans, the Asian Tigers and those non-EC Europeans, the Swedes and Swiss, are not sitting back. They are grabbing partners, and making the necessary investments and acquisitions. They recognize the potential rewards.

Managers must do their homework before marching into Paris or Prague. They have to gain self-knowledge about their own strengths and weaknesses. They must study potential competitors, suppliers and customers. It is a tall order — they have to move quickly *and* be well-prepared.

The free trade agreement with the United States should not blind us to other alliances. Many observers on both sides of the free trade debate agree that Canada needs strong business ties with the European Community. Advocates of free trade see another large market with potential customers and partners; critics see trade with Europe as our hedge bet against a risky overdependence on the U.S. economy.

There is a temptation to fall back on the tired, old rhetoric of Fortress Europe, and its portrayal of 1992 as a camouflage for protectionism. But the European threat is not of a defensive fortress. We should worry more about an offensive squadron of leaner, fitter European companies, that will be more intimidating in every market of the world, including Canada. It is an easy excuse to say the rules in Europe are stacked against us. The Europeans will not lock the door to outside companies. But they are saying that we should get inside the single market now, because the competition will be much tougher later.

We have an opportunity to take a place at the European table, to participate in the remaking of that continent. Our government can bring a perspective that is not American, not Asian — that has fewer axes to grind. In a turbulent world, we can be a strong and steady link from Europe to America and the Pacific. Or we can hang back, absorbed in North America, and miss this opportunity.

Index